The Idea of the City
in the
Age of Shakespeare

The Idea of
the City
in the Age
of Shakespeare

GAIL KERN PASTER

The University of Georgia Press

Athens

© 1985 by the University of Georgia Press
Athens, Georgia 30602
All rights reserved

Designed by Kathi L. Dailey
Set in 12 on 13 Linotron 202 Cloister

The paper in this book meets the guidelines for
permanence and durability of the Committee on
Production Guidelines for Book Longevity of the
Council on Library Resources.

Printed in the United States of America

89 88 87 86 85   5 4 3 2 1

Library of Congress Cataloging in Publication Data

Paster, Gail Kern.
The idea of the city in the age of Shakespeare.

Includes index.
1. Cities and towns in literature.   2. English drama—
17th century—History and criticism.
3. English drama—Early modern and Elizabethan, 1500–
1600—History and criticism.   I. Title.
PR658.C49P3   1985   822'.3'09321732   85-974
ISBN 0-8203-0785-8 (alk. paper)

Chapter 3 is based on an article by the author which
appeared in *Shakespeare Studies* (1978).

TO MY PARENTS, MY HUSBAND, AND MY KIDS

This publication has been supported by the National Endowment for the Humanities, a federal agency which supports the study of such fields as history, philosophy, literature, and languages.

Contents

Contents

Acknowledgments

A book that has taken as long to grow up as this wayward progeny has incurred significant debts on the way, some of them doubtless forgiven and forgotten long ago. In the category of nurture at a formative stage, I would put two early debts to teachers at Yale, to Maynard Mack but even more especially to Eugene M. Waith, without whose resolute direction and attentive friendship this book would never have grown up at all.

From early days, too, the Folger Shakespeare Library has provided safe harbor—no mean feat on Capitol Hill. I am as grateful to its resourceful staff as I am to its incomparable resources. Among its lesser-known treasures are its readers, many of them friends whose timely application of criticism and counsel has left me and this book chastened and improved. Virginia Callahan, Alan Dessen, Jeanne Addison Roberts, and Susan Snyder must be singled out from this company, for knowing how to help and when. I reserve a separate note of overdue appreciation for A. R. Braunmuller, for years of conversation and encouragement in various cities from New Haven to Washington and London. And I am grateful for the stamina and astuteness of those who read a long manuscript at various stages in its development and did their best to shape it, particularly my stalwart comrade-in-arms James Maddox, the clairvoyant Leeds Barroll, and the two readers whose enthusiasm made all the difference, Burton Pike and Lawrence Danson. Getting the manuscript ready for press has pushed other obligations temporarily aside; thanks to Paul Werstine for not minding. My colleagues at George Washington University have heard some of this book and have heard about it forever; thanks for listening go especially to Jon Quitslund and Judith Plotz.

Acknowledgments

This study has also been the object of welcome institutional benevolence. The National Endowment for the Humanities, which granted me a Younger Humanist Fellowship in 1973–74, now sees its patience rewarded. The Graduate School of George Washington University helped to defray expenses in typing, a welcome accompaniment to the even more welcome grant of a sabbatical year. And, as those who know him know, I am married to a one-man institution, not to say a one-man band. He has my thanks, too often implicit, always.

Note on Editions and Translations

Unless otherwise indicated, translations from classical writers come from the Loeb Classical Library (published by Heinemann in London, in Cambridge by Harvard University Press, or in New York by Putnam's). They are: Cicero, *De re publica* and *De legibus,* trans. Clinton Walker Keyes (1928); Cicero, *Philippics,* ed. Walter C. A. Ker (1926); Horace, *Satires, Epistles and Ars Poetica,* trans. H. Rushton Fairclough (1939); *Isocrates,* vol. 1, trans. George Norlin (1928); *Juvenal and Persius,* trans. G. G. Ramsay (1940); Plato, *Republic,* vol. 2, trans. Paul Shorey (1946); *Plautus,* 5 vols., trans. Paul Nixon (1924); Seneca, *Moral Essays,* vol. 2, trans. John W. Bashore (1932); Strabo, *Geography,* vol. 2, trans. Horace Leonard Jones (1923); Tacitus, *Annals,* 4 vols., trans. John Jackson (1937); Thucydides, *History of the Peloponnesian War,* vol. 1, trans. C. Foster Smith (1919); and Vitruvius, *On Architecture,* 2 vols., trans. Frank Granger (1934).

All quotations from Shakespeare are from the Arden Shakespeare (London: Methuen) as follows: *The Comedy of Errors,* ed. R. A. Foakes (1962); *Coriolanus,* ed. Philip Brockbank (1976); *Julius Caesar,* ed. T. A. Dorsch (1965); *Measure for Measure,* ed. J. W. Lever (1965); *The Merchant of Venice,* ed. John Russell Brown (1955); *Poems,* ed. F. T. Prince (1960); *Timon of Athens,* ed. H. J. Oliver (1959); and *Titus Andronicus,* ed. J. C. Maxwell (1953).

The edition of Jonson used throughout is *Ben Jonson,* ed. C. H. Herford and Percy and Evelyn Simpson, 11 vols. (Oxford, 1925–52). I have normalized *i, j, u,* and *v* and silently expanded abbreviations. Notes and commentary from other editions will be cited individually in the notes.

The standard edition of Middleton remains that edited by A. H. Bullen, 8 vols. (London: John C. Nimmo, 1886). I have used Bullen's text for Middleton's civic pageants, cited by page number in vol. 7, and for *Your Five Gallants* in vol. 3. Where possible, I have quoted from modern editions: *A Chaste Maid in Cheapside,* ed. R. B. Parker, Revels Plays Series (London: Methuen, 1969); *A Mad World, My Masters,* ed. Standish Henning, Regents Renaissance Drama (Lincoln: University of Nebraska Press, 1965); *Michaelmas Term,* ed. Richard Levin, Regents Renaissance Drama (Lincoln: University of Nebraska Press, 1966); and *A Trick to Catch the Old One,* ed. G. J. Watson, New Mermaids Series (London: Ernest Benn, 1968). The text of Middleton's *Honourable Entertainments* comes from the Malone Society facsimile, ed. R. C. Bald (Oxford: 1953).

The Idea of the City

in the

Age of Shakespeare

INTRODUCTION

The Arts Are Produced by Overcrowding

When literary criticism has turned its attention to the city, the city has often formed one half of a familiar contrast—with the country or the garden. Pairing the terms is not unique to literary criticism: the habit is as deeply embedded in Western consciousness generally, because together the terms sum up a whole range of human attitudes and possibilities. Country and city are powerful words, Raymond Williams suggests, because of "how much they seem to stand for in the experience of human communities."[1] Under the rubric of city vs. country, one can easily group some of the most familiar antitheses of intellectual discourse—art and nature, experience and innocence, classic and romantic, heroic and pastoral, everyday and holiday, the many and the one, society and the self. The course of human history or the course of an individual life can be summarized in the theme, as in the opening sentence of a well-known book on Alexander Pope: "Pope's poetry, like the book he was accustomed to call Scripture, begins with a garden and ends with a city."[2] Northrop Frye presents the city, along with the garden and the sheepfold, as one of the basic organizing metaphors of Christian symbolism. The garden and the sheepfold are the forms imposed by human desire on the vegetable and animal worlds; the city is the form imposed by human desire on the mineral world, the world of stone.[3] But the three terms reduce to two—the city vs. the natural world of unconscious life.

Thus, although Touchstone professes to find no differences between life at court and life in Arden, comparisons between opposed environments usually focus the defining characteristics of each. The physical alternation between the worlds of country and city provides the structural basis for an extraordinary amount of experience, in literature and outside it. We can generalize that the city reflects, as the garden does not, the urge to stand apart from the rhythms of the seasonal calendar. It defines time not as the cyclical revolutions of the natural year but as the linear sequence of historical process and visible time. Against literary celebrations of the country, which stress the integration of man with his physical environment, the city expresses human desire for ascendancy over nature through control of the environment by abstract, conceptual mental patterns—the square, the circle, the straight line.[4] The city signifies the ability to transcend the physical necessities of daily existence. It is a product of reason, a function of mind. And, when the desire for ascendancy over nature is regarded as rational in spirit, motivated by an eagerness to perfect rather than to ignore natural form, the city will appear as an ideal mode of social organization, or at least as a benevolent consequence of human aspiration.

When considered apart from the country, however, another way of looking at the city emerges. The city remains involved in dialectic, but now it contains its own antitype. Instead of the pairing, country and city, there are other polarities—between the city of man and the city of God, the earthly city and heavenly city, Rome and Jerusalem, whore of Babylon and bride of the Lamb, real and ideal. This idea of opposed cities is very old, and was already well established in classical and scriptural sources by the time St. Augustine gave it complete expression in *The City of God*. Nor does it exclude the other contrast between country and city. For example, the city, whether earthly or heavenly, is always deeply involved with the idea of historical time as the country is not. The earthly city is a creation of history, its visible record, while the heavenly city is a culmination of history, the goal of the earthly pilgrimage for the individual Christian and for mankind as a whole.

In the chapters to come I will be less concerned with the city-country contrast than with the idea of the city as its own antitype, although the considerable overlap between the two contrasts often makes them hard to disentangle. Either way of contemplating the city involves a dialectical formulation, as if the very idea of a city demanded it. And it is precisely this attribute of historical thinking about cities which explains the structure of this book and functions as a leitmotif in its pages. I will ultimately concentrate, in chapters 3 through 7, on the idea of the city as it appears in the work of three playwrights of the English Renaissance—William Shakespeare, Ben Jonson, and Thomas Middleton. I am also interested, however, in demonstrating that the urban dialectic has its own literary tradition that they in part reflect. Thus it is the double task of this introduction, no less than of the book that it precedes, to outline some ideas of the city and to explain why, in English literature, those ideas should first receive significant literary expression in the dramatic entertainments of Renaissance England.

From the literature of the city, therefore, two opposing attitudes emerge—the city as a visionary embodiment of ideal community (either on earth or in heaven) or the city as a predatory trap, founded in fratricide and shadowed by conflict. The differences between the two images are often quite specifically antithetical: the topics of urban panegyric are counterbalanced in satire, satiric comedy, and political tragedy. The ancient Rome that appears so often in Renaissance poetry or tragedy is often its own counter-statement—a doomed monument, a magnificent failure. One might diagram the literary appearances of the city as parallel lines of negative and positive charge which run beside each other yet never meet. As almost the deepest function of its nature, the city contains a large body of basic oppositions—the product of conflicting estimates of human nature and society and conflicting responses to time and change. Not surprisingly, therefore, the conventions of urban literature reveal an openness to antithetical statement, an affinity for paradox. Both tendencies are apparent, for example, in Thomas Dekker's apocalyptic response to Elizabethan London, newly released from an outbreak of plague: "Thou art the goodliest of thy neighbors, but the prowdest; the welthiest, but the most wanton. Thou hast all things in thee to make thee fairest, and all things in thee to make thee foulest; for thou art attir'de like a Bride, drawing all that looke upon thee, to be in love with thee, but there is much harlot in thine eyes."[5]

The recurring presence of such ambivalence in urban literature may explain the hold of the city over the collective imagination, especially for writers. In its practical need to order complexity, the defining tensions of the city correspond to their own. Urban literature usually stresses social complexity and weighs the possibilities of order through urban design. If complexity is seen as the forerunner of chaos, of course, the literary city will present no hope for order. But, when it does create order, the city can persuasively present its achievement as heroic in magnitude, resolving rather than ignoring contraries, promising maturity rather than innocence. The city is often the focus for themes of law, obligation, and responsibility; or, negatively stated, for themes of frustration, inhibition, and socially irresponsible aspiration. Such social complexity may obstruct self-discovery and frustrate desire. The importance of the love affair for the individual is subordinated to its importance for society—to guarantee the economic transfer of land, goods, and money, to renew the commonwealth, or to celebrate the social harmony of which marriage is the emblem.

Literary responses to urban complexity also divide sharply into a positive emphasis on variety of experience, individual development, and social commitment or a negative emphasis on crowds, dirt, change, and noise. Such positive and negative emphases cannot finally be separated. "The arts," says William Empson, "are produced by overcrowding."[6] The city arouses a profoundly ambivalent response in those who fear what it represents as much as they desire it. It stimulates and therefore comes to symbolize self-division and self-loathing. Such emotions are particularly apparent in conventional personifications of the city as a woman. Because the city is walled for most of its history, it is early associated with the female principle. Classical personifications of the city as a noble woman wearing a turreted crown carry over into Christian iconography, with the virgin assuming the functions of the classical city goddess.[7] As a fortified place subject to siege and assault, this personified city becomes associated with sexual possession. A comic version of this idea exists in *Lysistrata* where Athenian women deny their husbands sexual privileges at the same time that they barricade themselves within the city treasury on the Acropolis. Renaissance poets tend to treat the theme more soberly. After her rape by Tarquin, Lucrece compares herself to the fallen Troy, the city signifying wifely chastity. She defines betrayal and false appearance as the core of similarity between her fate and Troy's:

"For even as subtle Sinon here is painted,
So sober sad, so weary and so mild,—
As if with grief or travail he had fainted,—
To me came Tarquin armed to beguild
With outward honesty, but yet defil'd
    With inward vice. As Priam him did cherish,
    So did I Tarquin,—so my Troy did perish."
                [*Rape of Lucrece*, 1541–47]

In the third Sestiad of *Hero and Leander*, Chapman develops a similar comparison between the bewildered Hero—"Her maidenhead, her vows, Leander gone" (200)—and the English sack of Cadiz in 1596.[8]

Closely linked to the city as a woman is the idea of the city as a soul, the object of warfare among spiritual powers. In Donne's Holy Sonnet 14, for example, the city as soul and the city as violated woman come together in the poet's startling comparison of himself to a usurped town, longing for a violent repossession—by sack or rape—by the rightful spiritual lover-ruler. And, interestingly enough, Lucrece also imagines Tarquin's soul as a female city, not destroyed from the outside as Donne's is or as her chastity has been, but betrayed from within by rebellion:

She says her subjects with foul insurrection
Have batter'd down her consecrated wall,
And by their mortal fault brought in subjection
Her immortality, and made her thrall
To living death and pain perpetuall.

                [722–26]

All these tropes are variations on the Renaissance macrocosm-microcosm, itself based on the Platonic correspondence between state and man. Also implicit in these tropes of city as woman or as soul is an association of the city with sudden, violent reversals of circumstance or states of being: the city belongs to Fortune. Finally, therefore, the idea of the city reveals itself as a version of the idea of the hero—the sum of human nature in its communal form as the hero is the sum of human nature in individual form. The earliest heroes are the founders of cities, and city building—particularly among the humanist architects of the Italian Renaissance—is always treated as a heroic enterprise. The city-building architect becomes the new type of complete man, the Renaissance hero as "l'huomo universale."[9]

Renewed interest in the history and design of cities is one of the strongest manifestations of the Italian Renaissance, as we shall see in some detail in chapter 1. In Renaissance England, however, only London was a community large, rich, powerful, and self-conscious enough to qualify as a city in the terms of a modern urbanist or an Italian humanist. Only London was a densely populated community whose history, culture, buildings, and imaginative dominance over the surrounding countryside expressed high social and spiritual aspiration. Furthermore, it had only become a real city in this sense over the course of the sixteenth century due to a rapid growth in size and in a population drawn from elsewhere in England. As James Dougherty has noted, *city* would only have been a word on a page to an Anglo-Norman, and Chaucer's London would look to us like a large market town.[10]

One of the most significant pieces of evidence for the new status of Elizabethan London as world-city is, in fact, the establishment after 1576 of permanent theatrical companies and ongoing commercial dramatic productions. It demonstrates the existence of an audience of sufficient means, leisure, and civic tranquillity to support what must be considered a luxury trade. A new urban self-consciousness is apparent everywhere in Elizabethan writing, as can be seen in the verse of citizen-poets like John Taylor or in the London pamphleteering of Greene, Nashe, and Dekker with its fascination with London trades, occupations, and idioms. London was thus growing in importance not only as the dominant location for the production of English letters, but also as a dominant literary subject. Certainly for an ambitious young writer during Shakespeare's lifetime, there was no other place to be but London, just as there was no place but Rome for ancient writers like Horace and Juvenal. After the turn of the century, the rapid emergence of a new genre, city comedy, must also be seen in part as a response to this imaginative power in the contemporary urban scene. Elizabethan London had become part of the immemorial urban phenomenon—the city as magnet, as siren, as irresistible drawing card.

Yet London is only one of many cities—ancient and modern, actual and mythic—represented on the Elizabethan-Jacobean stage. Dramatists set their plays in Venice, Verona, Paris, Athens, Thebes, Troy, and of course Rome. And, even though they were writing plays to be presented on a mostly bare, unlocalized stage, playwrights were increasingly alert to the nuances of locale. We might therefore ask if the proliferation of city comedies is not just a response to social change in London but is also part of a larger awakening of interest, comparable to Renaissance civic humanism, in the idea of "the City." Certainly this was the hypothesis with which I began this project, as a study of the city in Shakespeare, Jonson, and Middleton, three figures who are representative of a spectrum of responses to and involvement in city life. Shakespeare, the provincial, constructed a life built around the antitheses, city and country. He avoided contemporary London as a subject for dramatic expression, yet set comedies in other cities and was profoundly interested in the subject of ancient Rome. Jonson and Middleton commonly used their native London as the setting for comedy and have been credited, by Brian Gibbons, with establishing the new city comedy form.[11] Furthermore, Shakespeare was one of the few playwrights of his time not to have written a civic pageant or entertainment on commission from the city livery companies, while Jonson and Middleton were much involved in the production of civic entertainments. Middleton held the post of city chronologer from 1620 until his death in 1627. And Jonson, of course, was increasingly employed as masque writer for the Stuarts during the same years that he was creating his greatest satiric comedies. His efforts at articulating the nature of ideal community in courtly terms were potentially relevant to the ideal urbanism so central to the Italian Renaissance from which the Stuart masque in part derives.

The major portions of this book, therefore, deal with those works of Shakespeare, Jonson, and Middleton which are to me most deeply preoccupied with the conditions and meaning of urban life—in ancient Rome, in contemporary London, in Venice and Vienna, and in the ideal city glimpsed in civic and courtly entertainments. Two chapters, 3 and 7, which treat Shakespeare's comic and tragic cities, might well have formed the nucleus of a separate book. Yet I wanted to treat the ancient cities of Jonson and Shakespeare together and to set Shakespeare's comic cities alongside the city satirized by Jonson and Middleton. Much the same reasoning applies to the two chapters that open the book and may, in some sense, be considered separable from it. Their subjects—the idea of the city in ancient and Renaissance sources and the idea of the city in three Roman writers—establish an essential context for the three Elizabethan writers. By this I do not mean that Shakespeare, Middleton, or even the polymath Jonson would have known all of the writers, architects, or citizens whom I cite in these early pages, although presumably they would all have been familiar with many, especially Horace, Juvenal, and Plautus whom I take up in chapter 2. I do mean, however, that the contrasts within the idea of the city which appear in the plays and entertainments reflect a way of thinking about cities which seems almost endemic. Burton Pike has made the point recently: "The widely varying historical cities of Western culture are the same city, a powerful archetype-emblem representing deep-rooted social and psychological constants." He finds, as I do, that the most enduring response to the city is ambivalence.[12] Although they did not have the word, Shakespeare, Jonson, and Middleton all find means of dramatic expression for the unresolved pride and guilt, fear and desire that ambivalence denotes. My reader may finally decide that Shakespeare is more profoundly responsive to the meaning of cities than either of his contemporaries or than any of his predecessors, known and unknown, whom I discuss earlier. But, only by considering the idea of the city in a variety of sources can the significance of his contribution and the fascination of theirs become clear.

Like the theme of country and city, the theme of two cities has its own broad critical history. I am thinking of books like Helen Rosenau's *The Ideal City* or Lidia Storoni Mazzolani's *The Idea of the City in Roman Thought* (both cited in full in notes) and more recently James Dougherty's *The Fivesquare City* and Burton Pike's *The Image of the City in Modern Literature*, mentioned earlier. Lewis Mumford's two magisterial studies on this subject, *The City in History* and *The Culture of Cities,* remain the indispensable starting point for anyone interested in the city in general and even the city in Elizabethan literature in particular.

CHAPTER ONE

Out of One City—Two

Like God, the city is an idea that provokes the sharpest kind of response. Even accounts of the founding of cities—let alone their subsequent histories—tend to expose conflicting attitudes about the social nature of man and the collective enterprise we call civilization. In the Renaissance, most urban theorists, holding optimistic views of the by-products of human collectivity, chose to ignore the scriptural tradition that Cain had founded the first city. The Counter-Reformation writer Giovanni Botero, for example, mentions the biblical account only to replace it with a socially more positive classical one:

> Cain was the first author of cities; but the poets (whom Cicero therein followed) fable that in the old world men scattered here and there, on the mountains and the plains, led a life little different from brute beasts, without laws, without conformity of customs and manner of civil conversation. And that afterward there rose up some who, having with their wisdom and their eloquence won a special reputation and authority above the rest, declared to the rude and barbarous multitude how much and how great profit they were like to enjoy if, drawing themselves to one place, they would unite themselves into one body, by an interchangeable communication and commerce of all things that would proceed thereof.[1]

The Elizabethan George Puttenham also prefers a benign urban etiology, although he turns Botero's argument around. Whereas the Italian uses the authority that humanism gave to orators to verify the greatness of cities, Puttenham uses the benefits of urban civilization to prove the value of poetry: "For it is written that Poesie was th'originall cause and occasion of [men's] first assemblies, when before the people remained in the woods and mountains. . . . Whereupon it is fayned that *Amphion* and *Orpheus*, two Poets of the first ages, one of them, to wit *Amphion*, builded up cities, and reared walles with the stones that came in heapes to the sound of his harpe, figuring thereby the mollifying of hard and stonie hearts by his sweete and eloquent perswasion."[2]

Associating the founding of cities with eloquence and poetry, however, had to ignore not only biblical tradition, but the founding myth of ancient Rome as well. That Romulus, like Cain, had been a fratricidal killer was an embarrassment of very long standing. The historians and poets of the Augustan age were eager for alternatives to the legend which made Romulus the murderer of his brother and which detractors of Rome used to trace the ruthlessness of the city to its very beginnings. Plutarch emphasizes another possibility, that Remus had died in a riot occasioned by his blasphemy in stepping across the sacred boundaries of the city. He is joined in this preference by Dionysius of Halicarnassus (*Roman Antiquities*, 1.87), by Ovid (*Fasti*, 4.809–56), and of course by Virgil (*Aeneid*, 1.292).[3] The *Aeneid* itself stresses the primacy of Aeneas—dutiful and only reluctantly ruthless—as the real founder of the city.

In terms of the foundation of a city—piety or murder, Aeneas or Romulus—lay the core of its identity.[4] Small wonder that Renaissance humanists too preferred the legendary city founders of antiquity to be poets, not murderers. For St. Augustine, however, there is more than a coincidental similarity in the fratricidal acts of the two most important city founders. His account of archetypal city foundings in *The City of God* makes no mention of Orpheus or Amphion, but broods instead on Cain: "The first founder of the earthly city was, as we have seen, a fratricide; for, overcome by envy, he slew his own brother, a citizen of the Eternal City, on pilgrimage in this world. Hence it is no wonder that long afterwards this first precedent—what the Greeks call an *archetype*—was answered by a kind of reflection, by an event of the same kind at the founding of the city which was to be the capital of the earthly city of which we are speaking, and was to rule over so many peoples."[5] Augustine's polemic against the earthly city requires him to stress the fratricide that city defenders would conceal. But, Augustine too sees in the idea of city founding the terms of a momentous choice. If identifying the city with fratricide or with poetry is a choice between finding savagery or creativity as more characteristic of human association, Augustine offers still more general alternatives, involving questions of ultimate belief and mutually opposed destinies: "I classify the human race into two branches: the one consists of those who live by human standards, the other of those who live according to God's will. I also call these two classes the two cities, speaking allegorically. By two cities, I mean two societies of human beings, one of which is predestined to reign with God for all eternity, the other doomed to undergo eternal punishment with the Devil" (15.1).

Augustine's metaphor for the divided nature of man is an image of enemy cities, mutually opposed organizations of the communal life that, like Cain and Abel, come from the same source but find antithetical destinies. The idea of two cities, one good and the other evil, is an old one, scholars having traced it back to ancient rabbinical sources.[6] *The City of God* is thus a late development of the idea in Christian terms, but it is also a powerful expression of the central theme of this book— that an idea of two cities is almost always implicit in expressions of the idea of one city. These two cities, two halves of a single urban idea, have the paradoxical relationship of the ideal and actual, bound together yet forever straining apart. A vision of one implies—leads almost inevitably to recognition of—the other. And, although characterizations of ideal cities are always criticisms, implicit or explicit, of life in the actual city, only the most wishful contemplation of the actual city is blind to the promise of a higher social order. This double image of good and evil cities reveals the city as a *coincidentia oppositorum*, the single archetype for warring social premises. Appearances of the city in literature, therefore, tend to be marked either by ambivalence or by a rhetorical vehemence that conceals deep social uneasiness. Great cities are founded by those who have murdered their brothers, probably *because* they have murdered their brothers: aspiration is compensation, shadowed forever by guilt.[7] But, the human challenge to time and nature that great cities also represent, whatever the legends of their origins, also nurtures a sense of kinship with the divine.

The City of God serves as an effective point of departure and return for the account in this chapter of the bipolar image of the city because it exposes the essential dialectic that other texts on the city conceal.

[11]

Stripped of its polemics, *The City of God* is a lexicon of the urban themes which this opening chapter presents. Augustine focuses on the love of self socialized by the promise of civic reward and secular immortality, on the nature of history, on power and temporal dominion, on the high arts of vanity and display. His doubleness in attitude about cities surfaces in the terms of his rejection of Roman civic life: his great otherworldly vision of the city of God is deeply rooted in the actual. Begun as a response to the Great Sack of Rome in 410, *The City of God* would demonstrate that the course of history depends not on the fate of Rome but on "an even greater city with an even greater founder: 'for he does not create from material which he himself did not make, nor does he employ any workmen, except those of his own creation'" (12.26).

By exposing the shallowness and ultimate futility of the Roman thirst for personal and national glory Augustine wants to diminish the prestige of Rome, especially that of the Roman past, and to demonstrate the proper object of love—the heavenly city.[8] For the material city, subject to decay, dissolution, and defeat, he substitutes an immaterial city that exists in and out of time as the ultimate goal of the earthly pilgrimage and as the symbol for a spiritual ideal to be achieved daily. But *The City of God* also reveals that, even for a committed citizen of God's city, the earthly city had an inescapable imaginative pull. In part, of course, this is due simply to Augustine's classical training. His definition of a city as a group of people bound together by a community of interests and an agreed-upon system of rights comes, via Cicero, from Scipio Major. His conception of the heavenly city is largely indebted to the Platonic vision of the city of justice, which Socrates beautifully enunciates in *The Republic:* "'Well,' said I, 'perhaps there is a pattern of it laid up in heaven for him who wishes to contemplate it and so beholding to constitute himself its citizen. But it makes no difference whether it exists now or ever will come into being. The politics of this city only will be his and of none other'" (9.592B).

Fundamentally, however, the great city was the symbol of phenomenal reality. St. Jerome lamented at its sack that "the whole world perished in one city."[9] The terms of existence, perhaps even of nature, had changed with the fall of Rome. For Augustine, the synonymity of Rome with the actual makes it serve as the negative pole of the essential dialectic: "That

City, in which it has been promised that we shall reign, differs from this earthly city as widely as the sky from the earth, life eternal from temporal joy, substantial glory from empty praises, the society of angels from the society of men, the light of the Maker of the sun and moon from the light of the sun and moon" (5.17). Such language shows that the earthly city sets the standards for the heavenly city to surpass. Because Rome was the only city the world had ever known which bound the human community together by the force of its civic idea, it alone could provide Augustine with a model for the heavenly city.[10] The whole book—indebted to Rome for its structure, its descriptive vocabulary, and its occasion for being—is in fact a long version of the classical *laudatio urbis,* dedicated like the others to proving how a particular city is uniquely worthy of praise.

Because it is part of the historical dialectic, Augustine never really tries to escape from the idea of Rome. The two cities exist together throughout time. Loyal citizens of the heavenly city use the earthly city as the arena for the struggle between good and evil, as the symbol of the life in time. Without it, there is no history, no opportunity for moral choice.

In view of Augustine's final repudiation of the earthly meaning of Rome, it is significant that the urban imagery of *The City of God* is thoroughly conventional in classical texts. Augustine transfers those classical urban topoi compatible with Christian ideology to the symbol of the heavenly city and brands the rest as superficial or futile. But the themes he takes over from Rome and redirects spiritually are, in fact, the major preoccupations of the earthly city—time and the historical process; the individual pursuit of a glorious immortality through common civic allegiance; and, above all, the overarching splendor of the city itself. This is not to deny the important differences between the Augustinian city of God and classical ideas about the city. For example, the diversity that both conceptions emphasize is for the ancient pagans largely a matter of class affiliation. Plato likens great discrepancies of wealth and poverty within a city to enemy cities, "the city of the rich and the city of the poor" (*Republic,* 4.423A). But for Augustine, any material diversity among earthly citizens collapses completely in the face of their common doom: "For all men who love pride and temporal dominion . . . are bound fast together in one fellowship; and even though they frequently fight one with another for these ends, still they are flung headlong by an equal weight of desire into the same abyss, and are united to one another by the likeness of their ways and deserts."[11]

The Christian, of course, could never agree with the Platonic Socrates that whether a perfect city exists or ever will exist does not matter. Furthermore, many of the ancient writers on the city did not recognize an antithesis between the actual and the ideal city. They tried to find aspects of the ideal in the city around them. Their perfect city was not a metaphor for the life beyond time, but a better ordering of worldly existence much on its own terms. Neither the Greeks nor the Romans ever conceived of anything other than the polis as the essential form of social life. Only with the facilities of the city—the marketplace, the place of assembly and center of worship, the gymnasium, and the theater—was it possible to live the life of reason.[12] Cities were the natural consequence of and the prudent response to human limitation. "The origin of the city," says Socrates, "is to be found in the fact that we do not severally suffice for our own needs, but each of us lacks many things" (*Republic*, 2.269B). C. Nicolet points out that the Latin word *civis*, related to the Indo-European word for family, means not citizen but fellow-citizen.[13] For the Romans, a city of one citizen was a contradiction in terms.

Thus citizenship in the fullest sense means not just the rights of a native, but a shared civility, allegiance to which during the Roman hegemony meant being a citizen of Rome. And, being a citizen of Rome gave one access to godlike being, as Seneca suggests to Marcia: "Consider that I am coming now to give you advice at your birth: 'You are about to enter a city,' I should say, 'shared by gods and men—a city that embraces the universe, that is bound by fixed and eternal laws'" (*Ad Marciam*, 18.1–2). Shared by gods and men, Seneca's city is two cities, one transitory in the life of its citizens, the other eternal.[14] The two cities are not antithetical, like Augustine's, however, but rather superimposed on one another to form a double image—the actual city blending into, yet distinguishable from, its ideal reflection. It thus partly transcends the conditions of earthly existence, as Cicero suggests in arguing that a city firmly founded will live forever: "Hence death is not natural for a State as it is for a human being, for whom death is not only necessary, but frequently even desirable" (*De re publica*, 3.23.34). When a city dies, however, the consequences are far greater than those of the death of an individual because the city is essential to the workings of the natural order in a way that the individual is not. The death of a city is like the dissolution of the universe. For Cicero, the reverse is also true: the act of mind which links the individual to his place in the universe is equivalent to citizenship: "When [the mind] realizes that it is not shut in by narrow walls as a resident of some fixed spot, but is a citizen of the whole universe, as it were of a single city—then in the midst of this universal grandeur, and with such a view and comprehension of nature, ye immortal gods, how well it will know itself" (*De legibus*, 1.23.61).

The city is both the bringer of order and the thing ordered, just as Rome, by extending citizenship to her conquered peoples, became both center and circumference of the civilized world. A fifth-century prefect belatedly praises Rome for having made "a city out of what was once a world."[15] In such a view the city is so integral to the proper workings of the natural order that it becomes not just a symbol for order but an expression of human mastery over time and nature as well.

To this theme of mastery, the ancients turn again and again. The Athenians, for instance, traditionally regarded as the first to found a Greek city, claimed duration itself as part of greatness.[16] The Romans extended their hegemony into the endless future of an eternal city. With the extension in time came an organization of space: the city was the *medius mundi locus*, a place at the center of the world. Thus Vitruvius sees the location of Rome as an ideal crossroads between north and south: "The divine mind has allotted to the Roman state an excellent and temperate region in order to rule the world" (*De architectura*, 6.11). Cicero, too, argues that "scarcely could a city placed upon any other site in Italy have more easily maintained our present widespread dominion" (*De re publica*, 2.5.10), a view that ignored the actual difficulties of the location of Rome for the sake of ideal portraiture.[17] Athens, even long after its real power had gone, could still be regarded by the second-century orator Aelius Aristides as a spiritual and aesthetic center: "From every extremity as to a device in the center of a shield, the signs of Hellas point to this region . . . the nation's common hearth" (*Panathenaic Discourse*, 13). Within the center there is a further concentration of centrality, circles within circles which culminate in the Acropolis, the soul of the city "where the high point and the center have coincided" (*Panathenaic Discourse*, 15). This physical centrality is important as a token of spiritual centrality: Aristides argues that Athens became the focus of Greek culture because she was farthest away from the barbarians.[18]

Although Aristides represents Athens as the drawing together of ever-smaller circles of spiritual perfection, when he turns to the praise of Rome there is an opposite kind of centrality, circles spreading outward from the center until the center and circumference are one. The Roman army is like a ring around the civilized world, a city wall "much greater and more impressive, in every way altogether unbreachable and inde-structible" (*Roman Oration*, 84), outshining any other.[19] The city itself is a center so inclusive that it resolves contraries, "the refuge and assembly place of all perioeci," of all those who dwell at opposite ends of the earth (*Roman Oration*, 61). This kind of centrality is geographic and concep-tual, so that if Rome spreads out to encompass the world, the world is also concentrated in Rome. For the geographer Strabo, the city replaces the world: "And again, if, on passing to the old Forum, you saw one forum after another ranged along the old one, and basilicas, and temples, and saw also the Capitolium and the works of art there and those of the Palatium and Livia's Promenade, you would easily become oblivious to everything else outside. Such is Rome" (*Geography*, 5.3.8).

This assumption of the centrality of the city elevated the actual com-ponents of the power of a city—its commercial life, for example—to the level of symbol and myth. In his praise of Athens, Isocrates transforms the Piraeus from "a market in the centre of Hellas" into a symbol of sufficiency: "the articles which it is difficult to get, one here, one there, from the rest of the world, all these it is easy to procure from Athens" (*Panegyricus*, 42). Aristides uses the mercantile topos in the *Roman Ora-tion* to demonstrate the city's command of times and seasons: "Whatever the seasons make grow and what countries and rivers and lakes and arts of Hellenes and non-Hellenes produce are brought from every land and sea, so that if one would look at all these things, he must needs behold them either by visiting the entire civilized world or by coming to this city" (*Roman Oration*, 11).

Beneath the hyperbole of panegyric, Rome seems genuinely mythic in its strength. The great city is god-like in its ability to give historical purpose to natural fecundity and to organize nature politically. The power itself has a tidal sweep, bringing together what lies within its embrace with the majesty, orderliness, and inevitability of natural law. The city rivals nature as a reminder and a touchstone of the real: "All meet here, trade, shipping, agriculture, metallurgy, all the arts and crafts that are or ever have been, all the things that are engendered or grow from the earth. And whatever one does not see here neither did nor does exist" (*Roman Oration*, 13). For Aristides, Rome is the beginning of the circle, source and destination. It contains the world while remaining whole itself. It merges with the sources of creation and moves beyond historical change. In the panorama of man and nature brought under harmonious and universal control, the expansive social fabric of the imperial city becomes a symbol of almost limitless possibility: "She has never failed them, but like the soil of earth, she supports all men; and as the sea, which receives with its gulfs all the many rivers, hides them and holds them all and still. . . . So this city has even sameness in common with the sea" (*Roman Oration*, 62).

The idea of Rome finally beggars even such overblown rhetoric. "Not only is it impossible to speak properly," Aristides confesses, "it is impossible even to see her properly" (*Roman Oration*, 6). And it is true that the Romans did have difficulty conceptualizing their unprecedented hegemony or reconciling the enormity of their power with the classical ideal of the orderly city-state.[20] The more extravagant accounts of the physical splendor of the city not only echo Aristides' rhetorical difficulties, but they also betray a latent uneasiness about the line between legitimate aspiration and dangerous aggression. The fifth-century prefect Rutilius Namatianus notes how the city dwarfs and absorbs the natural world: "Rivers are caught within your walls and buried underground: whole lakes are swallowed up by your mighty baths."[21] Claudian uses the grandeur of the city as part of its claim to ideal being and the right to rule, but his address to a fifth-century consul contains a sense that Rome has gone as far as it is possible to go: "Look round on the Seven Hills, whose gleaming gold challenges the sun's rays, on the arches carved with trophies, the temples that rise to the clouds, and all [that] Rome's many triumphs have built upon high. . . . Great consul, you are next to the gods, as you gaze over this great city, for no loftier on earth does heaven encompass!"[22]

Because they are ultimately self-praise, such accounts of the splendor of the city are particularly revealing of chronic urban ambivalence. They also suggest, in their leap toward ineffability, the difficulty of Augustine's task in countering the imaginative power of Rome. Even after the political power of Rome had greatly diminished, writers like Claudian continued to focus on the physical grandeur of the city. Through the evidence of its buildings, the city could remain a symbol of aspiration and creative control over nature, if not over time. In some ways, as we shall see in the Renaissance preoccupation with Rome's ruins, Rome was an even more evocative symbol in decline than she had been in prosperity. Her remaining physical splendor pointed simultaneously to undeniable human accomplishment and equally undeniable loss. The aspect of the city remained as a token of the human condition, its architecture a symbol of the challenge to mutability as well as of the power of change.

Throughout its history, then, the power of a city over the imagination is located in, as well as expressed by, its physical presence. The city, with its geometric, man-made forms, is a living, changing artifact, a work of art that is also the embodiment of the historical record. For the Romans in particular, the city was so closely identified with unfolding historical process that the best hopes for personal immortality lay in the physical aspect of the city. To identify oneself with the city by adding to its store of monuments was to identify oneself with forces working against nature and time. It was a way of becoming a monument, forging from nature what is greater than nature. To Cicero, for example, the exchange of a brief life for an enduring artifact was one of the greatest gifts of the city: "For to those that died in the service of the State our ancestors, as a return for the shortness of life, gave an everlasting memorial" (*Philippic*, 9.2.4).

Making the city more splendid was in itself a historical act, as Vitruvius suggests when he equates building and conquest as expressions of national glory. He tells Augustus that "the state was not only made greater through you by its new provinces, but the majesty of empire also was expressed through the eminent dignity of its public buildings" (*De architectura*, 1, pref. 2). Augustus himself thought building so important that he enumerated each of his efforts to beautify Rome in the *Res Gestae*. His example was telling: Tacitus records the tradition that Nero set fire to Rome because "he was seeking the glory of founding a new capital, and endowing it with his own name" (*Annals*, 15.40).

By bringing together events long separated in time into a shared and eternal present through the stasis of architectural form, the city challenges time in another way. The Romans were so impressed by the temporal challenge in urban architecture that specific architectural forms evolved for the one purpose of commemorating the single, culminating event in the heroic life—the triumph.[23] The architectural forms of the triumph—the column and arch—epitomized the city's challenge to time and its close identification with its heroes, for the triumph consummated a relationship between the city and the hero. The city thus turns the heroic act into architecture and architecture into history.

Like other kinds of urban symbolism, triumphal architecture demonstrates contrasting tendencies in classical thinking about the city—to see the city as the distillation of what is human or to make the city more divine than human, greater than the sum of its human parts. This unresolved contrast is perfectly captured in classical personifications of the city as a goddess, the symbol as well as the source of the *Tyche* or Fortune of the city. Usually, the nobly proportioned city goddess wears a crown of city walls and bears a cornucopia to symbolize bounty, abundance, protection, and prosperity. Like other, less concretely visual images of the city, the city goddess is the human figure idealized—lifelike, but also larger and far nobler than any merely human figure.[24] She is at one and the same time mother, mistress, and muse, as Pericles suggests when he tells the Athenians, "You must daily fix your gaze upon the power of Athens and become lovers of her, and when the vision of her greatness has inspired you, reflect that all this has been acquired by men of courage who knew their duty and in the hour of conflict were moved by a high sense of honour" (Thucydides, *History*, 2.43.1). Cato's dedication to Rome made him *"urbi pater urbique maritus,"* husband and father of the city. The title *urbi maritus* itself was more or less conventional praise for a dedicated citizen.[25] This dedication to the mother-mistress-wife figure,

Cicero tells us, is absolute: "For her it is our duty to die, to her to give ourselves entirely, to place on her altar, and, as it were, to dedicate to her service, all that we possess" (*De legibus*, 2.2.5).

And it is here finally that Rome and Jerusalem, the cities of Cicero and Augustine, come together—in this pull of the absolute to which the most influential characterizations of the city respond. Even without Augustine's belief in a city beyond time, the dedicated citizen of Rome articulates standards of commitment that are no less total and creates the idea of a city that is hardly less spiritualized. The power, size, and splendor of Rome so overwhelmed the individual observer that it took on mythic implications far outlasting the splendor itself, as the famous example of Petrarch's awed response to his first view of Rome makes clear. Only the contrary pull of his commitment to the city of God enabled Augustine to resist the centripetal pull of Rome, and he could not completely escape its influence. Thus the tendency of civic consciousness toward ideal urban portraiture carries with it inherent disadvantages. The force of convention and tradition over ideas of the city, combined with the imaginative power of cities themselves, creates strong currents of attraction and repulsion around the literary images of antithetical cities. To the citizen of another city, the splendid personification of mother-mistress-muse becomes the portrait of the city as whore.

The *locus classicus* of these antithetical female images is the Book of Revelation, the most powerful lexicon of urban imagery.[26] Even Augustine's antithetical rhetoric pales beside the violent polarities of John of Patmos, for whom the mystical imagery of the celestial city opposes the personification of earthly cities as harlots. Here is Jerusalem, "the holy city, new Jerusalem, coming down from God out of heaven, prepared as a bride adorned for her husband" (21:2). Here is Rome, "arrayed in purple and scarlet colour, and decked with gold and precious stones and pearls, having a golden cup in her hand full of abominations and filthiness of her fornication" (17:4). Far from denying the physical splendor of Rome, John combines the imagery of urban magnificence with a rhetoric of religious and sexual denunciation in a portrait filled with strong emotional currents. It is the beauty of Rome that makes her particularly treacherous, particularly evil. It singles her out for devastation at the end of time: "Thus with violence shall that great city Babylon be thrown down, and shall be found no more at all" (18:21–22).

Yet despite his ferocious distaste for Rome, John is still very much within her sphere of influence, unable to define an ideal city apart from Rome. The door opening in heaven at the beginning of Revelation leads to an apocalyptic version of the Roman tribunal, twenty-four elders seated in a semicircle round the judge's throne in a great basilica paved with glass and marble.[27] The celestial city itself is a perfect cube in form, classic in its symmetry. It testifies magnificently to the power and majesty of its prince and surpasses—because it cannot ignore—the splendor of Rome. Although it may not need the light of the sun and the moon, John does not forget to equip his city with the river of life or with the secure, defensive location of a mountain citadel. The nature and meaning of the celestial city, like the nature and meaning of Rome, manifest themselves through architectural allegory. Church and city unite: "And I saw no temple therein: for the Lord God Almighty and the Lamb are the temple of it" (21:22). The city, apotheosized, has become an artifact beyond time and change and nature.

With the reinterpretation of the ancient past in the Renaissance came a renewal of interest—both theoretical and practical—in the idea of the city and in the secular rewards of civic life. Like their predecessors in Greece and Rome, Italian urban theorists identified the city with the creative, civilized life free from molestation and with a historical record of renewed importance. The city afforded the men of the Renaissance, as it had afforded the ancients, a visible record of the passage of time, of human aspirations and achievement. Like Aristotle, the Florentine Remigio de Girolami found the city to be so essential an expression of man's best nature that "without a city the individual cannot achieve perfection at all."[28] Without a city, man is no longer a citizen and thus no longer a man, for he is by nature a civic animal. This social instinct generates the architectural instinct. In *De re aedificatoria*, the first architectural treatise of the Renaissance written about 1450, Leone Battista Alberti writes: "You shall find no body who has the Means but what has an Inclination to be building something . . . even when we are employed upon other

Things, we cannot keep our Thoughts and Imaginations from Projecting some Edifice."[29]

But building was part of a much larger program of social engagement, stimulated by finding models of active citizenship in the ancient city-states. The humanists of the Quattrocento quoted enthusiastically from a letter of Cicero: "There is a place reserved in heaven where all those who have laboured to preserve, augment and assist the fatherland, can enjoy eternal blessedness."[30] The chancellor of Florence, Leonardo Bruni, insisted that, like Socrates, whatever took place outside the walls of his city was of no interest to him.[31]

For these Italian urbanists, as for the citizens of the ancient city-states, the city was the significant arena for the historical actions of great men. The epitome of such a city was, of course, ancient Rome. Rome exercised so strong a hold over their imaginations as a symbol of the power and magnificence that a city ought to have that archaeology appeared almost simultaneously with philology as the first major interests of new learning. For a long time the greatest names in humanism were also the greatest names in archaeology, men like Flavio Biondo, Poggio, and above all Alberti.[32]

In their eyes, the Roman ruins were an evocative symbol of the instability of fortune. But they were also tangible proof of the former glory of the city and thus a symbol of human potential. Again and again, the architects argue that without the ruins, descriptions in classical texts of the power and beauty of the city would be incredible. Alberti writes in *De re aedificatoria:* "The Sepulchres and other Remains of the ancient Magnificence, every where to be found, are a great Inducement and Argument with us for believing many Things related by Historians, which might otherwise have seemed incredible" (p. x).

The humanists were awed by the ruins for their majesty and for the immediacy they gave to the past. Having been warned that he might be disappointed by the ruined city, Petrarch writes that "such reality I am happy to say has diminished nothing and instead increased everything. In truth Rome was greater, and greater are its ruins than I imagined. I no longer wonder that the whole world was conquered by this city but that I was conquered so late" (*Familiarium rerum,* 2:14). Although the ruins were an inevitable reminder of death and mutability, they were also an emblem of time past living on to confront and challenge the present. Thus they served not only to verify the historical record, but also to exemplify the importance of the ancient city as a model and inspiration for humanist activity. In particular, as Ricardo Quinones has argued, Rome served as a vivid exemplum for the Renaissance preoccupation with time. For Petrarch, the ruins demonstrated the heartening possibility of a limited triumph over time, reawakening his hopes for the worth of human endeavor. Late in his life he argues that, although the city, like everything else, decays daily, change alone cannot affect the idea of Rome. Time works physical changes, but the continuity of the historical record is located finally in the mind: "But Rome has not fallen to such ruin, and however seriously decayed, she is still something more than a name. Her walls and palaces are crumbling, but the glory of her immortal name remains. . . . The fame of the city will not be lessened until the end of the world; Rome will always be the world's high water mark."[33]

Joachim Du Bellay inherits Petrarch's preoccupation with the ruins of Rome, but he sees the city more soberly as a symbol of self-consuming glory. His reactions to the city in the sonnet sequence *Antiquitez de Rome* are deeply divided. On the one hand he is able to assert, like Petrarch, that Rome is not completely subject to time:

> Et que si bien le temps destruit les Republiques,
> Les temps ne mist si bas la Romaine hauteur,
> Que le chef deterré aux fondemens antiques
> Qui prindrent nom de luy, fust decouvert menteur.
> [Sonnet 8][34]

But against assertions like these runs a melancholy crosscurrent of awareness that time consumes everything except change itself: "Ce qui est ferme, est par le temps destruit, / Et ce qui fuit, au temps fait re-sistance" (Sonnet 3). In a curious way, however, Du Bellay's despair of mutability is separable from and has little effect on his historical estimate of Rome. He reiterates that the power of Rome at its height was limited only by "la mesme rondeur de la terre et de l'onde" (Sonnet 8). Like classical panegyrists, he makes the city universal by asserting that what-ever existed in the world—whatever Egypt produced, whatever wisdom Athens had, whatever riches came from Asia—could be seen in Rome

(Sonnet 29). Throughout the *Antiquitez*, Du Bellay elevates the city to tragic stature, an example of self-consuming greatness: "Rome seule pouvoit à Rome ressembler, / Rome seule pouvoit Rome faire trembler" (Sonnet 6). The *Antiquitez* advances several possible causes for the fall of Rome: fratricidal conflict caused by a surfeit of heroic men (Sonnet 10); "l'audace Romaine," which challenged the heavens (Sonnet 11); the natural course of growth and decay (Sonnet 20); or a tragic destiny forecast at the origins of the city when its walls were stained with brother's blood (Sonnet 24). Whatever the cause, Du Bellay makes the fall the consequence of forces within the city itself: only Rome could make Rome tremble. Like Cicero, he sees the death of the city as an example of the universal mortality but also one uniquely comparable to the final return to chaos, when everything "retourneront encor'à leur premier discord" (Sonnet 22). Alive, Rome was the ornament of the world; dead, it is the world's tomb. Like the ancients, like Petrarch, Du Bellay makes Rome a symbol for the sum of earthly potential: "tout ce qu'ont peu nature, / L'art, et le ciel" (Sonnet 5). But perhaps the most revealing image, other than the sight of the ruins themselves, occurs in Sonnet 19 when he compares Rome to Pandora, that quintessential gift from the gods:

> Tout le malheur qui nostre aage dedore,
> Tout le bonheur des siecles les plus vieux,
> Rome du temps de ses premiers ayeux
> Le tenoit clos, ainsi qu'une Pandore.

Because Pandora represents "an irresistible compound of good and evil," she is a particularly apt symbol for a city that provoked such profound ambivalence. Understood as a "consummate blend of blessing and curse," Pandora became among French humanists a conventional personification of a city.[35] Dora and Erwin Panofsky argue that Jean Cousin's design for the triumphal arch of Henri II's entry into Paris in 1549, which shows a kneeling Lutetia holding a classical vase containing blessings underneath the motto, "Lutetia Nova Pandora," was intended originally to contain two antithetical female figures, one portraying Rome as the first Pandora bringing nothing but evils, and the other, Lutetia, as a new Pandora of good omen.[36] With such an allusion, Du Bellay finds himself in the equally ambivalent company of the Revelation prophet and

St. Augustine. But the glorious past and ruined splendor of the city serve him finally as an emblem of the human condition: "Rome fut tout le monde, et tout le monde est Rome" (Sonnet 26). Although, for both Petrarch and Du Bellay, it is possible to find in the ruins the basis for humanistic faith and poetic aspiration, that faith always has to be tempered by the dismal contrast between past and present. The moral decay of Rome in the Renaissance was legion: there were enough prostitutes in the city to justify Revelation's name calling about the Whore of Babylon. A male visitor to the city was likely to go home with a case of syphilis.[37]

Beyond its ability to verify the past and to signify the power of mutability, Rome also provided the Renaissance humanists with a new way of regarding their own cities and an ideal upon which to model them. In Gasparo Contarini's historical treatise of Venice, *De magistratibus et republica Venetorum*, for example, ancient Rome lies constantly in the background as the city that Venice will challenge and surpass. On the one hand, Contarini is eager to give Venice those aspects of greatness for which we have seen the ancients praising Rome. The flow of trade is so great that it is as if "the City of *Venice* onely were a common and generall market to the whole world."[38] He finds the maritime situation of the city "so fitte and convenient for all things" that it seems the product of divine rather than merely human design. Contarini's Elizabethan translator, Lewis Lewkenor, is particularly struck with Venice as a miraculous work of art, marveling to "see such pallaces, monasteries, temples, towers, turrets, and pinacles reaching up unto the cloudes, founded upon Quagmires, and planted uppon such unfirme moorish and spungie foundations" (Preface, A3). But Contarini also contrasts Venice sharply with the example of Rome, arguing that greater longevity of Venice as a republic proves her to be founded on eternal principles of nature. He finds a greater civic devotion among Venetian citizens than among ancient Romans because the Venetians serve the city without expecting any secular reward of statues, tombs, or personal monuments. And the greatness of Venice is accomplished without the bellicosity of ancient Rome.[39]

Although equally eager to establish a relationship with the ancient city, the Florentines saw their city not as the contemporary rival to ancient Rome, but rather as the truest descendant and heir of republican Rome. The mythology of the city employs a particularly striking blend of Christian and Roman imagery. Often pictured as the repentant Magdalen, Florence was a daughter of the whore of Babylon whose repentance guaranteed her importance as the site of Christian renewal. Florence inherited Rome's centrality—in Savonarola's favorite image, as the umbilicus of Italy; her Cathedral would stand till the end of the world.[40] Although patriotic *laudes* had been a familiar medieval genre, rediscovered classical praises of the city furnished new urban themes and images. Thus Leonardo Bruni's description of Florence in the *Laudatio Florentinae urbis* (1403) specifically borrows from Aristides' praise of Athens. Using the recently rediscovered laws of perspective and optics, Bruni tries to discover why the Florentine landscape looks like one great scenic structure with the city appearing as the geometric center of four concentric circles. At the very center is the Palazzo Vecchio, the embodiment of central power in the republic. From a wider perspective the Palazzo reveals itself as the center of a larger center, the entire city looking from a distance like a castle towering over a larger Florence.[41] Bruni locates the special beauty of Florence in principles of symmetry and harmony, principles that architects later would use to make blueprints for ideal cities: "The city herself stands in the center, like a guardian and master; towns surround her on the periphery [of the picture], each in its place. A poet might well speak of the moon surrounded by the stars; and the whole is very beautiful to behold."[42]

For Bruni, Aristides' image of Athens provides a way of seeing a symbolic order in the actual configuration of Florence. Classical form had awakened new possibilities of meaning in the present. In medieval Florence Giotto had designed the Campanile as a monument that would rise over the rooftops to symbolize the great craftsmen of the city. But the Campanile was itself later dominated by the great classical dome Brunelleschi raised over the Cathedral to reflect the new earthly interests and aspirations of the Florentine humanists.[43] Thus the relationship between the values of the community and the physical constitution of the city became increasingly important, and in Florence in the late fourteenth and early fifteenth centuries comparisons between the republic's institution and its buildings were often made.[44]

The architects of the Italian Renaissance came to regard the entire city, and not just the Cathedral at its center, as a work of art. With architecture assuming the new historical obligation to embody the present while reviving the classical past, it was no longer enough for the city to be shaped by the haphazard growth of economies or populations. The irregular, vertical skyline of the medieval city with its heavenward orientation gave way to the uniform profile of the Renaissance plaza and the long, open vistas that stretched out to a vanishing point on the horizon.[45] The creation of a uniform urban beauty was a primary goal of the humanist architects.

Planners like Alberti and Leonardo sought to shape cities according to their understanding of the dictates of reason so that the city might be brought closer to the rational order of the cosmos. A well-designed city would be more natural, not less.[46] According to Palladio, to be natural is to be rational in structure and practical in design.[47] If the shape of cities, moreover, could conform to reason, it was only logical to conclude that an ideal city must be achievable on earth. This premise underlies the variety of urban blueprints in architectural treatises that existed in numerous manuscripts or went through successive editions throughout the fifteenth and sixteenth centuries. Franceso di Giorgio Martini and Giorgio Vasari designed octagonal cities, Fra Gioconda a circular one, and Dürer, the first city planner outside Italy, drew plans for a rectangular city resembling a Roman camp. Filarete creates the first, wholly planned ideal city, a star-shaped, sixteen-sided city plan that—however excessively geometric and unlikely it may appear to modern eyes—was, according to Pierre Lavédan, firmly grounded in reality.[48]

Several main directions of Renaissance urban planning existed amid this proliferation of ideal cities. The preoccupation with geometric form so striking in Alberti's *De re aedificatoria* or Palladio's *Quattro Libri* stemmed from a concern, ultimately Pythagorean in origin, with harmonic and mathematically exact interrelations of part and whole.[49] In the ninth book of *De re aedificatoria* Alberti outlines a complex theory of the proportion of numbers, the exact ratios determined by the kind and size of a building. Rudolf Wittkower argues that Alberti knew the individual could not perceive the correctness of proportion between height and length of a column, for example, or between section and whole of a building. Such harmonic perfection represented an absolute value, independent of the ability to perceive it, and an echo of the universal and celestial harmonies.[50] The idea had such profound associations that a cultivated Renaissance humanist like Palladio's patron Daniele Barbaro, under a Renaissance dome, might well experience a faint echo of the inaudible music of the spheres.[51] By constructing buildings, plazas, and even whole cities according to the absolute truths of mathematics, the Renaissance architect would demonstrate how art imitates the universal design and how human communities ideally could conform to natural law.

The architects' concern for proportion coincided on the one hand with a careful attention to practical requirements and on the other to a firm notion that the design of a city should express the social order. Alberti and Palladio write architectural treatises that are also handbooks for the builder. Although Filarete weaves an elaborate fictional framework around the architectural treatise he addressed to Francesco Sforza, he too does not fail to consider mundane matters. Clearly plans for octagonal, circular, or star-shaped cities are not tied to a particular site. Yet a closer examination of Filarete's plans for the imaginary city he calls Sforzinda does indicate how attention to symmetry and geometrical form could reflect political hierarchies and promote urban regulation. Like the centers of most ideal cities and many actual Italian cities, the center of Filarete's city is a large piazza containing those buildings at the heart of the political and social orders: the Cathedral, the Palace of Justice and possibly the prison, the Municipal Palace, and the Palace of the Signori. The emphasis within a political structure on different institutions determined the size and prominence of a new building. When the Medici rose to power in Florence, for example, the center of the city actually moved from the marketplace in front of the Palazzo of the Signori to the Casa Medici, much as the center of ancient Rome shifted from the old republican Forum Romanum to the imperial fora: the internal form of the city changes to mirror new realities.[52]

Alberti devotes a good part of the fifth book of *De re aedificatoria* to explaining how the buildings and situation of a republican city-state should differ from the buildings and situation of the city of a tyrant: "A good King takes Care to have his City strongly fortified in those Parts, which are most liable to be assaulted by a foreign Enemy: a Tyrant, having no less Danger to fear from his Subjects than from Strangers, must fortify his City no less against his own People, than against Foreigners" (bk. 5, chap. 1, p. 82).

The palace of a tyrant should stand entirely separate from all other buildings, "in a Manner out of the City and in it at the same Time" (bk. 5, chap. 1, p. 86). The ability of architecture to reify the social structure is even more clearly demonstrated in Leonardo's plan for a city on two levels, connected by steps. He attempts to distinguish architecturally between the workers and the governors by restricting shops, the movement of wagons and beasts, and all commerce to the lower level and giving over the upper level to the aristocracy.[53]

Filarete conceives of Sforzinda as an imaginative expression of the power and magnificence of his patron Francesco Sforza. Hence he designs the castello before he turns his attention to the piazza, the center of all civic life. From the piazza run sixteen wide roads, eight leading to towers at the outer, projecting angles of the city walls, eight to the city gates at each of the inner angles. These sixteen roads, eight of which run beside canals, are themselves connected by a road running like a ring around the middle of the city. This, in basic form, is the *ville radieuse,* the most common plan for the ideal city in the fifteenth century.[54] In Filarete's masterful design, the *ville radieuse* provides easy communication among parts of the city as well as direct access to and from the center of the city in order to facilitate commerce and defense.

Filarete has also carefully considered the relationship of his ideal city to the surrounding countryside, defining it not as the antithesis of landscape, but rather as the final product of a collaboration between man and nature. Since Filarete imagines Sforzinda as a new city created solely by agreement between prince and architect, he grants himself total freedom to imagine the relationship of city and country. It is interesting to notice, therefore, how closely his description resembles the relationships of actual cities to their environs. Filarete extends the organization of the *ville radieuse* outward to the country in a series of concentric circles of gradually larger tracts of land. Travelers to Sforzinda would pass through large tracts to smaller plots—that is, through a landscape of increasing density—until they reached the central unit: a city, like Florence, a circle within a circle, harmoniously compact behind its walls.

[29]

Sforzinda, planned city and work of art, must be filled and inhabited after the buildings are completely finished. But Filarete would hardly design an ideal Renaissance city without seeking at some point explicit authority from the ancients for its form and style. Hence he relates the archaeological discovery of an ancient golden book, which describes the ancient city that once stood on the site chosen for Sforzinda's port. Its buildings have foreshadowed the architectural style of the new city. Indeed Filarete's prince even decides that further building should proceed in outright imitation of the plans and drawings contained in the golden book. This discovery becomes the pivotal point of the entire treatise, for Filarete turns away from his fairly complete design for the structures necessary to maintain physical life in the city to describe new plans for an architectural allegory of the moral virtues and social values that underlie the spiritual order of the community. The monuments and statuary of Sforzinda become emblems for the intellectual traditions important to Renaissance culture. Here the city as a work of art reaches its fullest extension. Filarete's invention of the golden book provides him with the symbol that almost all Renaissance urbanists sought for models and authority to return to classical design—or to their version of it. Ancient cities were considered to be examples of the rational city: to imitate or better still to rebuild one was to obey both reason and nature. Filarete uses the golden book to make Sforzinda what Florentines and Venetians were trying to make their cities through historiography—ancient cities that had once existed and were now brought back to life.

One result of humanism's identification of the new polis with the old was a proliferation of arguments for the city as the ideal form of social organization. Not surprisingly, the arguments echo many of the themes we found in the ancients. Renaissance urbanists insist on the city as a civilizing force for otherwise barbarous human beings. It is the ideal home of all sacred and secular learning. The city is also an ideal way of recognizing and using the pluralism and diversity of the human community, as Renaissance republicans were quick to point out.[55] To an urbanist like Alberti, the pluralism of the city afforded a personal liberty and fullness of life unknown to country dwellers. Furthermore, because the city remained unified despite its diversity, it came to signify a kind of earthly completeness, as Castiglione suggests when he praises the Duke of Urbino for creating a palace so complete that "it appeared not a Palace, but a Citie in forme of a Palace."[56] Renaissance enthusiasm for the ideal potential of actual city life produced an equation of the city with the monastery through a common association with the city of God. Erasmus asks: "What else is a city but a great monastery?"[57] In their ideal manifestations both forms of social life prepared their inhabitants for life in the city to come.

Yet even in this apparently unequivocal celebration of a realizable ideal city it is possible to find a darker undertone. More's *Utopia* is a good example. Like the architects More grants himself a large measure of imaginative freedom to shape the conditions of life in the Utopian kingdom, enumerating the mundane elements of urban living with the thoroughness of an architect.[58] Like Sforzinda, Utopian cities are planned from the ground up. More importantly, they are identical "in language, traditions, customs, and laws" (*Utopia*, p. 113). "The person who knows one of the cities," says Hythloday, "will know them all" (p. 117). The uniformity and regularity we have seen in humanist urban blueprints come, in Utopia, to regulate every aspect of life. With time divided between work, devotion, and "profitable" recreation, with property held in common and competition allowed only in the creation of gardens, the cities of Utopia do resemble great monasteries. The austerity of Utopian law eliminates manifestations of individual freedom or idiosyncrasy in order to guarantee the righteousness of the whole.

Amid this overwhelming regularity, the most attractive features of urban planning in Utopia not surprisingly involve its harmonious and interdependent relations with the country. Citizens alternate between the two ways of life in a controlled sequence (although More does suggest that some prefer to reside permanently in the country). There is no sense here of city and country as hostile forces. The country provides food, the city provides learning and a center for worship. But More's recognition of the ideal potential of the earthly city created whole contains an irony highlighted for us by the contrast it offers to the architectural city plans. The physical orderliness of the architects' cities has for its ultimate goal the liberation of human creativity, the realization of social life as a work of art. Eliminating social disorder in More's cities, however, has the effect

[31]

of stamping out the very freedom and individuality that an urbanist like Alberti sees as the hallmark of urban life. With no room to grow, with little tolerance for cultural diversity, and with almost every aspect of life controlled in the rage for an order that is ultimately anti-urban, Utopian cities are the wrong kind of art. One leaves them with a sigh of relief.

CHAPTER TWO

Writers in the Ancient City: Horace, Juvenal, and Plautus

For writers, as for other inhabitants of the earthly city, the city offers simultaneously the best and worst possibilities in the world of experience. As the best hope for fullness of experience, the city would seem to provide the raw material of poetic creation. It is a model of form and an instance of content. But the city may also seem to oppose personal integrity in general and artistic integrity in particular. In the planned cities of the Italian Renaissance, this ambivalence manifests itself in the straight avenues leading to and from the central piazza. The plan allows citizen and visitor an efficient passage between the natural world outside the walls and the heart of the city within. Yet this spatial organization, which seems so beautiful an expression of urban sociability, is primarily military in function, allowing the speedy transfer of weaponry into and out of the city. As Lewis Mumford has argued, the city has always "combined the maximum amount of protection with the greatest incentives to aggression: it offered the widest possible freedom and diversity, yet imposed a drastic system of compulsion and regimentation. . . . The city had both a despotic and divine aspect."[1] At its best, the city is a common enterprise for the common good, but the solidarity of the commonwealth may come to look like the threat of the herd. Following the Socratic admonition to cultivate the city within is difficult enough in itself. But it becomes even more difficult when it can proceed only by means of an enervating struggle against the city without.

Accommodating the city within to the city without is thus part of the larger accommodation of the One to the Many, which is a central urban theme and a practical urban problem. Literary statements of the conflict assume comic, satiric, and utopian forms, and again ancient Rome provides the appropriate starting point for considering them. Horace and Juvenal are not the only major satirists of Rome; but they have given their names to two major branches of the satiric *gens*, with Horatian satire denoting greater moderation than its Juvenalian counterpart. Although their themes do not differ radically, as we shall see, Horace's Rome almost seems to be a different city than Juvenal's. Both writers call Rome a monster, but the label is far more accurate in Juvenal's nightmare city of seemingly limitless depravity. Thus I would like to apply the adjectives Horatian and Juvenalian not only to two different kinds of satire, but to two different cities whose importance lies precisely in the radically different estimates of human nature which they imply. For generations of writers, including those of the English Renaissance on whom we will later concentrate, Horace and Juvenal provide the two most influential models of contrasting poetic responses to urban life. Their ideas of the city compose the first half of this chapter. The second half is taken up by a discussion of the comic city of Plautus, because it too provides essential background for the comic cities of Shakespeare, Jonson, and Middleton to come. In Plautine comedy the conflict between the One and the Many takes on an obsessive character. But, in all three Roman writers, the idea of Rome generates dichotomies of characterization, language, and theme which are almost Augustinian in severity. As Romans, they do not escape from the notion that the city occupies a central position in any meaningful definition of human nature. But as imaginative artists, participant-observers by profession, they also stand somewhat removed from their culture to be alert to its incongruities. In the satires of Horace and Juvenal, Rome's greatness of being seems to prevent individual self-fulfillment, not to foster it. And, in the ostensibly Greek cities of Plautine comedy, the psychic penalties of Roman life stand revealed.

The Satirist as Citizen

This almost paradoxical urban combination of protection and aggression, of freedom and regimentation poses particular hazards for poets as deeply involved in urban life as Horace and Juvenal. At the simplest level, the very size and diversity of the urban world are problematic, offering both stimulus and distraction. More importantly, the satirist's relation to the city, almost by definition, demonstrates the ambivalence that we have been tracking in historical attitudes toward the city. Satire presupposes citizenship. The satirist is tied to the city not only because the city is always his subject, but also because the satirist can express the dissatisfaction that is the nub of satire only from a position within the society under attack.[2]

This social precariousness may also explain why the satirist so often commands a prominent position in his verse, for it is only by this act of self-inclusion that the poet can perpetuate his claim. As Maynard Mack has suggested, he must convince his listeners that he is moved to satire not by vindictiveness or vanity but by their shortcomings.[3] The ridicule to which he subjects the city, therefore, does not imply fidelity to a different city—unless implicitly to the city within—but to the ideal aspect of their shared everyday world. Like Augustine, the satirist recognizes the existence of two cities—the eternal Rome that exists as an ideal in the mind, an occasion for *laus,* and the Rome that is an everyday landscape, an occasion for *vituperatio.* Moved to satire by the discrepancy between them, his emotional source is recognizably akin to the millenary hopes of John of Patmos in the poetic amalgam of fascination and dissatisfaction, the conflict of quotidian citizenship and higher loyalties.

To many, Horace's portrait of Rome in the *Satires* and *Epistles* is remarkable for its subordination of politics and public life—what Niall Rudd calls a "conscious rejection of public life."[4] In the *Satires* the political world represented by Maecenas and Augustus exists at the horizon of daily consciousness, as a matter of reflection and constant but indirect pressure. Horace does not turn away, however, from the more inclusive preoccupation of every ancient citizen, his proper relation to society. Horace never underestimates the difficulty of this essential urban task, complicated as it is by the very size, wealth, luxury, power, and diversity for which panegyrists celebrate cities. Again and again in the *Satires* and *Epistles,* panegyric themes appear in a new guise, *laus* becoming *vituperatio,* reasons to glorify the city causing ethical confusion in her citizens. For the panegyrist, nature pales before the magnificence of Rome.

The monumentality of the city dwarfs the natural world in seeking to control it. For Horace, however, Rome's challenge to nature is a symptom of how far the city has moved from all that is natural: "est modus in rebus, sunt certi denique fines, / quos ultra citraque nequit consistere rectum." [There is measure in all things. There are, in short, fixed bounds, beyond and short of which right can find no place] (*Satires,* 1.1.106–7). For all kinds of life, nature represents an ethic of utility and sufficiency. Seamen and farmers saving for retirement claim to model themselves on the thrifty ant (*Satires,* 1.1.28–40). Even the poet aspires to sufficiency in every poem: "Iam satis est. ne me Crispini scrinia lippi / compilasse putes, verbum non amplius addam." [Well, 'tis enough. Not a word more will I add, or you will think I have rifled the rolls of blear-eyed Crispinus] (*Satires,* 1.1.120–21).

Significantly, Horace reaches the point of poetic sufficiency here not only when he has said enough, but when his audience has reached its limit. The natural and social standards unite. Horace's miser, however, betrays nature and man in his passion for accumulation, in his evasion of the idea of limit. When nature governs culture, Horace insists, money serves a natural function—to buy bread, greens, a measure of wine, "quis humana sibi doleat natura negatis" (1.1.75). The acquisitive man, however, finds himself in a spiral of material fears, lying awake to guard the treasure that was supposed to protect him. His indifference to nature extends even to neglect of the family that nature has provided, provoking in them a denial of the familial loyalty on which the social order depends.

Daily life in the city exhibits, even encourages, excessive behavior, extreme attitudes, and an immoderate use of material abundance that suggests indifference to the natural order. The wealth upon which the panegyrists of Rome dwell as proof that the city is the mythic reason for natural fecundity is, for Horace, a mixed blessing. The resources of the magnificent city and its monumental splendor produce in the individual the darker, more ambiguous qualities of an aggressive splendor, overweening pride and egotism, excessive self-interest, and an absurd overrefinement in matters of taste. The *Satires* abound in examples of distorted uses of the natural order. Thus in 2.2, the countryman Ofellus's most telling examples of absurd gourmandism display the triumph of misguided cultural standards over natural requirements. The men who eat peacocks rather than pullets, care where fish were caught, and require the largest of mullets are corrupted by the appearance of things: "jejunus raro stomachus volgaria temnit" [only a stomach that seldom feels hunger scorns common things] (38). The main objects of Horace's irony in the two major culinary satires, 2.4 and 2.8, are the absurd pedantry of the zealot gourmet Catius and the vulgarity of the arriviste host Nasidienus.[5] In demonstrating Rome's awesome material dominion, which was a central panegyric theme, they reveal its potential for abuse: the natural satisfaction of physical need has given way completely to ridiculous self-display.

Although it cannot be argued that Horace directly implicates the power of Rome in the distorted behavior of Catius and Nasidienus, he does link the city's enlargement of physical possibility to profound confusion. As the panegyrists claimed, Rome's dominion has turned the natural world into an object for Roman consumption. But, instead of being themselves enlarged by living in an urban world of such plenitude, the would-be connoisseurs Catius and Nasidienus are belittled and exposed by plenitude. They are almost betrayed by it. Catius elevates the recipe to a ridiculous metaphysical status, imagining that the rules that he is hastening home from a gastronomic lecture to write down have a force greater than that of Pythagorean or Platonic philosophy. The ambitious Nasidienus is far more harshly treated. The noble image of the Platonic symposia to which any later banquet poem implicitly alludes reminds us how far the *cena Nasidienus* stands from the conditions of ideal fellowship.[6] Status-oriented food has replaced philosophy, and social ambition has replaced friendship. In order to glorify himself in the eyes of Maecenas, Nasidienus would pervert the ideal banquet's conjunction of nature and culture. Horace hints lightly at the larger social implications of Nasidienus's behavior. When a canopy falls on the table, the host mourns as if his son had died. But the guests restore a sense of proportion to the whole episode by capping the revenge of nature with one of their own; they leave the banquet early, having tasted nothing at all.

Everywhere in the *Satires,* then, the abundance and diversity so integral to conventional definitions of the great city spread bewilderment among the citizens of Rome, robbing them of central principles, content, and a coherent sense of self. Urban restlessness comes in several forms. There is, first of all, the feverish physical pace of life in Rome, as when

Horace imagines himself in *Satire* 2.6 up at dawn to stand surety for someone, then hurrying back in a frenzy shoving aside those slower of pace. More significant, although equally symptomatic, is the discontent and envy that prompt the famous question which begins the *Satires*— "Qui fit, Maecenas." How comes it, asks Horace, that no one living is content with the lot that choice has given him or chance has thrown his way. The soldier would change places with the trader, the lawyer with the farmer, the countryman with the man in town. The theme is a commonplace. Horace is even more piqued by a similar, but more protean form of restlessness in the spectacle of people unable to persist for one hour in liking the same things. In *Epistle* 1.1 he takes care to distinguish this restlessness from the morally unexceptionable phenomenon of urban diversity, "men swayed by different aims and hobbies" (1.1.81). The Roman capacity for protean behavior is all the more alarming in that it transcends economic boundaries, affecting even the poor man who senselessly changes his garret, his bed, and his barber. Horace himself is not immune from this behavior:

> rides: quid, mea cum pugnat sententia secum,
> quod petiit spernit, repetit quod nuper omisit,
> aestuat et vitae disconvenit ordine toto,
> diruit, aedificat, mutat quadrata rotundis?

> You laugh: What, when my judgment is at strife with itself, scorns what it craved, asks again for what it lately cast aside; when it shifts like a tide, and in the whole system of life is out of joint, pulling down, building up, and changing square to round? [*Epistle* 1.1.97–100]

The architectural imagery that Horace uses to describe the upheaval in which he too feels caught suggests how urban a malaise he recognizes it to be. For Horace, the difficulty of finding a natural equipoise seems compounded by the sheer weight of social existence. The existence of others, in fact, is at the root of one form of urban behavioral extreme, that of the fools in *Satire* 1.2 who fall into one vice in an effort to avoid any association with its opposite. Such sinners come, naturally, in antithetical pairs, the reckless Tigellius contrasted with one who, fearing to be thought a prodigal, denies a starving friend; or the scent-box Rufillus contrasted with Gargonius, the goat: "nil medium est" (1.2.28). This preoccupation with others—with how one appears to others, with having what others have or doing what they do—implies a competitiveness governing urban life as relentless, all-absorbing and potentially hazardous as the image of the chariot race that Horace uses to conclude the first *Satire:* "In such a race there is ever a richer in your way" (1.1.113).

Throughout these early *Satires,* Horace weaves the texture of verse around the spectacle of urban extremes by using an organizational principle of antithetical social portraits that conveys a sense of urban disorder under rhetorical, although not social, control. However, Horace's urban world (unlike Juvenal's) is fundamentally capable of righting itself— although perhaps all the more perverse in that case for not doing so. As M. J. McGann has noted, Horace rarely portrays the world as given over to madness and those of his spokesmen who do, like the recently converted Stoic of 2.3, are discredited for us by their peculiarity of tone and attitude, and are kept at a distance from the poet himself.[7] Horace's more usual tactic is to adopt the reasonable tone of the *vir bonus* who points out that to insist upon extravagantly delicate foods, well-born sexual partners, rich togas, and a large house in town is to deny natural requirements in the act of fulfilling them. Quoting, in *Epistle* 1.10, one of the Stoic rules of life that to live agreeably to nature is our duty, Horace goes on to argue that system of profound reciprocity in nature wins out in any case: "Naturam expelles furca, tamen usque recurret, / et mala perrumpet furtim fastidia victrix." [You may drive Nature out with a pitchfork, yet she will ever hurry back, and, ere you know it, burst through your foolish contempt in triumph] (24–25).

Out of the oppositions of greed and prodigality, ambition and slavishness, over-refinement and crude sensuality, Horace builds a firm, prescriptive moral structure, an ethic of moderation for resolving the disharmonies between urban life and the natural order. Preserving one's integrity and self-content amid the ostensible blessings of wealth and power which the great city holds out is a matter of adopting the philosophic indifference that the poet outlines in the famous *Epistle* 1.6, "Nil admirari." The egotism, pride, and ambition bred by the applause of the crowd, high office, and splendid accoutrements ignore the inevitable limits nature sets on all things. By marveling at nothing, the individual accepts impermanence and change as the natural order even for cities.

For the bewilderment, envy, and inconsistency he sees as characteristic of urban life, Horace proposes the remedy of tradition and custom, and he offers his own life and poetry as evidence of the positive application of tradition and custom to contemporary culture. The strategy is a conventional one: the satirist, particularly if he wants to be accepted as a reasonable man, needs to cite someone as a positive test case. He can speak about no one with more authority than himself.[8] Self-deprecation thus becomes an inevitable, perceptibly ironic stance, and motifs of modest denial run throughout the satires. In 1.4, he thanks the gods for making him lowly in spirit ("pusilli animi") and demurs at reciting in public since many people dislike satire. He presumes to satirize less out of independent wisdom than out of respect for inherited social forms and poetic traditions, for his father's teaching on the one hand and the early satires of Lucilius on the other. "Contentus parvo," like "nil admirari," becomes a goal for the simple urban life demonstrable first of all in terms of poetic form and content. In both books of the *Satires,* for example, Horace demonstrates the inherently mixed nature of the Roman conception of satire by including a variety of rhetorical formats—diatribes, dramatic monologues, and dramatic dialogues; he also varies the role his personality plays from poem to poem. In so doing, he offers an alternative to the characteristically urban forms of pride and ambition which elevate the claims of the self above anything else. Such juxtapositions of dramatic monologue with formal verse satire, of the lecturer Horace of 1.1, for example, with the discomfited traveler and sexual victim of 1.5, demonstrate as a method of poetic organization the same doctrine of "nothing to excess" which the poet would like to find in human behavior and urban life. The manifest possibility of poetic self-restraint thus becomes evidence for the wider possibilities of social self-restraint in the city at large. Horace would not have us think either form of self-restraint particularly easy. He admits his own social and poetic failings, although claiming to have learned to avoid those that bring disaster (1.4.130). He also takes pains to dissociate himself from social ambition, reminding his audience in 1.6 of his modest parentage and insisting that his position within Maecenas's magic circle resulted from Maecenas's invitation and not from his own self-promotion. Admittedly, his rhetorical posture here and elsewhere communicates self-advertisement in the process of belittling it.

But he does strike a balance, both social and poetic, which we recognize as the key to *urbanitas*.

Because of such attempts to align poetry and nature, it is a significant mark of urban resistance to the natural order that Horace typically associates the city with forces hostile to poetic creation. The crowd displaying extremes of behavior and inclination, "all of these dread verses and detest the poet" (1.4.33). The crowd, furthermore, exerts an extremely strong pressure toward conformity, which represents a particular danger for the independent course a satiric poet must follow:

> Quod si me populus Romanus forte roget, cur
> non ut porticibus sic iudiciis fruar isdem,
> nec sequar aut fugiam quae diligit ipse vel odit,
> olim quod volpes aegroto cauta leoni
> respondit, referam: "quia me vestigia terrent,
> omni te adversum spectantia, nulla retrorsum."

> But if the people of Rome should ask me, perchance, why I do not use the same judgments even as I walk in the same colonnades as they, why I do not follow or eschew what they love or hate, I should reply as once upon a time the prudent fox made answer to the sick lion: "Because those footprints frighten me; they all lead toward your den, and none lead back." [*Epistle* 1.1.70–75]

The city swallows up the individual in the greedy embrace of the crowd and, for the loss of personal control and sense of self, offers nothing in return. Horace asks the "many-headed monster": "nam quid sequar aut quem?" [What am I to follow or whom?] (*Epistle* 1.1.76). He associates the city with dependency and obligation, with lack of freedom and the inability to write poetry. The poet as citizen is hardly a poet at all. Thus in *Epistle* 2.2 he writes to Julius Florus:

> Praeter cetera me Romaene poemata censes
> scribere posse inter tot curas totque labores?
> hic sponsum vocat, hic auditum scripta, relictis
> omnibus officiis; cubat hic in colle Quirini,
> hic extremo in Aventino, visendus uterque.

> Besides all else, do you think I can write verses at Rome amid all my cares and all my toils? One calls me to be surety, another, to leave all my duties

and listen to his writings. One lies sick on the Quirinal hill, another on
the Aventine's far side; I must visit both. [2.2.65–69]

He goes on to describe the dizzying whirl of activity in Rome and suggests that writing under such conditions could only be an attempt to
curry favor at the expense of self-respect. Real poets love the grove and
flee the town. And, in addition, Horace describes the ironic burden of
being Maecenas's friend—finding oneself the obsessive object of poet-
asters like the bore of *Satire* 1.9. The comedy here lies in Horace's
exaggerated discomfiture and helplessness in the face of relentless im-
portunity, as the bore spots the poet's unhappiness yet still refuses to go
away in the hope of being introduced to Maecenas. The very interest that
Maecenas had shown in poetry—an ideal collaboration between art and
the great man of the city—makes Horace a social victim. The entire
encounter, in fact, is presented ironically as a comic collision between art
and the social code. Horace even attempts to make use of the network of
social obligation, conjuring up a sick friend who must be visited at the
other end of town. But the bore cannot be put off. Horace's lightness of
tone throughout the poem suggests that no one is to feel sorry for him:
Apollo not only finally rescues him, but provides him with a poetic by-
product of the encounter as well.

Like Rome, Horace discovers the ironic wages of too much success.
The bore's curiosity about Maecenas's circle implies the possibility that
writing poetry in the city may become simply another form of competitive
behavior, with no better claim to moral value than stockpiling money,
which it would come eventually to resemble. The poetry of accumulation
would turn from the natural order rather than seek to promote it. Thus
the ambivalence that Horace displays toward Rome when he writes those
Satires that take Rome for their subject becomes even more pronounced
when Horace reflects on the city from the vantage point of his farm at
Tivoli. In book 2 of the *Satires* and increasingly in the *Epistles* written a
decade later, Horace finds a focus for his ambivalence about Rome in the
life he discovers on the farm. In *Epistle* 1.7, Horace answers Maecenas's
request that he return to the city by outlining a statement of artistic
independence as the only source of poetry which has earned Maecenas's
patronage in the first place. The country fosters a self-sufficiency that

allows the poet to continue to accept and deserve Maecenas's favor only because he can surrender it at any time. In Rome his attachment to a powerful patron may bring him comfort and civilized companionship but it also exposes him to unwelcome curiosity and even attack. Horace may write in *Epistle* 1.2 that one's state of mind matters far more than location, yet the evidence of the poems suggests that for Horace the farm at Tivoli provided an alternative to urban confinement essential to his integrity. The farm, he tells his discontented foreman in *Epistle* 1.14, returns him to himself, and frees him for the self-examination necessary for discovering the life agreeable to nature. He describes the farm as a finished form to which nothing can be added or subtracted. It is the essential incarnated:

> Hoc erat in votis: modus agri non ita magnus,
> hortus ubi et tecto vicinus jugis aquae fons
> et paulum silvae super his foret. auctius atque
> di melius fecere. bene est. nil amplius oro.

> This is what I prayed for!—a piece of land not so very large, where there would be a garden, and near the house a spring of ever-flowing water, and up above these a bit of woodland. More and better than this have the gods done for me. I am content. Nothing more do I ask. [*Satires*, 2.6, 1–4]

The farm at Tivoli becomes for Horace a kind of personal myth representing the union and collaboration of art and nature, a landscape of self-definition and self-expression. Tivoli provides all that is vital to life and art. It, not Rome, is the landscape of personal fulfillment.

Horace, though, never ceases to acknowledge the strong fascination that Rome holds for him—at Tivoli longing for Rome, and at Rome loving Tivoli (*Satires*, 2.7). In the course of his career as a poet, he moves from a deep involvement with city life in the *Satires* to relative retirement at the end of his life in the *Epistles*. But, within this gradual movement away from Rome, there is another pattern—that of a productive alternation between Rome and Tivoli.[9] The farm provides a perspective for seeing the city whole. The city is to be identified with Maecenas and Augustus, and thus with the political order underlying Augustan poetry —the intelligent and humane use of power, the maintenance of a productive social order, and, of course, the gift of the farm itself. Horace's removal from the actual city allows him to perceive and to render a portrait of the ideal city of Maecenas and Augustus which daily life in Rome had obscured.

For Juvenal, writing nearly two centuries later, there is neither an alternative landscape nor any reason, apparently, to feel grateful to mother Rome. His satires, like Horace's, articulate a rejection of public life, although not out of any preference for private life. The personal bitterness into which Juvenal occasionally lapses suggests that he rejects Rome because Rome has already rejected him. He can find no satisfactory way of remaining faithful to the idea of Rome; he has neither Augustus nor Maecenas. Nor does he offer up his own life for contemplation, as does Horace, largely because he lacks incentive to do so. Juvenal, insisting that almost everyone in Rome has reached new heights of monstrousness unknown in Horace's time, distances himself from the city morally and explodes any hope of reformation.[10]

The themes of his *Satires* recall Horace's—extravagance, greed, waste, unbridled sensuality, extreme forms of sexual preference, the tumult of urban life, and the antipathy of Rome to all learning, but to satire in particular. Juvenal, however, invests urban life with an all-pervading monstrousness that makes his city an altogether different place from Horace's. Lacking a present alternative to Rome and unable or unwilling to leave the city, Juvenal can only perceive another Rome in the irretrievable past of the city. Juvenal agrees with Horace's dictum in the *Ars Poetica* that the poet should be *utilis urbi*—useful to the city.[11] But, in the city in which he now finds himself, the poet can no longer be the advocate of nature and reformer of society. He rather becomes a sardonic malcontent who writes invective because the city does not allow him to channel his energies in a more constructive way. Throughout most of the *Satires,* particularly the earlier ones, his tone is explicitly negative, as if there were no other mood left given the quality of contemporary life:

> difficile est saturam non scribere. nam quis iniquae
> tam patiens urbis, tam ferreus, ut teneat se,
> causidici nova cum veniat lectica Mathonis
> plena ipso.

It is hard *not* to write satire. For who can be so tolerant of this monstrous city, who so iron of soul, as to contain himself when the brand-new litter of lawyer Matho come along, filled with his huge self? [1.30–33]

Like the panegyrists, Juvenal portrays Rome as the center of historical process, but reverses their interpretation of splendor. He makes the conventional Roman celebration of the agrarian past into a personally held myth of national decline.[12] "Et quando uberior vitiorum copia? quando / maior avaritiae patuit sinus?" When was Vice more rampant? When did the maw of Avarice gape wider? he asks in the first *Satire* (87–88). But he would also like to use Roman history to find the source of moral corruption. He thus questions the god of Rome: "O pater urbis / unde nefas tantum Latiis pastoribus?" [O Father of our city, whence came such wickedness among thy Latin shepherds?] (2.126–27). The monuments and landscape of the city become particularly useful for Juvenal as meeting places where an honorable past confronts the sordid present. In the third *Satire,* he meets his friend Umbricius who is leaving Rome by the "dripping archway of the old Porta Capena":

hic, urbi nocturnae Numa constituebat amicae,
nunc sacri fontis nemus et delubra locantur
Iudaeis, quorum cophinus faenumque supellex
(omnis enim populo mercedem pendere iussa est
arbor et eiectis mendicat silva Camenis).

Here Numa held his nightly assignations with his mistress; but now the holy fount and grove and shrine are let out to Jews, who possess a basket and a truss of hay for all their furnishings. For as every tree nowadays has to pay toll to the people, the Muses have been ejected, and the wood has to go a-begging. [3.12–16]

In the first *Satire,* Juvenal establishes his closeness to everyday urban life by placing himself and the reader on a busy streetcorner to watch the parade of urban life, which at this moment includes an obese lawyer, a forger, an informer, and a "matrona potens" who teaches women to poison their husbands as she has poisoned hers. The rhetorical balance so apparent in Horace gives way to closely packed sentences and an extreme diction which, as Gilbert Highet has suggested, move the reader along as if he were being buffeted and mauled by street traffic.[13] The effect of this accumulation of particular details—which is Juvenal's primary rhetorical technique throughout the *Satires*—is to elevate the world of everyday to the level of symbol in order to overwhelm the reader with an impression of monumental viciousness.[14] Like the panegyrist Aristides, although for opposite reasons, Juvenal wants to show the difficulty of finding a vantage point from which to see Rome properly, or to see Rome whole. From his perspective within the "monstrous city," no orderly survey of daily life is possible because the poet has become part of the tumultous subject matter.[15] The poet must mirror the disorder and confusion around him as a way of making his satiric point: that indignation *is* making his verses.

The discomforts, strife, and importunities of urban life which Horace could accommodate within an essentially comic vision become for Juvenal actual perils in a city that presses in from all sides. Umbricius, Juvenal's spokesman in the third *Satire*, portrays the social structure of the city in as extreme a state of collapse as its physical structure:

> nos urbem colimus tenui tibicine fultam
> magna parte sui; nam sic labentibus obstat
> vilicus et, veteris rimae cum texit hiatum,
> securos pendente iubet dormire ruina.

> But here we inhabit a city supported for the most part by slender props: for that is how the bailiff holds up the tottering house, patches up the cracks in the old wall, bidding the inmates sleep at ease under a roof ready to tumble about their ears. [3.193–96]

Juvenal's is the nightmare vision of urban outrage, which dwells relentlessly on the ugliest detail—particularly on sexual detail—in order to transform the familiar topography of ancient Rome into grotesque panorama. If Horace attributes the accumulation of wealth to a human inability to rest content with little, Juvenal finds wealth springing from a criminality so pervasive that it taints all possessions and subverts all relationships. To be somebody in Rome today, he insists in *Satire* 1, one must be willing to commit an outrageous crime. The urban competition for honors and riches which Horace found so foolish has changed to a competition in vice. Nature has been dumbfounded:

> nona aetas agitur peioraque saecula ferri
> temporibus, quorum sceleri non invenit ipsa
> nomen et a nullo posuit natura metallo.

We are living in a ninth age; an age more evil than that of iron—one for whose wickedness Nature herself can find no name, no metal from which to call it. [13.28–30]

Juvenal succeeds so well, in fact, in reversing our customary standards for normative human behavior that the bisexual gigolo Naevolus presents himself in the ninth *Satire* as an exemplum not of sexual degradation but of ingratitude: he has been spurned by his patron. Sympathy and disgust uneasily combine as Juvenal ironically sets up two kinds of relationships—the sexual and the client-patron relationship—and reveals their perversions through Naevolus in a way that incongruously makes each compete for our moral attention.

Juvenal is especially bitter about the neglect and perversion of the patron-client relationship around which the life of the city had long centered. He advises a friend in *Satire* 5 not to accept a dinner invitation without checking to find out what services it is supposed to repay: "tantine iniuria cena, / tam ieiuna fames, cum possit honestius illic / et tremere et sordes farris mordere canini?" [Is a dinner worth all the insults with which you have to pay for it? Is your hunger so importunate, when it might, with greater dignity, be shivering where you are, and munching dirty scraps of dog's bread?] (5.9–11). He is also outraged by the effect of upstart slaves from the provinces and of suddenly moneyed tradesmen on the traditional social hierarchy of the city. A characteristic attitude is class-oriented racial prejudice, a dislike of newcomers to the city, like the Jews and Egyptians, who balked at cultural assimilation.[16] Clearly Juvenal lacks sympathy for the cosmopolitan view of Roman citizenship which we saw in chapter 1. Far from attesting to the city's greatness of spirit, the racial diversity of Rome threatened to move the city even farther from the simple agrarian past that Juvenal equates with *romanitas*. In a city overrun by foreigners and debased by appetite, the life of the mind has no place. Letters must starve. Horace, Juvenal reminds us, had a full stomach (7.62); Virgil had a slave and a roof over his head (7.69–70). The rich man of today prefers to keep a lion rather than a poet, and the contemporary poet must pawn his clothes in order to keep on writing.

Despite the force of Juvenal's outraged tones, it is important to remember just how conventional some of his rhetorical strategies are, just how much poetic control is being applied to the creation of emotional intensity. By accumulating example after example of monstrous depravity and by passing rapidly from one subject to another, Juvenal creates an overwhelming impression of limitless vice and bewildering disorder in the scene around him. But the accumulation also serves to create a critical distance, if not between the satirist and his scene, then between the satirist and his audience. Repetition, the mainspring of humor, serves here to move us away from his apparent indignation and closer to a kind of amusement. In fact, the pleasurable recognition of irony in Juvenal often derives from this refusal on his part to draw moral distinctions among the vices that fill his page, thus inviting us to temporize as he, in general, will not. Whatever the particular focus of any one satire—women, gluttony, sexual perversion, greed—the accumulation of details and case histories points to a single overarching theme: the baseness and degradation of life in the imperial city. But it is a baseness and degradation from which Juvenal will not turn his fascinated eyes or go into exile.

Gilbert Highet reminds us, usefully, that only a world-city like Juvenal's Rome merits this kind of obsessive fascination.[17] Although satirists typically tend to argue that they set acid pen to paper because folly or vice has reached its apogee, satiric attacks on city life reach full force only when the city itself has become a magnet for the whole world, a Spenglerian Megalopolis filled with the babel of a dozen tongues.[18] Jerôme Carcopino warns against taking Juvenal too literally, arguing instead that Rome during Juvenal's lifetime was an overcrowded, but still fairly orderly and liveable place, thanks to imperial donations of cheap food, wine, and amusement, to a short working-day, a high rate of literacy, and a relatively firm social structure.[19] But the immense size and power of the city are equally undeniable and play the largest part in the intense dynamics of Juvenal's relation to his subject. Horace continually balances alternatives—Rome vs. Tivoli, the attractions of his civilized community of friends vs. the timelessness of nature, the tumult of Rome vs. the solitary life on the farm. But there are few virtuous figures in the Juvenalian populace and, particularly in the early *Satires,* no effective alternatives for the poet between a life of independent destitution or a life of humiliating dependence on a cruel patron who cares nothing for letters.

As a poet, then, if not also as an individual, Juvenal is inescapably attracted and repelled by the city that is almost exclusively the setting and subject of his verse.

Perhaps because of this willed poetic myopia, Juvenal's view of Rome eliminates almost all traces of normality from the city. Indeed, the freakishness of the city is all the more extreme because Juvenal is uninterested in looking inside the consciousness of urban man. Juvenal allows only the out-of-work pathic Naevolus to tell his side of things; and only in the thirteenth *Satire* does Juvenal imagine the existence in Rome of guilt and remorse. As E. Courtney remarks, "Juvenal is more interested in the external horrors of behaviour than the internal moral horrors of the mind."[20] The *Satires* imply that behavior in Rome is Juvenal's only subject matter because it is the only subject matter that really counts:

> haec quota pars scelerum, quae custos Gallicus urbis
> usque a lucifero donec lux occidat audit?
> humani generis mores tibi nosse volenti
> sufficit una domus.

> What a mere fraction these of the crimes which Gallicus, the guardian of our city, has to listen to from dawn to eve! If you would know what mankind is like, that one court-house will suffice. [13.157–60]

Rome is coextensive with reality; but reality has become a nightmare.

Juvenal does, however, create his own dichotomy of the two Romes by a rather sentimental idealization of the past. Since contemporary Rome has become a concatenation of horrors, inspiring an extreme ambivalence, Juvenal dwells nostalgically on the history of the city. Horace's Rome, better still the elder Cato's Rome or even the city in its earliest manifestations, takes on the dim outlines of an ideal city that, like Astraea, has left the earth and now exists in memory. Not surprisingly, Juvenal's view of the past differs considerably from Horace's. In *Satire* 1.3, Horace following Lucretius equates the foundation of cities with the rule of law. He proposes an evolutionary scheme in which fist fighting yields gradually to the uses of language: "dehinc absistere bello, / oppida coeperunt munire et ponere leges." [Thenceforth they began to cease from war, to build towns, and to frame laws] (1.3.104–5). In such an ameliorist view, the rule of law thus begun remains a standard applicable even to contemporary man.[21] For Juvenal, however, virtue itself is essentially a thing of the past except as the enforced possession of the simple poor. When the world was young, he says in the sixth *Satire*, chastity dwelled in caves with unkempt wives and belching husbands. After the withdrawal of Astraea at the end of the Golden Age, poverty enforced virtue in Rome. In the *Satires* Umbricius seems to be the only living embodiment of true *romanitas* and his withdrawal from the city, echoing Astraea's, leaves the city without an in-dwelling spirit, leaves Rome without *romanitas*.[22] In a city without a living past, the moral man can find no place for himself and none of the benefits of community and solidarity. As the only present landscape, the giant city offers all goods and all evils, but its blessings, located only in the past, can no longer be experienced. Thus, after considering the claims of fame, beauty, and longevity in the unusually reflective tenth *Satire*, Juvenal finally outlines an ethical posture of minimal desire which in its Stoicism bears some resemblance to the Horatian "contentus parvo":

> orandum est ut sit mens sana in corpore sano;
> fortem posce animum mortis terrore carentem,
> qui spatium vitae extremum inter munera ponat
> naturae.

> You should pray for a sound mind in a sound body, for a stout heart that has no fear of death, and deems length of days the least of nature's gifts.
> [10.356–59]

It is a prayer that has specifically turned away from the erstwhile social blessings of a wife and son, of the foundation of a family which is the city in small compass. Juvenal's prescription for the good life makes no claims on the state, allows the individual to harbor no expectations from his fellow men. One survives, finally, despite, not because of, Rome.

The City of Plautus

Compared to the *Satires* of Horace and Juvenal, the comedies of Plautus would seem at first glance to be far less interested in the fundamental ethical relationship of the individual to the city of Rome. The plays are not set in Rome, for one thing, and they also are absorbed in ludicrous incident for its own sake.[23] But Erich Segal has returned Plautus to serious consideration by arguing that, like Shakespeare's festive comedies, Plautine comedy derives its raison d'être not from ignoring the conditions of contemporary urban existence but from deliberately flouting them.[24] In Plautus's lifetime, Rome really did resemble the straitlaced city evoked by Juvenalian nostalgia. Its moral severity and ethical constraints are summed up in the forbidding figure of the elder Cato. Plautus recognized the civic holidays on which comedies were performed as occasions for libidinal release. That his representation of city life should contrast with Horace's or Juvenal's is hardly surprising: their points of view are almost diametrically opposed. The satirists call for the reinstallation of norms in a society that has departed dangerously from them. The festive comedian celebrates the evasion of norms and subversion of the status quo, although with an ethical escape clause built in: Plautus's citizens are never Romans.

The question of the characters' civic status suggests one way in which Plautine comedy differs significantly from Shakespeare's festive comedies. In Shakespeare, the emotional contrast between everyday and holiday finds topographical expression in an outward movement from court or city to the pastoral world. Plautus achieves a similar emotional contrast within an urban framework by giving Greek names to his characters and their cities and by dramatizing behavior distinctly forbidden to his audience. The idea of an idyllic rural life hardly occurs in Plautus, perhaps because it pales by comparison with the psychic appeal of an idyllic urban life.[25] Only by placing his characters in a specifically urban context can Plautus make comic action a meaningful denial of the absolute claims of the ancient city, for whom it was the supreme glory to die.

Plautus's challenge to the status quo is all the more significant given the formal restrictions of Roman comedy, set before a fixed architectural facade and unable to present the Roman girl of good family onstage even though the plays often hinge on her romantic fortunes. Yet the very need to emphasize the offstage dramatic existence of characters and situations which could not be presented directly has the almost paradoxical effect of making more of the city seem to be involved in the action.[26] Parts of the city which lie offstage take on a vivid reality they rarely do in plays with more flexible stage conventions where exposition is a tiresome narrative

[51]

chore, perfunctorily dispensed with. Vivid descriptions of urban detail sometimes stand out from the action as virtuoso set pieces with their own unity and inner life. Examples abound: there is the vibrant picture of returning soldiers tramping through streets crowded with captives, excited relatives, and eager harlots (*Epidicus*, 208ff.); the street scene of cloaked, book-laden Greek tutors and ball-playing slaves (*Curculio*, 280ff.); the spectacle of prostitutes from all over the city worshipping at the temple of Venus (*Poenulus*, 265–70); or the pimp's long monologue about the tradesmen from whom he is demanding birthday tribute (*Pseudolus*, 133ff.).

The concreteness of such word painting makes clear that, although the urban stage-street has little importance in itself, it does serve as the point of conjunction for the worlds of the forum, the harbor, and the household which lie out of view. That is, the comic mise-en-scène focuses attention on the potential ethical significance of comic action because it is staged precisely where the public and private spheres intersect. All action behind the housefront produces a reaction on the street; all roads in the Plautine city lead onstage. Thus the characters in Plautine comedy, whether they walk onstage or remain a verbal presence only, are presented as having an essential relation to the urban dynamic. Like the Romans who watched them, they are always participants in the common life.

The essential contrast in Plautus's plays is not, therefore, as it often is in Shakespeare's, between city and country, but between two kinds of cities: the imaginary Greek city within the play and the actual city outside it. Imaginative tension between the two cities provides much of the thematic interest of the plays, as it does later for the city comedies of Jonson and Middleton set in Jacobean London. But the Roman audience, despite their ready recognition of Plautus's urban imagery, would initially have been struck by the differences between the two cities, imaginary and real. The typical plot of New Comedy is familiar: a young man, blocked in his erotic pursuits by parental disapproval, financial difficulty, or other disabling obligation, enlists his slave in a successful scheme to win the girl. In the joint triumph of *adulescens* and *servus*, normative social values topple: *industria* gives way to *voluptas*; patriarchal sanctions give way to amoral wit; individual freedom overcomes self-restraint. Comic anarchy replaces the entire ethical system known as *mos maiorum*. The extreme hedonism embodied in Plautine comedy functions as a compensatory mechanism

for Roman society: the entire city shut down on holidays and re-
assembled for the civic entertainments at an amphitheatre constructed
especially for the purpose. A slave society as repressive as third-century
republican Rome needed the psychic release afforded by saturnalian experience, whether vicarious or actual.[27]

As a result of these cultural dynamics, however, the city in Plautine
comedy is fundamentally no more desirable an image of collective experience than the actual city to which Plautus's audience belonged. It is
neither more complete nor more balanced. It has simply replaced the
obsessions of the actual city for obsessions of its own, and in the process exchanged one kind of psychic cruelty for another. For example,
even after allowing for Plautus's deliberate inversion of Roman norms,
the absence of familial affection in his plays is striking. The Plautine
son not only wants to dupe his father, but he is also quite capable of
wishing for his father's death. Philolaches in the *Mostellaria* wishes "for
news now of my father's demise" (233) so that he can disinherit himself
in favor of his mistress.[28] Strabax in *Truculentus* adds a wish to eradicate his mother (662), and the father Demaenetus tells his son as they
carouse together with a courtesan that when his wife is near, "periisse
cupio," he wishes for a death in the family (*Asinaria*, 901). Plautus delights in exposing pillars of the state not only to their sons' parricidal
desires, but also to the contempt of their wives and slaves and to the
public ridicule of sexual humiliation. The slave Epidicus spies his master with a friend—"just such a pair of old dotards as I want" (*Epidicus*,
185). The wife Artemona, who imagined her husband as "a paragon of
men" (*Asinaria*, 856) wearied out by his daily labours in the Senate,
discovers him with a courtesan:

ibi labore delassatum noctem totam stertere:
ille opere foris faciendo lassus noctu ad me advenit;
fundum alienum arat, incultum familiarem deserit.

He wearied out by his labours there, there, that he spends the whole night
snoring! It is business away from home, that makes him turn up at night
all weary—the business of ploughing other people's fields and leaving his
own uncultivated. [*Asinaria*, 872–74]

Plautus never introduces the spectacle of aged lust as a gratuitous humiliation: the lustful *senex* is invariably his own son's rival, thus offending

against the dual proprieties of age and family. Such rampant familial discord results, in part, from Plautus's interest in breaking Roman taboos; the lack of remorse in the parricidal Plautine son underscores by contrast the collective power of guilt and remorse in Roman society. But, within the plays themselves, the absence of family loyalties results more directly from the characters' obsessive pursuit of pleasure to the exclusion of any larger interest. Often, in fact, Plautus's many references to urban life point up the narrowness of his characters' mentality. Diniarchus, one of three romantic rivals in *Truculentus*, has just returned from a state mission to Lemnos. Aware of the uses of *pietas*, he comments that pimps, harlots, and prodigality would soon disappear if young men would only confide in their elders and learn the fruits of their wisdom. His own independence of mind, however, along with his patrimony, has been lost to Phronesium and, while he recognizes the irrationality of such behavior, he is unable to control it:

> si iratum scortumst forte amatori suo,
> bis perit amator, ab re atque ab animo simul;
> sin alter altri propitiust, idem perit:
> si raras noctes ducit, ab animo perit;
> sin crebras ducit, ipsus gaudet, res perit.

> In case the hussy chances to get angry at her lover, the lover's a double wreck, in fortune and in peace of mind together. Yet if all goes smoothly with them, he's still a wreck: having her seldom, his peace of mind is wrecked; having her often, he's happy, but his fortune wrecked. [*Truculentus*, 46–50]

In *Mercator*, the *adulescens* Charinus melodramatically prepares to leave Athens, "ubi mores deteriores increbrescunt in dies," where vice grows daily (838). His despair at Athens disappears immediately, however, when he learns that his girl has been returned to him. But the lustful *senex* is equally single-minded; Lysidamus fumes at having been called to the forum:

> Stultitia magna est, mea quidem sententia,
> hominem amatorem ullum ad forum procedere;
> in eum diem quoi quod amet in mundo siet.

It's perfectly asinine—that's what I call it—for any man in love to set out for the forum the day his sweetheart is all in trim for him! [*Casina*, 563–65]

Such single-mindedness and sexual aggression with the family extends outward to the city at large. The plots of several comedies—*Aulularia, Truculentus, Cistellaria,* and *Epidicus*—turn on the reclamation of wronged (even raped) women. In the *Truculentus,* however, Diniarchus has no sooner pledged to marry the woman he has wronged than he reassures his courtesan, "Operae ubi mi erit, ad te venero"—when my opportunity comes, I'll be with you (883). Plautine courtesans, however, restore the sexual balance with a cold calculation of their lovers' sexual and financial weaknesses, seeming as delighted by their lovers' gullibility as the wily slave is by that of his old master. Indeed Plautus sometimes employs martial imagery to describe the relations of lover and mistress, of slave and master. The maid Astaphium tells Diniarchus that a lover is like a hostile city, the sooner he can be stormed and sacked the better (*Truculentus,* 170–71). Pseudolus uses the imagery of siege and assault to launch his plot against the pimp Ballio (*Pseudolus,* 585–90); thus the slave Toxilus describes his victory over the pimp Dordalus (*Persa,* 753–57), and Palaestrio the plot against the *miles gloriosus,* Pyrgopolynices (*Miles Gloriosus,* 1154–58).

We do not need to employ modern sexual or social standards to find Plautine societies marked by selfishness and aggression. A Plautine husband or son wishes for the convenient death of wife or father as an anticipation or expression of their own intense erotic pleasure. The self-sacrifice of the Roman ethos changes to the sacrifice of others for self. Usually in Plautus it is the slave who bears the brunt of human indifference, managing the intrigue amid a barrage of threats of whippings and beatings. Erich Segal has argued that the threats rarely lead to actual punishment. In the inverted moral order of the Plautine world, the slave wins his freedom and ends triumphant over a submissive and humbled master. The verbal violence of these threats is quite specific, however:

advorsum stetimus lamminas, crucesque compedesque,
nervos, catenas, carceres, numellas, pedicas, boias
inductoresque acerrumos gnarosque nostri tergi.

we have defied hot irons and crosses and gyves, and thongs, chains, cells, shackles, fetters, collars, and painters—painters keen as can be and intimate with our backs! [*Asinaria*, 549–51]

In a world created by words, we cannot discount such verbal violence. Since this verbal violence hardly ever results in action, it is in a sense all the more gratuitous, accepted as a stage idiom of social intercourse the way obscenity will be in the London of Jacobean city comedy. It is a rather cruel kind of fun, appropriate to a milieu in which the young men for whom intrigues are undertaken are wholly absorbed by eros. The exchange between the slave Epidicus and his young master Stratippocles is typical. Epidicus has succeeded in buying a slave girl at Stratippocles's urgent request, only to find out that Stratippocles has a new object of affection. To Epidicus's objections that he is being victimized and will surely be punished, Stratippocles airily replies: "Quid istic? verba facimus. huic homini opust quadraginta minis / celeriter calidis, danistae quas resolvat, et cito." [Come, come! this is mere chatter. I am a man that needs a hundred and sixty pounds piping hot, in a hurry, to pay off a money-lender, and no time to lose] (*Epidicus*, 141–42).

The point is not that Plautus asks us to care a great deal about whether Epidicus or his fellow slaves ever get the beatings they are threatened with, but that on the contrary there is very little emotional involvement with any of the characters or their situations.[29] If Plautus seldom allows anyone to take threats of whipping seriously, he can hardly expect the audience to take seriously the moral sententiousness that is also part of the Plautine character's vocabulary. Moral behavior in these plays is as rare as violence, and sententiousness is often given an ironic context, as in lines from *Mercator* quoted earlier where Charinus condemns Athens because his father has appropriated his mistress. In these comedies, characters tend to think of each other in functional terms— parents being useful for the money they control, slaves for the wit and energy they bring to bear on the problem at hand, and pimps for the women whose fates they direct. Yet the very functionality of its citizens in the service of eros guarantees the comic self-perpetuation of the Plautine city and becomes the subverted civic norm.

This eventual triumph of undutiful sons and witty slaves thus constitutes an implicit criticism of contemporary society. Like other urban playwrights, Plautus recognizes the psychic cost of institutionalized dedication to the mother city and replaces her with the object of a compensatory devotion—the courtesan who personifies pleasure. In refusing to sentimentalize the courtesan, Plautus underscores her appeal. She may, like the city, exact a sacrifice from the young man whose devotion she accepts, but the sacrifice (usually financial) will not be exalted. In its amorality and aggressiveness, in the absoluteness of its libidinal release, however, the Plautine city is no closer to ideality than the city it periodically replaces. The Greek cities of Plautus are founded in a negative ethic: they only make sense as the antithesis of Rome.

CHAPTER THREE

To Starve with Feeding:
Shakespeare's Idea of Rome

The immense prestige of classical Rome throughout the Renaissance and the abundance of its narrative remains made the ancient city almost as inevitable a subject for Shakespeare as it was for Horace and Juvenal. As the archetypal earthly city, Rome offers Shakespeare what it offers other writers moved by its appeal—a powerful symbolic locus for the warring social premises summarized in chapter 1 as the double image of Cain or Amphion, fratricide or creativity, city wall or city gate. Like the Elizabethan historians who associated the city with civil war, Shakespeare is particularly drawn to those moments in the Roman past which brought the internal order of the city to a point of critical change, when one kind of city was giving way to another.[1]

There are however clear differences among the Roman plays in the part the city has to play in the action. In *Antony and Cleopatra*, for example, Rome is not *urbs* but *imperium*, and because of this I have omitted the play from consideration here. In *Titus Andronicus, Julius Caesar,* and *Coriolanus*, Shakespeare uses Rome to mean "the City," that "morphological entity operating much as the human body does, bound by duties to the whole and subject to demands by its members."[2] In all three plays, the relation between the *urbs* and the hero enacts a central urban paradox: the social mandate for heroic self-sacrifice collides with the heroic mandate for self-realization conceived in civic terms. Like the city of the Florentine humanists, this city is the essential instrument of individual perfection, but that perfection comes only through death. In all three plays, Rome represents collectively held ideals of individual aspiration and creates the conditions for achieving them. But its political processes reveal a predatory savagery that seeks out and destroys the hero at the moment when he most completely embodies the ethos of the city. The city bestows secular immortality by exacting a sacrifice that diminishes what it preserves.

The emblematic opening of *Titus Andronicus* resembles a ritualistic re-enactment of the social and political origins of cities, a subject that deeply interested Renaissance political theorists.[3] The tribunes and senators of Rome enter first, "aloft"—presumably on the city walls. Two groups, headed by the rival brothers Saturninus and Bassianus, then enter from opposite doors to a position below the walls. Each brother comes to claim the right to rule the city. This choreographic balance then becomes verbal, as each brother states his political principles in short, rather colorless speeches with the older Saturninus arguing for primogeniture and Bassianus for personal fitness to rule. That Bassianus is the worthier brother cannot yet be apparent, especially perhaps to an audience whose culture was strongly primogenitural.[4] With each brother arguing out of self-interest, what may be best for Rome remains unclear, particularly since neither brother claims to be his emperor-father's choice.

In its formality and balance, this dramatic picture of armed rival brothers beneath the walls of Rome must have reminded some in the audience of the legendary founding of the city. Here, the city lacks a fixed rule of succession not because Shakespeare wanted to leave the historical setting of the play unclear but because he wanted to present a city in the act of reconstituting itself.[5] The meaning of the city as social life protected by walls, which we will discover again in *Coriolanus*, is never clearer than at this moment early in *Titus Andronicus*.[6] The process of pacifying the brothers is fundamentally a question of who is allowed within the walls and who must be kept without. Standing beneath the walls to articulate their claims, the brothers acknowledge the life within. And in so doing, they introduce Rome as the essential object of rivalry in the events to come.

The actual election results turn the attention of the audience from the origins of Rome to its ethos; fratricidal conflict is replaced by fraternal reciprocity in service to the state. The long formal panegyric of Titus Andronicus, "surnamèd Pius," by his tribune brother Marcus is less the portrait of a credible individual than a personification of essential *romanitas*:

> Ten years are spent since first he undertook
> This cause of Rome, and chastised with arms
> Our enemies' pride: five times he hath return'd
> Bleeding to Rome, bearing his valiant sons
> In coffins from the field.   [1.1.31–35]

That Titus appears more monumental than actual in this formal heroic portrait is very much to the point. His return suggests a process exactly the reverse of what we found in Juvenal's third *Satire*, where the departure of Umbricius, itself reminiscent of Astraea's, leaves the city soulless. Titus—symbolizing tribal power, the potency of Priam, ceremonial piety, and brutally self-denying service to the state—returns *romanitas* to Rome. "For her it is our duty to die," says Cicero, "to her to give ourselves entirely, to place on her altar, and, as it were, to dedicate to her service, all that we possess" (*De legibus*, 2.2.5). What Titus possesses is sons.

Marcus's portrait of Titus as ethical icon also demonstrates the ideal functioning of the city. By giving itself a new father, the city seeks to pacify the imperial brothers and avert civil war. Indeed, there is a kind of Orphic magic in the idea of Titus so that, by words alone, both brothers are tamed: without resistance, each in turn relinquishes his claim, commits himself "to the love and favour of my country" (58), and is drawn up into the city in order for civic life to commence anew.

Given Saturninus's behavior later in the first act, it is possible to see dramatic irony in the brothers' ready response to the will of the Roman people. To do so, however, ignores the emblematic function of this opening scene, which stands against the horrors to come. The initial movement of drawing into the city under a single, persuasive rule the factions threatening its walls demonstrates the function of law as the political ground of civil society, ordering the city's fundamental understructure of tribal families.

[60]

Titus's refusal to rule the city is catastrophic, much as Lear's similar abdication will be. It represents a betrayal of the Roman ethos and a denial of Titus's own history. This first error leads inexorably to the second, choosing Saturninus as emperor instead and bringing into the city the dangerous individual appetites and fraternal jealousies earlier kept outside its walls. Saturninus and Bassianus immediately reenact their initial fraternal strife, as the Goth brothers will at the beginning of act 2, with Lavinia replacing Rome as the contested prize.

Anticipation of horror should not blind us to the importance of this opening image of civilizing forces. Although Shakespeare does go on to identify the city with the universal woes of the Iron Age, the city first exhibits a significant capacity for orderly self-renewal out of its own ethical resources.[7] This image of normative civic process, created and destroyed, is so self-contained, in fact, that it might well stand as a counter-image for the tragic action in *Julius Caesar* and *Coriolanus* as well. They too open with a small mirror scene that encapsulizes the tensions between the city and its hero which will dominate the action to come.

The attention of the opening crowds in *Julius Caesar* and *Coriolanus* is fastened on the figure of the great man—to celebrate, flatter, or revile him. Their expansive physical presence creates an almost pressing sense of the urban milieu—the "felt solidity" of Rome.[8] In *Julius Caesar*, Shakespeare uses the initial conflict between the tribunes and the plebeians celebrating Caesar's triumph to characterize the city and its *romanitas* in a number of ways. In rebuking the citizens for leaving their work, the tribunes accuse the plebs—as the conspirators will accuse Caesar—of not knowing their place and function in the social order. The tribunes' rebuke also evokes the normal urban rhythm of everyday and holiday which the plebs have disrupted. Their reminder of the everyday laboring city—for an audience that had also taken the afternoon off to see Caesar—establishes a genuine connection between the impulses of the ancient city onstage and those of the actual city on the other side of the Thames.

Marullus's long and angry response to the plebeians' explanation of their purpose becomes an opportunity to set this opening action against a wider perspective—the enduring, destructive ambivalence between the

[61]

hero and the city. He reminds the plebs how they climbed to the rooftops just to wait for a glimpse of Pompey:

> And when you saw his chariot but appear,
> Have you not made an universal shout,
> That Tiber trembled underneath her banks
> To hear the replication of your sounds
> Made in her concave shores?
>
> [1.1.43–47]

By making these few plebs representative of the universal shout, Marullus converts their present impulse into a continuum of heroes and cities—celebration yielding endlessly to ingratitude. But the plebs' use of the city as a vantage point for seeing the great man culminates in an image of urban collapse—Tiber's trembling shoreline. All the essential elements of the final moments of the play in Rome are here at the opening—the memory of the great man, partisan rhetoricians, and a volatile crowd. Marullus's speech establishes the basic morphology and social dynamic of the city. Pompey's power as totem has passed to Caesar, but the polarized emotions that both great men have aroused underlie the action of the entire play.

The starving plebs who come onstage at the beginning of *Coriolanus*, resolved rather to die than to famish, seek Marcius's death for a specified social end: "Let us kill him / and we'll have corn at our own price" (1.1.9–10). The crowd is moved by the vision of a city radically polarized into us and them, good citizens and poor citizens, surfeit and misery, gain and sufferance. They see a closed system of deliberate economic imbalance and particular oppression: "the leanness that afflicts us, the object of our misery, is as an inventory to particularise their abundance; our sufferance is a gain to them" (1.1.18–21). Their immediate purpose, like that of the crowd in *Julius Caesar*, is deflected by another entrance, here of the patrician Menenius. In the exchange that follows, Shakespeare first establishes a fundamental contrast between Rome as a concretely realized setting and as a city located in the mind, a symbol of human possibility, and then demonstrates dynamic interplay between the two Romes. The plebeians' grievances are based on physical necessities. But Menenius invokes an idea of the Roman state as historical process in language that stations itself firmly in the abstract:

> . . . you may as well
> Strike at the heaven with your staves, as lift them
> Against the Roman state, whose course will on
> The way it takes, cracking ten thousand curbs
> Of more strong link asunder than can ever
> Appear in your impediment.   [1.1.66–71]

The suggestions in Menenius's speech of awesomely disinterested power and his association of Roman history with the will of the gods make the city heroic. His words were also intended, I suspect, to remind the Elizabethans of the future greatness of Rome in the more familiar imperial period that Shakespeare had already dramatized. Here, more explicitly than in *Julius Caesar,* republican Rome becomes part of a long, celebrated continuum of men and events which distinguishes the present citizenry from the urban *res publica* that is allied with the workings of fate. Furthermore, Menenius's reminder of the historic future of the city this early in the play makes possible an ironic perspective on approaching threats to the existence of the city: whatever else may happen, it is not Rome that will be destroyed.

Menenius goes on to deliver his famous fable of the belly in a dialogue with the citizens which acts out the political mutuality he is espousing.[9] Whether or not we take the fable as an ideal image of civic life, its reiterated rhetorical status as a fable distinctly sets it apart from its context, just as Menenius has set the idea of Rome apart from the individuals who live there. The fable of the belly not only makes the city a body, but it also makes the body a city with storehouses, workshops, rivers, offices, and a central court and almost suggests intricate topography in the winding distribution of the general food supply. Even in this metaphoric exchange of attributes between body and city, there is some hint of the mutuality that is Menenius's ostensible message, for the fable brings together an idea of the political process as hierarchical distribution of function with the concrete actuality that idea seeks to regulate. Linked now with the inexorable processes of nature and history, the idea of Rome would seem to command allegiance. The fable is followed, however, by Coriolanus's abrupt, bellicose entrance that breaks up the moment of equilibrium and returns the dramatic situation to its discordant beginnings. Like the opening scene of *Julius Caesar*, this becomes a brief, introductory enactment of the characteristic rhythms of the play and evidence for the continual forward momentum of civic life.[10] Coriolanus's harsh catalogue of plebeian unworthiness dissolves the metaphoric accord between an idea of the city and its multitudinous inhabitants which Menenius had so patiently evolved. The moment of urban stability that the relentless major action leaves behind, isolated and unresolved, is a sign of the division between idea and actuality, between the comedy it is possible to imagine and even at moments achieve, and the tragedy it becomes impossible to prevent. Like the city itself, Menenius's fable cannot finally accommodate the intractable individuality of the hero.

Thus, the opening actions of all three plays present critical ambivalence in the relation between the city and its designated hero. The tension between the force represented by the Many and that embodied in the One is clearest at the beginning of *Coriolanus* because the Roman citizenry there has singled out Caius Marcius for destruction, not praise. In *Titus*, as we have seen, the idea of the city is introduced rather abstractly in action and language as the city goes through the rites of political succession and expresses its identity by choosing Titus as the new emperor. Having become symbols of the Roman ethos by standing like the city victorious in mourning weeds, the Andronici continue to incarnate the city in the sufferings to come. There is no such simple identification of family and city in the two later plays, yet the opening situations of all three have important similarities. In each, Shakespeare presents a city in political crisis at a moment when the governing order is undergoing either challenge or change. The crowds that open *Julius Caesar* and *Coriolanus*, embodying the urban raw material of their societies, demonstrate their fascination with the great man whose individual fortunes are at stake in the general crisis. The enthusiasm of the would-be celebrants in *Julius Caesar* is mirrored antithetically by the destructive impulse of the rebellious plebs in *Coriolanus*. In both, their present action is set in a wider perspective of historical continuity which serves to underscore the city as a separate dramatic idea.

Each of these plays can be understood in part, therefore, as an examination of what a city is or ought to be. "What is the city but the people?" asks the tribune Sicinius in *Coriolanus*, as if uttering an accepted commonplace (3.1.197). In fact, however, definitions of Rome in each play split sharply, sometimes between classes or families, but often within them. The opening of *Titus*, as we have seen, is a painstaking evocation of *mos maiorum*, especially when the action slows to center around the Andronici family monument. The tomb—a visual symbol like Titus himself of the demands of the Roman way—reveals the centrality of death to the Roman ethos.[11] The Roman ethos of patriarchal authority and filial self-sacrifice is thrown into even greater relief first by the resistance to it from the defeated Goths and then by a rebellion within. Titus denies Tamora's pleas to abjure the customary Roman sacrifice of defeated prisoners because it is as an act of tribute to the Andronici dead who have achieved Rome's ideal of ultimate self-sacrifice. Marcus makes this even clearer by addressing the dead and the living, hardly distinguishing between them:

> Fair lords, your fortunes are alike in all
> That in your country's service drew your swords;
> But safer triumph is this funeral pomp
> That hath aspir'd to Solon's happiness
> And triumphs over chance in honour's bed.
>
> [1.1.174–78]

Indeed, his rather prolonged tribute to the dead represents a brief moment of Roman unity: only the Goths question the sacrifice, for the Romans are at one in their absolute valuation of the patriotic dead. It is not surprising, then, that Titus's subsequent refusal of the crown reintroduces questions about the nature of the city and leads to a rebellion against the patriarchal order he symbolizes. In giving Lavinia to Saturninus when he must know that she is already betrothed to Bassianus, Titus abrogates the ideal of fidelity to custom to which he had sacrificed Tamora's sons. If Titus's motivation is left unclear, what is clear is his presumption about the absolute primacy of patriarchal authority in Rome. The contest over Lavina is, indeed, a conflict about the meaning of Rome when law collides with the patriarchal will. Its immediate consequence is

[65]

an ironically distorted reimposition of *pietas* and reenactment of Andronici family history—the sacrifice of yet another son. The confrontation of outraged father and rebellious son, in such a context, is thus a dramatic emblem of Rome embarked on self-destruction, its weapons unsheathed within the walls. "What, villain boy?" shouts Titus the moment before he slays Mutius, "Barr'st me my way in Rome?" (1.1.290–91).[12] The family monument, so recently the dramatic focus of Roman triumph and unity, becomes the focus of Rome's lacerating self-division as the vault opens again.

In this succession of events which seems to bring resolution to the unfolding dramatic crises only to collapse, Shakespeare uses repetition to reveal the rapid breakdown of the city. Saturninus replaces Titus; Tamora replaces Lavinia; the burial rites of sons slain in the service of their state are followed by rites for a son slain by his father. Even the initial confrontation of brothers over the rule of Rome, repeated after Titus refuses the crown, is grotesquely parodied in act 2 by the entrance of Tamora's sons Chiron and Demetrius quarreling over Lavinia. Only Aaron, his blackness announcing his irreducible otherness in opposition to Rome, stands apart from the action to predict its consequences: "This siren that will charm Rome's Saturnine, / And see his shipwrack and his commonweal's" (2.1.23–24).

This conflict over the meaning of Rome expressed through the warring families of *Titus Andronicus* is treated in the republican world of *Coriolanus* as an issue of class. Definitions of the city split so sharply along class lines that one is reminded of Socrates' comment in the *Republic* that, in a city where there are divisions of wealth, there is more than one city: "The city of the rich and the city of the poor, and in each of these there are many" (4.422E–423A). The patricians tend to identify the idea of Rome exclusively with themselves—"our Rome," Volumnia says. Her identification of Rome with her class is so complete that she can ask Coriolanus in act 3 to use policy and strategy in his relations with the plebs as he would against a warring city. He calls them "scabs," sores on the body politic that healing, presumably, would take away. Only when the physical survival of the city is at stake does the pronoun shift in favor of the plebs: "He'll shake your Rome about your ears," shouts Cominius to the frightened tribunes (4.6.99).[13] The concordance is revealing: Marvin

Spevack counts eighty-eight uses of the word *Rome* in *Coriolanus,* the highest frequency of all the Roman plays. But the anonymous Roman plebs never use the word, and even the tribunes between them account for only six instances: "Rome" belongs to the patricians.

The play is so firmly grounded in the public arena that only three scenes clearly take place inside a private house, and Coriolanus is the only character to appear by himself onstage. Yet his first words while alone in 4.4 are, significantly, an address to the city of Corioli, so that in a way he is not alone and does not feel himself to be alone at all.[14] Meetings between Coriolanus and his family all take place in full view of the Roman populace, or at least of the Roman senate. At the climactic final meeting, Coriolanus makes sure that Aufidius and the Volsces hear what he says to his family: "For we'll / Hear nought from Rome in private" (5.3.92–93). In this exclusion of private moments and settings, Shakespeare dramatically embodies the sacrifice of self which Roman citizenship involves in *Coriolanus* no less than in *Titus Andronicus.* The patricians present Rome as a standard for individual conduct, an idea of human greatness with which Coriolanus strongly identifies. Indeed, he verbally expels the plebians who care more for grain than glory from the collective ideal, as they will later expel him physically from the actual city:

> I would they were barbarians—as they are,
> Though in Rome litter'd; not Romans—as they are not,
> Though calv'd i'th'porch o'th'Capitol—   [3.1.236–38]

Extreme civic consciousness prevails even in the one ostensibly domestic scene of the play. After two noisy military conferences, first in Rome and then in Corioli, 1.3 introduces a quiet, almost passive mood as Volumnia and Virgilia begin to sew. This mood quickly changes, however, as Volumnia articulates the grim conditions of honorable citizenship for Roman mothers and their sons. Motherhood is a civic obligation, a part of the historical process. As she tells a horrified Virgilia, she has in her imagination already offered up the life of the son she has and the putative lives of the sons she might have had to Rome as the rightful exacter of sacrifice. Her identification with the state is so absolute that she makes no distinction between biological continuity and fame, that life of the name which only the community can bestow. To Virgilia's question, "had he died in the business, madam," the mother replies:

> Then his good report should have been my son, I therein would have found issue. Hear me profess sincerely: had I a dozen sons, each in my love alike, and none less dear than thine and my good Martius, I had rather had eleven die nobly for their country, than one voluptuously surfeit out of action. [1.3.20–25]

Romanitas in Volumnia is Andronican in severity: the mother here glories in the number of her son's wounds, as the father there gloried in the number of sons slain for Rome. Like Marcus Andronicus, Volumnia gives the dead—here imaginary—larger attention than the living. Virgilia's quiet articulation of an intensely personal ethos represents the only possible alternative here to the predominant code of public commitment.

The absence of private moments in the play takes on greater significance for the idea of Rome through Shakespeare's use of ceremony as a key structural device. John Holloway has spoken of Shakespeare's use of ceremonial actions in *Coriolanus* to plot the hero's movement from being the cynosure in triumph to being an outcast after the ceremonial expulsion from Rome. Ironically, Coriolanus has another triumph in his final return to Corioli just before his ritualized death at the hands of the mob, but even that death has been forecast in the images of ritual sacrifice (3.2.1, for example) and in the actual threat of ritual sacrifice when the crowd demands that Coriolanus be thrown from the Tarpeian Rock. There are also the important ceremonies attached to the election of consul, although as Holloway points out, these are not triumphal rites but rites of supplication which Coriolanus would prefer to forgo.[15] There is, finally, one ceremony or ceremony *in potentia* which has received little attention and which I shall discuss in more detail later. This is the moment of Volumnia's triumph as she is hailed as "our patroness, the life of Rome" (5.5.1), and borne away to a celebration offstage.

Together, the sacrifice of private time and space and the prominence of civic ceremony suggest how thoroughly and intensely civic the life of this city is and how little room remains in Rome for the gigantic individual figure of Coriolanus. The report of Coriolanus's triumph is a description not of the returning hero, but of the city pressing upon him its almost violent welcome. One thinks of Pompey's and Tiber's trembling shores. Here Rome's

> stalls, bulks, windows,
> Are smother'd up, leads fill'd, and ridges hors'd
> With variable complexions, all agreeing
> In earnestness to see him.   [2.1.208–11]

That the triumph figures importantly in all three plays suggests the depth of Shakespeare's interest in the accommodation of Roman militarism and Roman citizenship—his interest in how Achilles behaves in the Forum.[16] The Roman plebs in *Julius Caesar* come onstage to celebrate Caesar's military victory as they have celebrated Pompey's, but without distinguishing between victory over a foreign enemy and victory "over Pompey's blood" (1.1.51). In fact, the distinction is crucial. Romans fight only Romans in this play, as if there were no other enemy. The questions that dominate the opening events do not concern the value of military accomplishment, as in *Coriolanus,* or its cost, as in *Titus.* They rather concern a central paradox of *romanitas,* which functions like synecdoche here for the nature of social existence. What can being a Roman mean if *romanitas* stands for a common order of being and for the highest pitch of individual accomplishment? In *Julius Caesar,* Rome is a city obsessed with the nature of individuality, perceiving difference as comparison. As in *Coriolanus,* Shakespeare defines the importance of class distinctions so sharply that patricians and plebeians are a virtual lexicon of antonyms. Thus, if the plebeians demonstrate a persistent shortness of memory, the patricians habitually measure themselves and the present moment against a long historical continuum. The tribunes remember Pompey; Caesar cites the Roman elders in encouraging Antony to touch the barren Calphurnia; and Cassius climaxes his first persuasion of Brutus with an involuted historicism, remembering their fathers' evocations of the past:

> O, you and I have heard our fathers say,
> There was a Brutus once that would have brook'd
> Th'eternal devil to keep his state in Rome
> As easily as a king.   [1.2.156–59]

Even more characteristic of the patricians is the complementary habit of histrionic self-regard, the first circle of an interest that widens to include the present natural order and a future unknowable except in its preoccupation with them. Thus Cassius boasts of presenting himself "in the very aim and flash" of "cross blue lightning" (1.3.50–52). Thus Brutus urges the conspirators to daub themselves with Caesar's blood in order to give a memorable finale not only to the assassination but to its staged enactments in time to come:

> CAS. Stoop then, and wash. How many ages hence
> Shall this our lofty scene be acted over,
> In states unborn, and accents yet unknown!
> BRU. How many times shall Caesar bleed in sport,
> That now on Pompey's basis lies along,
> No worthier than the dust!   [3.1.111–16]

Caesar exhibits patrician theatricality in a fatally exaggerated form, telling Antony rather "what is to be fear'd / Than what I fear" (1.2.208–9) about Cassius, boasting to the conspirators of his constancy.

If the plebeians in *Julius Caesar* represent the physical city, as they do in *Coriolanus*, the patricians attach their loyalties to an abstract conception of Rome and act as if they are agreed about what it means—or ought to be. That it means, for all of them, participating in a common order of long-standing greatness is implicit not only in the many references to the past, but also in the fact that the word *Roman* is always an honorific one, bestowed as praise or as self-praise. Even more significant perhaps is an assumption common in the play that the word *Roman* establishes the essential common ground between men. Such an attitude is at the heart of Antony's attempt to reassure Caesar about the lean, hungry, and thereby dangerous Cassius: "He's not dangerous. / He's a noble Roman, and well given" (1.2.193–94). To be a Roman, at one level, is to be one in a community of like-minded individuals, with the word *Roman* guaranteeing a harmony of traits and interests that overarches all other differences in character and renders them insignificant. But, as L. C. Knights has pointed out, this ideal of assumed like-mindedness is jeopardized from the very beginning of the play by the intimate knowledge that the patricians have of one another and by their habit of using that knowledge in interpreting political events.[17] Much of the early dialogue is given over to a particular rendering of a character's distinguishing traits, always with the inference that such traits are politically meaningful. Brutus refuses to see the Lupercalian race because "I am not gamesome: I do lack some part / Of that quick spirit that is in Antony" (1.2.27–28). Cassius is dangerous, according to Caesar, in part because "he loves no plays, / As thou dost, Antony; he hears no music" (1.2.200–201). Brutus and Cassius expect Casca to tell them what happened at the Capitol "after his sour fashion" (1.2.178). Later in the dark of the storm, Cassius recognizes Casca by his voice alone. Characters note changes in one another, as Cassius does in complaining of Brutus's unaccustomed neglect and as Brutus does in commenting rather lightly about Casca: "What a blunt fellow is this grown to be! / He was quick mettle when he went to school" (1.2.292–93). This same habit informs Brutus's train of thought when he contemplates killing Caesar not for what he is, but for what he might become: "He would be crown'd: / How that might change his nature, there's the question" (2.1.12–13).

The play is so strongly pervaded by this personalism (to borrow Knights's term) that it becomes, ironically, the most significant belief the patricians have in common. Preoccupation with one another is, at one and the same time, evidence for patrician like-mindedness and a cause for the jealousy and factionalism that tear them apart. Together they belong to a patrician order of inherited tradition, theoretically as equals. As individuals, they are preoccupied with the differences between them and how those differences affect personal relationships. With community and individuality set at so delicate a balance, republican *romanitas* is overtaken by paradox. The very qualities that distinguish an individual may bring him honor and recognition, the goals of a Roman life. But they will also seem to set him apart from and dangerously above the rest. That Caesar's honors appear threatening in just this way is clear from the beginning of the play in the tribunes' anxiety that Caesar "would soar above the view of men / And keep us all in servile fearfulness" (1.1.74–75). This imagery of height and lowness, growth and disproportion reappears in Cassius's description of Caesar. Nowhere in the play is the dangerous tension between community and individuality more striking. Cassius insists that he and Brutus are no different than Caesar:

> I had as lief not be as live to be
> In awe of such a thing as I myself.
> I was born free as Caesar; so were you;
> We both have fed as well, and we can both
> Endure the winter's cold as well as he.
>
> [1.2.94–98]

For Cassius, Caesar's personal triumphs represent a threat not only to freedom but to identify itself: "and this man / Is now become a god, and Cassius is / A wretched creature" (1.2.114–16). Caesar's deeds have not enlarged Rome because what enlarges one man dwarfs all the rest and makes them ridiculous:

> Why, man, he doth bestride the narrow world
> Like a Colossus, and we petty men
> Walk under his huge legs, and peep about
> To find ourselves dishonourable graves.
>
> [1.2.133–36]

Caesar's greatness crowds everyone else out of the city, until the city is no longer a city at all but a private chamber: "Now is it Rome indeed, and room enough, / When there is in it but one only man" (1.2.154–55).

The problem for Rome in *Julius Caesar*—as it will be in *Coriolanus*—is how to remain a city, an idea of the collective spirit, and still accommodate the city's most splendid product, the heroic individual. The hero's drive to self-realization may make community impossible by challenging other claims to selfhood. In *Julius Caesar*, Shakespeare is interested in the problem from the point of view of the challenged lesser selves like Cassius whose stake in keeping the common good common is greatest of all.

Throughout the play characters describe and redescribe one another almost obsessively, giving knowledge so subjective a cast that our own position vis-à-vis the political events of the play mirrors that of the characters themselves. The conspirators, in calling upon Brutus in act 2, cannot agree among themselves about the points of the compass, arguing about where the day will break. With even this kind of knowledge in dispute, it is surely significant that we never hear from Caesar himself of the nature of his ambition. The most telling evidence of it—Casca's narration of events at the Capitol—is strongly qualified by Brutus and Cassius's characterization of the speaker. The unity of the city is thus made problematic not only by the intense singularity of Caesar, but more fundamentally by the hermeneutic complexities of urban life. The Romans think they know one another because they are all Romans.

Of the three plays with which we are concerned here, only *Julius Caesar* is pervaded by so strong a sense of the complexities of social experience, primarily because it is centrally concerned with the effect of Caesar's life on other men in the community-at-large. In all three, however, Shakespeare develops the idea of the city through imagery that closely identifies characters with setting in order to reveal the dark, primitive underside of civic life. *Titus Andronicus* lacks the architectural references so conspicuous in the two later Roman tragedies. But the effect of its imagery is similar in revealing the horrific intimacy of life in Rome, the urban interconnectedness that makes any event political. The inexorable arithmetic of replacement in the first act of the play—Saturnine for Titus, Tamora for Lavinia, living sons for dead ones—obtains also in the imagery. Once Titus has helped to dismantle the structures of civic order in Rome by allowing the political triumph of the Goths, the city becomes the forest. The physical and spiritual center of the city—the Andronici family tomb—gives way to its horrible counterpart, the pit that becomes the death chamber of Bassianus and a trap for two Andronici sons.[18] Repeatedly described in strongly sexual imagery as a "subtle hole" (2.3.198), a "detested, dark, blood-drinking pit" (224), a "fell devouring receptacle" (235), the pit becomes a predatory womb, taking rather than giving life. Death in the monument, presented as a spiritual state of noble cessation after the sacrifices that make civic life valid and beautiful, gives way to death in the pit presented farcically as a savage butchery. The womb-pit is also linked to the emergence of Tamora over Lavinia as the feminine personification of Rome, the bride become whore. In act 2, Shakespeare insists on the identity of political revenge and sexual violence by staging the entrapment and false accusation of Quintus and Martius Andronicus while their sister's rape and mutilation occur offstage. As in *Lucrece,* Shakespeare defines rape politically. The asexual

Lavinia must be raped and widowed because, as "Rome's rich ornament" (1.1.52), she personifies the sanctity of the culture for whom the Andronici males wage war.[19]

The Andronici themselves consistently define their suffering as the result not of personal vengeance or private lust, but of civic ingratitude. Titus in his madness would send Pluto a petition for justice "from old Andronicus, / Shaken with sorrows in ungrateful Rome" (4.3.16–17). Marcus urges his kinsman to "join with the Goths, and with revengeful war / Take wreak on Rome for this ingratitude" (4.3.32–33). Thus the mutilations are precise, if horrific, symbols of a society in collapse.[20] Rome's rich ornament, raped, becomes an emblem of the spiritual truncation of the city, for in losing her hands and tongue Lavinia loses the physical components of civility. Having hands means serving Rome; serving Rome, for the Andronici, has always meant self-expression. But, as Titus declares on seeing Lavinia, serving Rome now means becoming her victim: "Give me a sword, I'll chop off my hands too; / For they have fought for Rome, and all in vain" (3.1.73–74).

This harrowingly specific association of self-mutilation and political despair—one hand helping to cut off the other—links other images in the play to the tragedy of Rome. Hostile nature from which city walls offer protection ravages the Andronici in ruling their city, now a "wilderness of tigers" (3.1.54). Titus sees himself environed not with walls but "as one upon a rock, / Environ'd with a wilderness of sea" (3.1.93–94). The grieving Andronici become living monuments of the spiritual death of the city, the shrunken vessels of its heritage. Marcus describes Lucius as "struck pale and bloodless" (3.1.257) and sees himself in grief, Niobe-like, as "a stony image, cold and numb" (258); and Lavinia, "thou map of woe" (3.2.12), moves dumbly through the action like a totem, her power as symbol residing in her monumental muteness. The messenger who brings Titus back his hand with the heads of his sons finds his sufferings emblematic of *pietas*: "Woe is me to think upon thy woes, / More than remembrance of my father's death" (3.1.240–41). In such a context, even the return of the hand and two heads is a demonic parody of political recognition and reciprocity, a grotesque reenactment of the sacrifice of sons. Rome cannibalizes the Andronici.

That the cost of such suffering is civilization itself becomes clearer in

[74]

the last acts of the play through imagery of aesthetic acts. Marcus's rather literary lament upon seeing Lavinia's mutilation mourns the destruction of civilized pleasure, even of art itself. She could sew like Philomel, play the lute "to make the silken strings delight to kiss" her hands (2.4.46), and, like Orpheus in Hades, remove danger in "the heavenly harmony / Which that sweet tongue hath made" (48–49). The literary past becomes the dramatic agent that moves the Andronici from passive suffering to active revenge and political rebirth. Ovid gives Lavinia what Chiron and Demetrius had taken away—the capacity to communicate the truth of her defilement. Ovid also provides Titus with the design of a hideous revenge, myth as a model to surpass: "For worse than Philomel you us'd my daughter, / And worse than Progne I will be reveng'd" (5.2.194–95). He hopes the banquet, where Tamora like the earth will swallow her own increase, will "prove / More stern and bloody than the Centaurs' feast" (202–3).

It is important to see the cannibal banquet as an appropriate device for unifying the various image patterns of the play. Cannibalism, or more generally eating and feeding, return as important images for the city in *Julius Caesar* and *Coriolanus*. Here, Shakespeare presents a mother devouring her sons as an emblem of the purgation of Rome. Because of the play's sustained identification of sexual appetite with political disorder, Tamora's punishment precisely reverses the action of the play. Throughout the play, the contrast between Tamora and Lavinia has been a contrast between two cities as absolute, as powerful as the parallel contrast in Revelation between the whore Rome and the bride Jerusalem. The same contrast obtains, as we have seen, in the central physical symbols of the play: the Andronici family tomb and the deep predatory pit in the forest, both of which ingest sons. In this grammar of imagery, the predatory cycle completes itself. Titus's murder of Lavinia and Tamora's cannibalism are parallel horrors, emblems of the filial sacrifice central to the tragic meaning of Rome. If the Andronici have died in service to the state, Titus's revenge upon Tamora makes her sons too die in service to Rome. Appetite must be turned upon itself if Rome is to survive. Although the entire Andronici family serves as the ritual scapegoat, it is Titus, of course, who stands at the center of the prolonged sequence of destruction and self-destruction. He gains immortality, finally, in two ways—as a tragic hero through suffering and as a patriarch through the diminished survival of his family in Lucius and young Lucius. As the chief exemplar for the stern Roman code, Titus is necessarily its principal victim.

This is also true of the titular figures of the two later Roman tragedies. Even in the far more historically accurate setting of *Julius Caesar*, imagery of ritual sacrifice and predation focuses upon Caesar. The two warring families of *Titus Andronicus* give way to warring members within a class; political fraternity takes the place of family ties in the dangerous intimacy of civic life. Here, as in the other plays, there is no line dividing private and public, no way of distinguishing between personal and political. Marital encounters are full of anxiety about the world of affairs; domestic meetings end inconclusively, interrupted by representatives from the world outside. Poor Calphurnia cannot even keep the interpretation of dreams within the family: Caesar turns to Decius Brutus for exegesis of her dream, just as earlier he had made public his anxiety about his wife's barrenness.

Most important, as in *Titus*, civic relationships become increasingly predatory, even cannibalistic, as the conflict comes to center on the body of the hero as symbolic battleground. As *Titus* links images of eating and self-mutilation, so *Julius Caesar* links images of eating and architecture: the political reciprocity between the individual and the state becomes the demonic reciprocity of the cannibal feast. Caesar, the focus of imagery, is monumental prey and predator. At the opening, the tribunes will pluck down Caesar's images lest he soar like an eagle above them. And the irony by which the prey turns on its predator reverberates throughout the play. Caesar comes to us first as an image, a problematic work of art in the city landscape as well as a problematic idea in the city's consciousness. Shakespeare's fascination with the interplay between the man and the monument is most apparent in Cassius's first speeches in 1.2, contrasting the god-like Colossus who bears the palm alone with the weak epileptic drowning in the Tiber or feverish in Spain. With a dizzying shift of proportion which implies Cassius's uncertainty about comparative human scale, he focuses first on Caesar's coward lip, pale eye and tongue, and then on the huge legs of the Colossus. He imagines his body bending before Caesar's and the patricians walking fearfully under Caesar, peering about "to find ourselves dishonourable graves" (1.2.136). Like the tribunes, he also presents Caesar as a predator, here of monstrous dimension: "Upon what meat doth this our Caesar feed, / That he is grown so great?" (147–48). But the question is rhetorical: Caesar's meat is other Romans.

The question of who is predator and who is prey depends on political loyalties. Cassius tells Casca that Caesar is a wolf to the Roman sheep, a lion to the Roman hinds. But Caesar, offering the crowd his throat to cut when they cheer his refusal of the crown, depicts himself as sacrificial object and does fall down before them, choked by their stinking breath. It is symptomatic of Brutus's divided loyalties that he tends to regard Caesar as prey rather than as predator at the same time that he justifies the assassination. He describes Caesar as a sacrificial animal to be carved "as a dish fit for the gods" (2.1.173). Although Cassius has focused on Caesar's threatening physical monumentality, Brutus imagines the conspirators to be standing up "against the spirit of Caesar" (2.1.167). Only on these grounds can he justify the assassination as sacrifice rather than butchery, ennobling Caesar in the act of killing him. Sparing Antony, then, who is but "a limb of Caesar" (2.1.165), becomes a way for Brutus to avoid being a murderer himself, to respect the body he would kill. Antony echoes Brutus's sacrificial imagery when he sees Caesar's body lying in the Capitol, but changes its emphasis. Caesar is not a sacrificial animal ennobled by the purposes of its killers, but a prey whose own nobility is confirmed by sacrifice:

> Here wast thou bay'd, brave hart;
> Here didst thou fall; and here thy hunters stand,
> Sign'd in thy spoil, and crimson'd in thy lethe.
> [3.1.204–6]

Most important, predatory imagery is linked to Caesar as monument in Calphurnia's dream. The image of Caesar's statue spouting blood confirms him as an architectural image around which Romans cluster. It anticipates not only the cluster of assassins in 3.1 but also the plebeians in the next scene who ring Caesar's corpse. The image also suggests what becomes clear in the funeral scene—the totemic power of the corpse as monument. As long as Caesar is alive, the contrast between Caesar as man and idea can persuade the conspirators that Caesar is "such as thing as I myself" (1.2.95)—*semblable* and *frère*. After the assassination, the idea absorbs the man and makes him sacred—irrevocably different. In these terms, the relationship between Caesar and the conspirators represents a variation of what René Girard has called the fratricidal myth of Difference, in which a society reaffirms its cultural integrity by sacrificing or expelling one twin brother and incorporating the other.[21] The Roman preoccupation with individual difference reaches a critical point in the relation of the conspirators to Caesar: they must deny any difference of kind in him for the sake of their individuality, yet the act of killing him can only confirm it. The process is suggested in Decius Brutus's interpretation of Calphurnia's dream because, when he tries to make the dream-image flattering and reassuring, the statue becomes oddly maternal, suckling "great Rome" with "reviving blood" (2.2.87,88). The flattery lies in the critical role reversal, Caesar exchanging places with mother Rome as the source of civic benefit. We recognize, though, that the power ascribed to the statue requires death as a precondition and ironically that the dead Caesar will have far greater power than the living. Caesar is not maternal at all, but the primal father of whom Freud speaks in *Totem and Taboo*, "the feared and envied model of each one of the company of brothers" who, by killing him, give him greater power over them.[22]

There are, then, several ironies in Caesar's fall at the foot of Pompey's statue. The most obvious is the image of Pompey standing over the hero celebrated earlier for triumphing over Pompey's sons, another revolution in the cycle of celebration and ingratitude. Yet the transformation from man to monument, represented visually by Pompey's statue, yields ironies for the conspirators as well. Once the dead hero becomes a monument, the political idea that he represents becomes part of the permanent physical history of the city. He is now, like Pompey, beyond the threat of assassination. Brutus can only kill Caesar's body. In doing so, however, he frees Caesar's spirit from physical confinement and consummates the movement toward monumentality that Caesar displayed so arrogantly in life. The conspirators, by daubing themselves with Caesar's blood, confirm Decius Brutus's prophecy about Caesar as ritual object, for they, like Antony at the funeral later, make his blood symbolic. When he joins them, Antony is immediately moved by the sight of the corpse to a self-forgetful apostrophe. Later, he uses its power as a reliquary object to inflame the crowd:

> Let but the commons hear this testament,
> Which, pardon me, I do not mean to read,
> And they would go and kiss dead Caesar's wounds,
> And dip their napkins in his sacred blood.
>
> [3.2.132–35]

The bodily infirmities that Cassius had found so unworthy of a leader of Romans now bring about an ironic revenge. Caesar's body becomes a kind of historical or narrative emblem, its mantle a reminder of victory, its blood invested with sentimental pathos, until the power of Antony's eloquence has been transferred to the corpse, putting "a tongue / In every wound of Caesar that should move / The stones of Rome to rise and mutiny" (3.2.230–32). The dead Caesar achieves an anti-Orphic power, not to raise a city, but to destroy one. And the sacrificial object turns out to be Rome after all, its physical state inseparable from Caesar's: "Pluck down benches. / Pluck down forms, windows, any thing" (3.2.260–61). The action that had begun with plucking down Caesar's images in loyalty to the fallen Pompey is now complete.

A similar identification of character and setting in *Coriolanus* sets up competing monumentalities—the body of the city against that of the hero. Throughout the play, Rome's physical features provide images for assessing its spiritual state so that the physical survival of the city depends upon the fates of the human agents onstage. G. Wilson Knight has noted the imagery of building and building materials: "The present civilization is clearly a hard one."[23] More significant, perhaps, is the architectural imagery of desire or accomplishment. Cominius speaks of the "spire and top of praises vouch'd" (1.9.24); Volumnia exults to her son that she has lived "to see inherited my very wishes, / And the buildings of my fancy" (2.1.197–98). The patricians use city imagery rhetorically to symbolize what is at issue in the conflict between Coriolanus and the plebeians. Cominius images the popular revulsion against Coriolanus as consul in act 3 as "the way to lay the city flat, / To bring the roof to the foundation" (3.1.202–3)—to collapse form into chaos. Coriolanus, by contrast, becomes increasingly associated with monumental form. Just before the news of Coriolanus's decision to spare Rome, Menenius describes him as the massive creation of the military architect, a walking colossus:

> When he walks, he moves like an engine and the ground shrinks before his treading. He is able to pierce a corslet with his eye, talks like a knell, and his hum is a battery. [5.4.18–21]

Volumnia and Menenius, in fact, identify Coriolanus with the Capitol itself. After his banishment, Volumnia rebukes the tribunes in an architectural equation: "As far as doth the Capitol exceed / The meanest house in Rome, so far my son, . . . does exceed you all" (4.2.39–42). Later Menenius assesses the chances of Coriolanus sparing Rome by comparing him to the Capitol:

> If it be possible for you to displace it with your little finger, there is some hope the ladies of Rome, especially his mother, may prevail with him. [5.4.4–6]

We, of course, know them to have done just that, and Menenius's speech is laden with dramatic irony. The city has been spared, but at a cost, which, as Coriolanus tells his mother, will prove most mortal to him. If to move Coriolanus is to move the Capitol, then to move the Capitol (here a heroic symbol of fixity and permanence) is inevitably to bring it down when Coriolanus himself falls. But a city without a Capitol is a city without a center, with a dead place where once the symbol of extraordinary accomplishment stood.

In *Coriolanus*, as in *Julius Caesar*, a collocation of images—of predator and prey, of animals, eating, body parts, and cannibalism—reveals the underside of urban life, the horror and savagery that breaks finally in a brief, uncontrollable moment of violence. Anatomical imagery, which underscores the literal significance of the body politic, is given sustained comic elaboration in Menenius's fable, the ostensible purpose of which is to provide a way of seeing the parts of the social organism in relation to the whole. But, as Leonard Barkan has explained, imagery of the body in *Coriolanus* suggests the fragmentation of society because Coriolanus and the many-headed multitude manifest a compelling tendency toward division and inner disharmony.[24] In the first act alone, we hear of Coriolanus's lips and eyes; brows bound with oak and bloody brows; Hecuba's breasts and Hector's forehead; Aufidius's head, knee, and neck; Aufidius washing his hands in Coriolanus's heart; the buttocks of the night and the forehead of the morning. Body parts are seen in isolation as separable units. Although the effect of the pervasive body imagery may be to anthropomorphize and make fully dramatic an abstract conception of the commonwealth, the tendency among the characters to see human beings rather primitively as component parts is a constant reminder of the physical vulnerability of the body. It serves to qualify the divinity and monumentality with which Coriolanus is increasingly associated after his expulsion from Rome until the final moments when the tropes of fragmentation become literal.

This anatomical imagery takes on its final terrifying significance for the idea of the city in relation to the recurrent, related emphasis on animals and eating. At several points in the play, images of animals eating or preying equate the predatory relationships of animals with the political relations between heroes and their cities. As in *Julius Caesar*, Coriolanus and his opponents are variously imaged as predator and prey. The plebeians describe Coriolanus as "a very dog to the commonalty" (1.1.25–26), but for Aufidius much later Coriolanus is a noble predator who will be to Rome "as is the osprey to the fish, who takes it / By sovereignty of nature" (4.7.34–35). Although Coriolanus complains to the plebeians that "he that trusts to you, / Where he should find you lions, finds you hares; / Where foxes, geese" (1.1.169–71), many explicitly predatory images in the play link the plebeians with the predator. Menenius for instance speaks of them as a wolf devouring the lamb Coriolanus (2.1.9–10). Later Coriolanus speaks of Rome in a riddling Hamlet-like image as the "city of kites and crows" (4.5.42), carrion birds who have devoured everything but his name.

These images of predatory nature provide the thematic link between animal imagery and the images of food and eating which recur throughout the play. Maurice Charney suggests that most food imagery in the play associates the plebeians negatively with appetite and the patricians, by contrast, with temperance, asceticism, and, in the case of Coriolanus, with an aristocratic disdain for physical necessity.[25] But the plebeians are not alone in having appetites. They see themselves figuratively as food for the patricians, eaten up either by war or repressive statutes, a suggestion that Coriolanus unconsciously confirms by welcoming war as a "means to vent / Our musty superfluity" (1.1.220–21). Images of predatory feasting describe the activities of a warrior, too, for Coriolanus shares with Aufidius, Cominius, and other military figures an appetite for battle. Cominius images battle as a feast, when he praises Coriolanus's conquest of Aufidius: "Yet cam'st thou to a morsel of this feast, / Having fully din'd before" (1.9.10–11). Later, Aufidius's servingmen imagine the newly reconciled warriors sharing a common table and feasting together at the coming battle, "as it were, a parcel of their feast, and to be executed ere they wipe their lips" (4.5.222–24). These images of feasting do not merely, as Maurice Charney suggests, make war a devourer of men;[26] they make men the devourers of other men and war the social occasion for aristocratic feasting.

The imagery of food and animals, related thematically in images of prey, provides a way of seeing analogy in the otherwise discrete conflicts of city with city, warrior with warrior, hero with city, patrician with plebeian. If Coriolanus devours his opponents on the battlefield, Rome in banishing Coriolanus devours all of him but his name. The cannibalism that is literal punishment in *Titus* remains metaphor in *Julius Caesar* and *Coriolanus*. Even so, it is clear that Shakespeare found a deeply disturbing analogy between the predatory order in the natural world and the social relations among men in cities. The predatory order comes full circle at the end of each of these political tragedies, validating the survival of the community while, at the same time, underscoring its hideous cost.

Thus, the closing action of *Titus Andronicus* includes and reenacts the opening events. Lucius, returning to Rome with his army of Goths, confronts Saturninus and Tamora and each disputes the political power of the other. Again Marcus mediates the confrontation, here by inviting the opponents to share Titus's feast, that archetypal image of communal harmony. Titus, to whom the city initially turned over political power, now comes forward briefly to resume political power, once again by exacting a personal revenge that reconstitutes the political order. And the sacrifice of sons—celebrated at the opening of the play, exacted of Tamora, and grotesquely parodied in the middle acts—now achieves its final meaning. Titus, who already has killed one child onstage, now kills another as a climactic self-punishment, "for me, most wretched" (5.3.45). It is as if the patriarch can only punish himself for killing one child by sacrificing another. For Tamora, demonic mother, Queen of Rome, the punishment for lawless appetite is not merely the deaths of her sons but the knowledge that she has consumed them. Her action is thus a horrible parody of the sacrificial order upon which Rome is founded, transforming the pit in the forest back into a family tomb. For Titus, the cost of absolute civic obligation is not only his own death and Lavinia's, but also a violent psychic metamorphosis.[27]

Titus himself can no longer live in Rome, for his actions move beyond what is possible for the civic order to justify and accommodate. He is the savior of Rome, but he is her ultimate sacrificial victim as well. His death, along with those of Lavinia, Tamora, and Saturnine, allow the city, once again, to live. That it will do so is clear when Marcus Andronicus turns from the horrors to speak to the city in an image of commonweal that, like epic simile, evokes a seasonal world far removed from present carnage:

> O, let me teach you how to knit again
> This scattered corn into one mutual sheaf,
> These broken limbs again into one body.
>
> [5.3.70–72]

The address to the people of Rome in a play that leaves them out of the action suggests how completely the Andronici have concentrated in themselves the political suffering of an entire city. Thus the slaughter at the end of the play is truly purgative, truly complete. Three Andronici survive, in three generations, representing past, present, and future—the nucleus of the historical order, the nucleus of a city. Lucius becomes the city founder, another Aeneas obliged to build a city on the bodies and ruins of the old. Marcus goes on to reaffirm the *mos maiorum* in the continued willingness of the Andronici to sacrifice themselves to the Roman will:

> Have we done aught amiss, show us wherein,
> And, from the place where you behold us pleading,

[83]

> The poor remainder of Andronici
> Will hand in hand all headlong hurl ourselves,
> And on the ragged stones beat forth our souls,
> And make a mutual closure of our house.
>
> [5.3.129–34]

Instead of a new order for Rome, there is only a solemn restoration of the old under Lucius whose merciless disposition of Aaron and Tamora echoes his father's actions early in the play. Rome is again victorious in its mourning weeds, having survived a war within. Indeed, as Hunter argues, even though the play presents the Roman ethos of self-denying loyalty to family and city in an extreme form, that ethos remains the only possible alternative in the world of the play to the chaos of lawless appetite.[28] The recurrent references to Troy suggest that no city is immune to threats from without or within, no citizen is exempt from the continuous struggle to preserve order. But the city is capable of restoration as long as it grants immortality through honorable burial to those who die for its sake and leaves unhallowed those who war against it. Thus even the necessity of disposing of bodies onstage becomes a final dramatic vehicle for the definition of civilization and returns the monument to a central place in the symbolic vocabulary of the play. For Titus and Lavinia, Lucius provides honorific entombment, the play's metaphor for the achievements of the civilized order, but condemns Aaron to starve to death and Tamora to be left to the cyclic ravages of the predatory order, her devouring flesh devoured:

> No funeral rite, nor man in mourning weed,
> No mournful bell shall ring her burial;
> But throw her forth to beasts and birds to prey.
>
> [5.3.196–98]

The funeral rites for Caesar bring the Roman scenes in that play full circle, too. The plebeians' urge to destroy the city, coming as it does at the end of a prolonged funeral sequence, is the perceptible climax to the cycle of celebration and ingratitude adumbrated at the very beginning of the play. The plebs forgot Pompey for Caesar, were ready to let Brutus be Caesar, and are moved by Antony's oratory to celebrate the memory of Caesar, once again, in mob violence. Although act 4 begins, ostensibly, in Rome, the world and people of the play have in fact changed with the death of Caesar. Shakespeare's depiction of the Rome of Cassius, Brutus, and Caesar, then, is circumscribed by the mob, just as the mob surrounds and threatens the men whose task it is to govern them. It is ironic that Brutus, who had thought to avoid changes in the political structure by killing Caesar, helps to bring about changes that are far more complete. But he has not changed the nature of the mob, who will go on celebrating, forgetting, and avenging its dead heroes.

Caesar, like Titus, is the consummate prey of Rome because, in his now immortal monumentality, he is the central symbol of the individuality which for all the patricians exemplifies *romanitas*. The conspirators, otherwise preoccupied by personality, threats to identity, and subjectivity, become a single and united power under Brutus only in their decision to murder Caesar. But the hands that clasp to seal the conspiracy wound Caesar separately, perhaps even wounding each other in a competition to inflict injury. So Antony would have it accusing them later of hacking one another in the sides of Caesar (5.1.40). The murder itself serves only to bring permanent divisions among the conspirators. Most of them drop from the play, so removed have they become from their leaders and the fortunes of Rome. Brutus and Cassius, of course, are forced to flee "like madmen through the gates of Rome" (3.2.271), having turned all of Rome against itself.

Thus *Julius Caesar*, like *Titus*, demonstrates a central political paradox—the city as *discordia concors*, abiding and unstable at the same time. The concern for individualism and for immortality in the historical record, gives permanent human significance to the ongoing earthly city because the city in giving meaning to the past enshrines the present. For these Romans, only the city can erect structures of consoling order, monuments against the flux. But the pitch of accomplishment which the city encourages and which, properly directed, makes the city great endangers it, too. The social bonds forged by common allegiance to *romanitas* can be strengthened or weakened by the social intimacy so characteristic of the patricians in this play. Cassius urges Brutus to join the conspiracy by adopting "that opinion of yourself / Which every noble Roman bears of you" (2.1.92–93), but Caesar's greatness—his opinion of himself—engenders suspicion, jealousy, and factionalism. Caesar is the most Roman of them all because he exhibits in the most extreme way the characteristic strengths and weaknesses of the city, asserting an immortal greatness without regard for evident bodily infirmity. Of all the Romans, he is the shrewdest judge of character and the quickest to find political significance in the ingredients of individual temperament. But, as the most spectacular example of the strong and self-conscious individuality of *romanitas*, he destroys *romanitas* in everyone else, making part of Rome turn against him and bring on full-scale civil war. Brutus, initially with himself at war, turns that self-division outward to the community-at-large. The self-contradictions in *romanitas* reveal themselves to be founded in the self-contradictions of individual character, rendering commonweal the more noble and the less practicable. The central irony of the play is that Caesar exemplifies and destroys *romanitas*. Once he is dead, the ascription of honor becomes an incitement to riot, the enemy becomes a fellow Roman to be damned with a spot. In killing Caesar, the conspirators can only enact paradox: Caesar's death no less than Caesar's life has dwarfed them all.

In *Coriolanus*, however, Shakespeare's understanding of the paradox that is *romanitas* reaches its full development.[29] The meaning of Rome becomes clearest in the rise of Volumnia to triumphal celebration in a penultimate action, a rise that in turn determines our response to the death of the hero. From her first appearance onstage in 1.3, Volumnia has been associated with birth and death, with the continuation of life through issue and the sacrificial death of that issue. If, as Leonard Barkan suggests, Coriolanus sees his body as an extension of the state, Volumnia sees Coriolanus as an extension of her body.[30] From her flow those qualities of Coriolanus of which she approves: "Thy valiantness was mine, thou suck'st it from me / But owe thy pride thyself" (3.2.129–30).

It is Volumnia's function to stand like a signpost pointing the tragic way forward for her son and the city. The first to mention him as a candidate, she congratulates him for his victory at Corioli by telling him what he can do next to please her:

> only
> There's one thing wanting, which I doubt not but
> Our Rome will cast upon thee.   [2.1.198–200]

His response—"I had rather be their servant in my way / Than sway with them in theirs"—signals a division that will culminate in act 3 in the beginnings of a civil war prevented only by Coriolanus's banishment. In that division, Volumnia becomes the unofficial spokesman of the Senate for the sacrificial code of Rome. As she had first sent him off to war to sacrifice his youth and at least potentially his person for Rome, so she would send him off to the marketplace to beg for office. But this time—such is the inevitable progression of sacrifice—she asks him to offer up the absoluteness of being which is the core of his greatness. Volumnia subsumes the fundamental contradiction in giving up the source of greatness ostensibly for the sake of greatness to the absolute demand for further sacrifice:

> I prithee now, sweet son, as thou hast said
> My praises made thee first a soldier, so,
> To have my praise for this, perform a part
> Thou has not done before.   [3.2.107–10]

"Come all to ruin" (3.2.125), she exclaims before he relents, and she invokes the destruction of the city again when he is expelled from it: "Now the red pestilence strike all trades in Rome, / And occupations perish" (4.1.13–14). But her final speech to the tribunes underscores even more pointedly the dramatic effect of her presence for she invests herself with mythic significance in images of feeding and preying that adumbrate the crisis to come: "Anger's my meat: I sup upon myself / And so shall starve with feeding" (4.2.50–51).

This image of paradoxical appetite echoes Menenius's image of "renowned Rome" as an "unnatural dam" like Tamora eating up her own children (3.1.288,90). It also looks forward to the moment when Volumnia, pleading for "the country, our dear nurse" (5.3.110), prevails most mortally with her son. Now, cut off from the son whom she regards as the biological and historical extension of her life, Volumnia can only feed upon herself and die. But it is an image that applies in an important way to the city, too. Having cast out Coriolanus in order not to "cleave in the midst, and perish," the city finds that, without him, it is still faced with destruction. Thus, always the embodiment of motherhood, Volumnia be-

comes increasingly the embodiment of mother Rome. She makes Coriolanus see her as the city by insisting that to march on Rome would be to
tread "on thy mother's womb" (5.3.124). The claims of city and family
are absolute and only annihilating paradox can result when the two come
unnaturally into conflict:

> for how can we,
> Alas! how can we for our country pray,
> Whereto we are bound, together with thy victory,
> Whereto we are bound? [5.3.106–9]

For Coriolanus to march against Rome is to turn against the sources of
his life. He cannot renounce his city because he cannot change his mother,
cannot alter the fact of his parentage. Thus Volumnia argues that to
destroy Rome is to destroy his beginning and his end, to replace fame
with "a name / Whose repetition will be dogg'd with curses" (5.3.143–
44). It is fitting that Coriolanus relents at the reminder of the future in
his son. The action that began by Volumnia leading the young Marcius
by the hand ends by Coriolanus taking the hand of his mother. But, when
he does so, the irony of Volumnia's appeal becomes evident. The promise
of life for Rome means death for Coriolanus; the sacrifice of her issue
which she has already imagined and accepted in 1.3 is, through her
efforts, close to fulfillment:

> O my mother, mother! O!
> You have won a happy victory to Rome;
> But for your son, believe it, O, believe it,
> Most dangerously you have with him prevail'd,
> If not most mortal to him. But let it come.
> [5.3.185–89]

That the source of life—now mother and city, nature and history—
should be the instrument of death makes the scene unnatural. The claims
of love become the claims of death. And Volumnia, as Rome, has become
the unnatural dam eating up her children in order to survive, starving
with feeding. To Coriolanus's prophecy of death, she makes no reply.

The two final scenes of the play create a last, ironic perspective on the
meaning of Rome by juxtaposing the rise of Volumnia with the fall of her

son. Coriolanus predicts that rise, as he predicts his death: "Ladies, you deserve / To have a temple built you" (5.3.206–7). Our last view of Volumnia, in one of the several mirror scenes of the play, is a deeply ironic echo of Rome's earlier welcome of Coriolanus when Rome was first saved from the Volscians. This time the mother has replaced the son as cynosure and become the almost deified patroness of a joyful city that lights fires and strews flowers in her path. The scene is resonant with classical associations, looking back to the long tradition of deified women representing the *Tyche* or fortune of ancient cities in statues and on medals and cameos.[31] Volumnia, "the life of Rome," becomes hedged about with this traditional significance, but with the addition of an untraditional irony. It is the city's desire to "unshout the noise that banish'd Martius; / Repeal him with the welcome of his mother" (5.5.4–5). And, in a sense, the welcome of his mother is his repeal because, in exacting sacrifice, she has become the instrument of his immortality, as she had wanted to be. It is the only future life he will have. Volumnia has moved Coriolanus to make a choice we cannot wish otherwise, and this in itself is a key to understanding the meaning of the city. As in *Titus Andronicus,* Shakespeare cannot deprive Rome of its central importance. It is worth saving because the city as mother is the source of nurture, training, and ideals, the achievement of common humanity, and the seat of the heart's affections, which it is impious, unnatural, and perhaps impossible to deny. For all its ties to the higher order of ideals and aspirations, though, the city is also tied to the natural world represented in this play by animals, eating, and parts of the human body. Like other aspects of nature, the need of the city to maintain its physical integrity demands the sacrifice of its best and most characteristic product—the hero. Coriolanus's decision to spare Rome and die—in a way, to starve with feeding—reveals the community to be in truth the mother who eats her children.

Thus, for Volumnia and Rome, the end of this play is comic, a dramatic fact that Shakespeare chooses to highlight by presenting them finally moving joyfully to an offstage celebration in conventional comic fashion. The community will survive, as it always does in comedies and as it must, always. But our recognition that tragedy will follow comedy gives this scene a heavily ironic cast. Because of the evident fragility of community harmony in Rome, its unresolved class differences and the inevitable fickleness of the crowd, this penultimate allusion to comic form suggests the endless regeneration of a political process whose violent workings we have already seen and are reminded of once again at the end.

Like the Romans, the Volscians in this last scene begin by welcoming Coriolanus and end by turning against him. The Volscians also have cause to celebrate Coriolanus and cause to kill him as well. Here the crowd swings violently from celebration to revulsion in a concentrated repetition of the dynamic of the play. The pendulum swings back again after Coriolanus's death and the play ends in a mood of remorse: "My rage is gone," says Aufidius, "And I am struck with sorrow" (5.6.146–47). Fittingly, then, Coriolanus is celebrated once again, this time in a nascent ceremonial of mourning: "Beat thou the drum that it speak mournfully; / Trail your steel pikes" (5.6.149–50). Only Coriolanus is dead; the community will go on, in the endless tragicomic cycle of regeneration, devouring the heroes it nurtures and immortalizes because it is in its nature to do so. If he cannot help being greater than they are—and in his greatness alone—they cannot help being less. Although we would not have the community die for Coriolanus, it survives diminished, starved by such feeding.

CHAPTER FOUR

"Some High-Vic'd City":
Timon of Athens, Sejanus,
and *Catiline*

The cities named Rome in *Titus Andronicus, Julius Caesar,* and *Coriolanus* each possess deeply valued qualities that Shakespeare sets against the endemic horrors of civic life. The subdued retrospection in the final moments of those plays serves to weigh loss and preservation, to express a measured relief at what must survive whatever the cost. When we turn, however, to *Timon of Athens* (1607–8), and to Jonson's two Roman tragedies, *Sejanus* (1603) and *Catiline* (1611), we find cities of such corruption and degeneracy that the rather stately poise of tragedy must give way, at least in part, to satire.

I have chosen to treat these three plays together because of their common bleakness of social vision. In them, Shakespeare and Jonson are less interested in the cycle of tragic interdependence, which characterized the relations of hero and city in the plays discussed earlier, than they are in the causes of the collapse of a city. What Larry S. Champion, speaking of *Timon,* calls "the social dimensions of tragedy" are also the satiric dimensions of tragedy.[1] The strongest emphasis in each play is on decline, arguably the universal complaint of a satirist. Ideal, even normative urban polity, no longer exists as a hope in the general restoration of the close. Instead, it recedes even further within the borders of dim possibility, to be remembered with Juvenalian bitterness as part of an increasingly unreal and irrelevant past.

The familiar details of urban life, those touches of local color provided by plebeians in varying moods that help to bring Rome to life onstage in *Julius Caesar* and *Coriolanus,* are largely missing from Timon's Athens and Jonson's Rome. In this respect, all three plays more closely resemble *Titus Andronicus,* where an insistent reiteration of the word *Rome* and the problems of political succession in act 1 establish the city's stake in the action. The idea of Rome is embodied in the Andronici, especially in Titus and Lavinia. In Jonson's plays, Rome is represented on stage by meetings of the Senate as a way of dramatizing the state of mind of an entire society.[2] This is also a sign of Jonson's preoccupation with the verifiable historical record, conforming to the "truth of argument" which he regarded as an office of the tragic poet.[3]

In all three plays, the opening actions are specifically shaped by the perspective and subjects of satire to show how far the play worlds stand from the social norms of a healthy society. Thus two pairs of characters—poet and painter, jeweler and merchant—walk onstage at the beginning of *Timon of Athens,* representing in art and commerce two conventional hallmarks of a specifically urban civilization. The succeeding dialogue develops the visual juxtaposition further as each man praises the object he hopes to present to the great man of the city, the munificent Timon. Indeed, Shakespeare shapes the action to show a deep perversion of the poet's social and moral functions of which Sidney's *Defense of Poesy* had given the classic English formulation. Athenian materialism is so profound that it has infected those traditional guardians of the spirit of the city—its artists.[4] The poet comments on the force that has drawn all four to the place: "Magic of bounty, all these spirits thy power / Hath conjur'd to attend" (1.1.6–7). Theoretically, he understands the danger that gold represents for the integrity of poetry: "When we for recompense have prais'd the vild, / It stains the glory in that happy verse / Which aptly sings the good" (15–17). But he exempts his poetic allegory, warning Timon of the fickleness of Fortune and the ingratitude of society. Like Sidney, he speaks of the noble independence of poetic inspiration and the freedom and majesty of his calling, which "flies an eagle flight, bold, and forth on, / Leaving no tract behind" (49–50).

Of course, the poet's description of his poem has the primary function of foreshadowing Timon's fall. But his hope of material gain from the man he claims to be instructing undercuts the moral validity his work might otherwise have had. The painter disputes the primacy of words for moral instruction by a standard that is merely quantitative, claiming knowledge of a thousand moral paintings "that shall demonstrate these quick blows of Fortune's / More pregnantly than words" (93–94).

The artists' refusal to see themselves in the moral light they cast on others is further underscored by the entrance of the misanthropic Apemantus. Apemantus conflates the merchant's material offering and the poet's artistic one by preferring "plain-dealing which will not cost a man a doit" (210). To him, poet and painter, jeweler and merchant are all alike in their servile relation to the prodigal nobleman at the center of this rapacious social order. He even refuses to participate in Timon's banquet, that conventional image of communal harmony, rightly seeing in it the cannibalistic behavior that we have come to associate with Shakespearean cities: "I eat not lords" (204).

Shakespeare's emphasis here on the perversion of high civilization becomes clearer when we recall the demonstrations of orderly civic process, achieved and destroyed, at the openings of *Titus* and *Coriolanus.* This time there can be no doubt of the moral deficiencies of the Athenian polity.

The idea of civic corruption is equally clear—and even more harshly presented—in the opening moments of Jonson's *Sejanus* and *Catiline.* In both, he mocks the possibility of normative social order by presenting opening situations that harshly parody it. The initial conversation among the Germanican party in *Sejanus* (much of it translated from Juvenal) creates the discomforting perspective of a world turned upside down, morally, as these old-fashioned Romans describe their allegiance to virtue in a rhetoric of negative constructions:

> We want the fine arts, and their thriving use,
> Should make us grac'd, or favour'd of the times:
> We have no shift of faces, no cleft tongues,
> No soft, and glutinous bodies, that can sticke,
> Like snailes, on painted walls.   [1.5–9]

Jonson uses this negative rhetoric again in *Volpone* when Volpone and Mosca describe the normal activities and relationships Volpone does not engage in. Here it perfectly conveys the edginess, the chronic sense of peril peculiar to life under a tyrant. The Germanicans' only hope of survival is to remain choric, to do nothing to attract the notice of the emperor at the destructive center of the action. By the end, the dramatic and moral impossibility of such a task is revealed when, of the Germanicans who appear onstage in act 1, only Arruntius is allowed to survive. And even his survival is designed to further the political ends of Tiberius and Sejanus, as the latter explains:

> By any meanes, preserve him. His franke tongue
> Being lent the reines, will take away all thought
> Of malice, in your course against the rest.
> We must keep him to stalke with. [3.498–501]

Isolated in the present, they feel cut off, too, from the past: "There's nothing *Romane* in us; nothing good, / Gallant, or great" (1.102–3). This sense of inner emptiness is mirrored without by the recent murder of Prince Germanicus, who was once a bridge between past and present and whose death, therefore, signifies a terrible break with the past. They eulogize him as an exemplary compound of *romanitas* with "POMPEI's dignitie, / The innocence of CATO, CAESAR's spirit, / Wise BRUTUS temperance" (150–52)—an ideal city in himself, a city of the honored dead.

This sober insistence on the spiritual qualities of the Roman past, as exemplified by the highly idealized masculinity of the dead Germanicus, emphasizes the shamelessness of the present, which Jonson represents through an imagery of sexually debased body parts. Jonson uses bodily imagery not only to prefigure the horrific dismemberment of Sejanus in act 5, but also to show the dismemberment of the Roman body politic.[5] In this respect, the imagery closely resembles body imagery in *Coriolanus* and *Titus*. Jonson emphasizes parts of the body not just to reduce "the pretensions of the Roman world" but to bring down upon that world an audience's strong emotions of sexual revulsion. Thus the spiritualized Germanicus's opposite is Sejanus, whose path to power lay in submitting sexually—which Jonson equates with being cannibalized. As a serving boy, Sejanus "prostituted his abused body / To that great gourmond, fat APICIUS" (214–15). His fame as "noted *pathick* of the time" (216) parodies Rome's ideals of self-denying service, giving one's body to the state.

In such a social order, interdependence between the citizen and the state can only invert heroic self-sacrifice. In this city, only one activity—

an absolute sycophancy—is really acceptable to the emperor to whom it is directed and thus represents a parody of the mutuality we have already seen in *Coriolanus,* in Menenius's fable of the belly. Mutuality here is the exquisite mechanical responsiveness and highly exaggerated effeminacy of parasites who

> Laugh, when their patron laughes; sweat, when he sweates;
> Be hot, and cold with him; change every moode,
> Habit, and garbe, as often as he varies;   [33–35]

The climactic parody of the masculine Roman ethos occurs at the arrival of Tiberius himself, whose physical self-debasement provides the central analogue with the state.[6] Ironically, it is Tiberius's articulation of the political ideals of the Roman state which most effectively reveals their utter extinction in him. His speeches to the patricians, translated from Tacitus (*Annals,* 4.37,38), are a pastiche of Roman pieties, concluding in a secular prayer beautifully expressive of the noblest goals of the individual Roman life:

> We then
> Make here our suite, alike to gods, and men,
> The one, untill the period of our race,
> T'inspire us with a free, and quiet mind,
> Discerning both divine, and humane lawes;
> The other, to vouchsafe us after death,
> An honourable mention, and faire praise,
> T'accompanie our actions, and our name:
>   [490–97]

This wily speech, with its stately diction and balanced clauses, testifies to the irony of a state in which the nature of social perfection is easy to agree upon but hopelessly out of reach. Says one Germanican,

> If this man
> Had but a mind allied unto his words,
> How blest a fate were it to us, and *Rome?*
> We could not thinke that state, for which to change.
>   [400–403]

If Sejanus represents the abuse and contempt for the body, subordinated to the unnatural demands of power, Tiberius represents abuse and contempt for the integrity of language, perverted like the body to his own carefully hidden ends. The link between the abuses of the body and the abuses of spirit becomes clearer when Tiberius asks the patricians to erect to him "temples, and statues, reared in your mindes / The fairest, and most during imag'rie" (485–86). This beautiful expression of self-effacing *romanitas* is completely destroyed, however, by Tiberius's subsequent revelation—his intention to place a statue of "our SEJANUS" in Pompey's theater. Arruntius's outraged reaction, that this is to "bruise the name of *Romanes* into dust" (546), makes the physical desecration moral, a bruise upon a name.

In Tiberius's placing the "shame of souldiers, / Above the best of generalls" (544–45), we are reminded of the crowd at the opening of *Julius Caesar*, forgetful of Pompey in their adulation of Caesar, or of Caesar's death at the foot of Pompey's statue in the Capitol. Jonson also wants us to regard the statue as an ironic symbol of life and death, immortality and desecration, counting on us to remember Tacitus's description of Sejanus's fall and dismemberment. Tiberius knows how easily statues come down:

> For those of stone, or brasse, if they become
> Odious in judgement of posteritie,
> Are more contemn'd, as dying sepulchres,
> Than tane for living monuments.   [487–90]

This cycle of celebration and ingratitude would seem to depend entirely on Tiberius.[7] More obvious than this, however, in the contrast between Pompey and Sejanus is Jonson's emphasis on catastrophic social decline. Even the presence of the noble Drusus among his father's listeners here makes any idea of political reformation a bitter illusion because we have already heard Sejanus plotting to destroy him.

The terms of Jonson's anatomy of Rome change between 1603, when *Sejanus* is produced, and 1611 when he returns to Roman material to compose *Catiline*. The significant historical shift—from imperial Rome with its corruption emanating from and symbolized by ulcerous, anointed Tiberius to republican Rome without a hereditary head and thus prey to electoral factionalism—occasions a change in Jonson's dramatic imagery. Rome is now not a debased body, but a debased mother. As in *Coriolanus*,

Rome is insistently personified in *Catiline* as a *matria*. Here, it is mother Rome's tragic condition to have produced good children and bad, equally legitimate issue who bear a distressing family resemblance and upon whom the fortunes of their great parent wholly depend. As in *Titus*, the factional struggles in such a city have the unnatural ferocity peculiar to family warfare, although Jonson keeps the violence verbal. He wittily parodies the Roman ethos in terms of sexual violence committed within the family. Thus the Senecan ghost of Sulla who stands as prologue describes himself as a succubus come to produce the monstrous child, Catiline. Like a proud parent, overmastered by his prodigious offspring, Sulla enumerates Catiline's sexual and familial crimes, a *curriculum vitae* proving his eligibility for "the ruine of thy countrey; thou wert built / For such a worke, and borne for no lesse guilt" (45–46). There is a similar effect of strain in Catiline's opening words, a rather hysterical *machismo* that asserts a greatness equal to Rome yet betrays a deep dependence upon her for recognition. Catiline's intentions for revenge are puerile— "I will, hereafter, call her step-dame, ever" (91)—and grotesquely in-fantile, imaged as a sexually aggressive return to the womb and weighty rebirth.

All the speeches of Catiline and his co-conspirators in this opening act have an absurd, puffed-up quality, from Catiline's complaint about the tediousness of organizing a conspiracy to the conspirators' nostalgia for "the dayes / Of SYLLA's sway, when the free sworde took leave / To act all that it would!" (229–31). There is a bravura quality in their blood-thirstiness, as they remember Sulla's creation of an inverted social order in which licensed violence subsumed all rational social distinctions: "Sonnes kild fathers, / Brothers their brothers" (232–33); "Virgins, and widdowes, matrons, pregnant wives, / All dyed" (243–44). This night-mare city even had its own grotesque monumental architecture, the co-lossus Slaughter who

> bestrid the streets, and stretch'd himselfe
> To seeme more huge; whilst to his stayned thighes
> The gore he drew flow'd up: and carryed downe
> Whole heapes of limmes, and bodies, through his arch.
> [235–38]

The colossus stretching to seem more huge, whom Jonson found in Lucan (*Pharsalia*, 2.103–6), betrays the same quality of strain as the conspirators themselves. And, against this litany of horrific violence, incest, and catastrophic destruction, Jonson works an undercutting irony. He insists, largely through the conspirators' subsequent glorification of Sulla, that Catiline is not a unique phenomenon as he himself grandly assumes but a recurrent one. Under Sulla, everyone behaved as Catiline wants to now. Thus the strain in the conspirators' ferocity makes it seem insubstantial and vainglorious. And, when seen as a parody of the Roman code of secular reward for self-sacrificial public service, the designs of Catiline and Aurelia to attract and reward the conspirators seem more ridiculous than frightening. For the "slight ayrelings," Catiline will provide dogs and horses. For the others,

> if they venter lives,
> For us, AURELIA, we must hazard honors
> A little. Get thee store, and change of women,
> As I have boyes.   [169–72]

This verbal anticlimax becomes even more darkly comic when the conspirators justify this low estimate of them. Much of their early discussion, for example, is taken up by mutual recriminations about who overslept for the meeting. The details of the scene—meeting at dawn, the presence of a boy servant, the choleric impatience of Cethegus, the ritual oath-taking, and especially the portents that interrupt the conclave—are designed to remind an audience of the analogous scene in Brutus's orchard in act 2 in *Julius Caesar*.[8] Thus Catiline's barely disguised contempt for his conspirators contrasts sharply with Brutus's earnest disinterestedness and the idealization of his fellows before the assassination of Caesar. Indeed, the contrast between the two scenes, by underscoring the Catilinarian conspirators' seriocomic deficiencies, gives their bloodthirstiness an adolescent quality and makes the self-pretension of Catiline's aspirations to monumental evil more obviously hollow.

Ironically, it is Jonson's emphatic deflation of the conspirators as political agents that ensures our sense of their threat to Rome. For the effect of parody here is to insist upon a disturbing resemblance between the parody and the thing parodied. Catiline's long speech to his conspirators, closely translated from Sallust, has the ringing authority, the conservative social outlook, and the bitter envy of Juvenal at his fiercest. From a speaker of such carefully portrayed degeneracy, however, the speech becomes a parody of ethical satire that is itself rather closely echoed one hundred lines later by the first-act Chorus. This verbal mirroring of Catiline and Chorus gives a special dramatic significance to the Chorus's summary judgment of collapse from within, the city become "both her owne spoiler, and owne prey" (586).

The point is partly, as Geoffrey Hill has noted, that Jonson carefully builds upon "the stress and counterstress . . . evoked from the conflicting connotations of words such as 'liberty' or 'freedom' ": the conspirators' call for the "freedom we all stand for" is clearly a call for anarchy.[9] But Jonson also uses this rather peculiar amalgam of near-farce and sensationalism to create a satiric distance from the events and personalities to come. To miss the witty incongruities of this first act, to see in the portrayal of Catiline only "a hard monotony of mood" leads to a simplification of Jonson's subtle discrimination of Catiline and Cicero and finally to a flattening-out of the political import of the entire play.[10]

That the playwrights' greatest initial interest in each of these three plays is directed less toward character than toward unsparing social analysis becomes clear when we note how careful they are in each case to particularize social corruption. In each, as in *Hamlet,* the nature of its disease *is* the world of the play, although the diseases here are ethical rather than metaphysical. This is true even in *Timon,* although the play lacks a fully particularized sense of place. Part of the rough brilliance of the first act of *Timon* lies in its portrayal of the unhealthy needs that bind Timon and his city together in pathological interdependence. The mentality of Athens is so narrowly materialistic that the bonding agent in this social fabric is not love, as it is in *Lear,* but rather money. (Shakespeare plays on the word *bond* as a tie of fellowship between men and as a formal document specifying terms of financial indebtedness here as in *Merchant of Venice.*) Indeed this city seems untouched by the desire for power which wreaks such destruction in the other plays. The "magic of bounty" which has drawn all the characters onstage in act 1 reveals what passes in Athens for common humanity—a desire for Timon's bounty leveling usual urban distinctions of rank and occupation.

The common ingredient in all the opening transactions of the play—enumerating the claims of moral poems and paintings, equalizing the weight of bride and groom, establishing the price of Ventidius's freedom and that of a much-praised jewel—is this materialistic city's persistent transformation of all its people and products into the means of Timon's bounty. Here is the political reciprocity of the classical city at its most reductive: Athens's eagerness to receive Timon's bounty is matched by his eagerness to bestow it, the appetite to receive met and fulfilled by an equal appetite to give. That Shakespeare describes the relationship between Timon and his society in cannibalistic terms should not surprise us, after the prominence of cannibalism images in *Titus, Julius Caesar,* and *Coriolanus*.[11] What sets Timon apart is his astonishing willingness to be cannibalized: "Th'art an Athenian," he tells Apemantus, "therefore welcome. I myself would have no power; prithee let my meat make thee silent" (1.2.35–37). It is madness, says Apemantus, for the victim to "cheer up" the many who dip their meat in his blood. In this context, Apemantus's initial refusal to join the banquet that ends the first act is not a denial of the symposium as an ideal of fellowship. It is rather a refusal to succumb to the universal cycle of predatory appetite which really underlies the event. Thanks to Apemantus, it is impossible not to recognize the aggressive potential of eating or eating as a sublimated aggression:

I wonder men dare trust themselves with men.
Methinks they should invite them without knives:
Good for their meat, and safer for their lives.

There's much example for't; the fellow that sits next him, now parts bread with him, pledges the breath of him in a divided draught, is the readiest man to kill him. [1.2.43–49]

Our polarized perception of festivity and aggression also informs the masque, one that links social love and warfare by presenting Amazons led by Cupid. In the macabre perspective created by Apemantus's commentary, even aristocratic dancing—the social expression of cosmic harmony, the moving image of high civilization—is set against Apemantus's reductive vision of physical necessity, the elemental predatory struggle that turns dancers into murderers:

> Who lives that's not depraved or depraves?
> Who dies that bears not one spurn to their graves
> Of their friends' gift?
> I should fear those that dance before me now
> Would one day stamp upon me.   [1.2.136–40]

The tension between the onstage festivity and this predatory imagery is made significant by Timon's reiterated gratification at being the cynosure. He notes the competition for his favor, telling his friends: "Why have you that charitable title from thousands, did not you chiefly belong to my heart?" (1.2.88–90). Like the Old Athenian, he sees the possession of money—specifically, the dispensation of it—as virtual definition of self, what sets him, with rather hypocritical anxiety, apart: "Why," he tells the first lord, "I have often wish'd myself poorer that I might come nearer to you" (98–99). From this point of view, interpretations of *Timon* in the context of the Elizabethan economic crisis, nicely summed up by Rolf Soellner, are less important than the evident psychological truth: Timon's ego cannot function apart from Athenian greed.[12] It is thus beside the point to argue that Timon's wealth has bred Athenian corruption or that Timon has been the victim of his society's "pursuit of false values."[13] Shakespeare seems far more interested in holding up the social phenomenon of destructive interdependence for the light it casts on psychic need and economic behavior. And, although the interdependence of Timon and Athens cannot clear the Athenians from accusations of ingratitude any more than it frees Timon from "the vanity of giving," it does point to the reasons for the bewilderment of the Athenians when the bankrupt Timon suddenly changes the rules of a game conducted heretofore for mutual benefit and makes plausible their gullibility at the second banquet.[14]

I do not mean to suggest that Shakespeare is solely interested in the psychopathology of Timon's relations with Athens or even that the more generous interpretations that Timon's behavior has elicited cannot coexist with my own.[15] The number of laudatory comments like those of the steward Flavius which run throughout the play prevent us from seeing Timon only as satiric object.[16] Furthermore, it is important to the idea of the city here that Timon's acceptance of the roles of patron, benefactor, and bountiful host implies his allegiance to a vision of ideal community based on friendship. Timon's interpretation of the first banquet, although severely limited by naiveté, runs counter to Apemantus's as a reminder of the idea of noble fellowship which Apemantus's doctrinaire cynicism rules out. Timon's graciousness to the cynic makes Apemantus's surliness particularly repellent. Thus Apemantus's grief at seeing "so many dip their meat in one man's blood" (41) receives an effective counterstatement in Timon's emotional celebration of friendship: "We are born to do benefits; and what better or properer can we call our own than the riches of our friends? O what a precious comfort 'tis to have so many like brothers commanding one another's fortunes" (1.2.99–103). However, in *Timon* the hopeful vision of ideal society, which is never quite eradicated in *Julius Caesar, Coriolanus,* or even *Titus Andronicus,* becomes instead the symptom of naiveté. Timon has been a naive utopian in his inability to recognize that he shares his social idealism with no one or that the idealism itself is nurtured by vanity. A city of one citizen is no city at all.

Shakespeare dramatizes Timon's psychological transformation from naive philanthropist to intractable misanthrope with a sequence of emblematic actions that makes Timon an antitype of Orpheus, unbuilding the city in a rhetoric of destruction. Oddly, by moving out to an isolated cave, Timon remains the most expressive symbol of his city. The retreat to the cave becomes a dramatic metaphor for the state of uncivilized, presocial existence which Apemantus had earlier insisted upon as the nature of Athens. Timon's cave becomes an imaginative symbol not only of his own misanthropic isolation but also of the underlying realities in the city he had left behind, realities that Athens itself must confront in the face of destruction by Alcibiades.

The necessary first step in this deconstruction is that of self and home. Timon presents himself as a man dismembered sacrificially at his own house, his body substituting for the fortune he has squandered: "Tear me, take me, and the gods fall upon you" (3.4.98). At the second banquet, Timon interrupts the appetitive cycle into which he and Athens were locked with a ceremonious presentation of water that mocks his guests' appetite for his bounty, denies them sustenance, and expresses the insubstantiality of civilization. Timon has replaced Apemantus as the banquet's priest and apostle of death:

> The rest of your fees, O gods, the Senators of Athens, together with the common leg of people—what is amiss in them, you gods, make suitable for destruction. For these my present friends, as they are to me nothing, so in nothing bless them, and to nothing are they welcome. [3.6.77–82]

This negative mirror image of communal emptiness, treachery, and death at the second banquet takes over as a symbol of the actual city just as the first banquet had been intended as the image of an ideal one.

The structural device of antithetical mirror scenes which Shakespeare employs here to shape the hero's psychic change and turn of fortunes also accounts for a number of episodes in the last two acts. Rolf Soellner has described Timon's behavior in these acts as a "symbolic reenactment of the history of mankind," his withdrawal from Athens analogous to a fall from the utopian innocence of the golden age and his existence in the woods an accelerated movement from the iron age to the last days.[17] That Shakespeare intends to suggest something like this is clear, I think, from the primal quality of Timon's activities, especially the digging for roots which leads ironically to the discovery of gold. But, although Timon's psychic transformation is indeed a fall from imperfect innocence, we have seen in Athens itself the materialism and decadence of high urban civilization, with artists looking for commissions, merchants in luxury trades, even masquers—a corrupt efflorescence characteristic of a late stage of human development. Timon's retreat from the city to a primitive setting and a presocial existence thus suggests a backward movement in time to the rough but virtuous subsistence living that Lovejoy and Boas call hard primitivism.[18] It is a bitter twist on the pastoral theme that the spiritual growth Timon now seeks is a growth in hatred:

> Timon will to the woods, where he shall find
> Th'unkindest beast more kinder than mankind.
> The gods confound—hear me, you good gods all—
> Th'Athenians both within and out that wall;

> And grant, as Timon grows, his hate may grow
> To the whole race of mankind, high and low!
> [4.1.35–40]

Like some other pastoral sojourners, however, Timon finds neither isolation nor solace in nature. And, although he gains a new perspective upon the urban world, Shakespeare will not allow us simply to accept it. Shakespeare presents Timon's gradual achievement of full-scale misanthropy as a rejection not only of mankind and the idea of a city but of nature as well. Timon's first diatribe (4.1.1–41) moves outward from private relationships to the correspondences in the public sphere, stating in negative terms what the Renaissance expected in a healthy society. Timon's curse is actually a prophecy of the inevitable, a warning about "those evils which were certain to beset a state when the divinely ordained structure was impaired or corrupted."[19] He invokes a permanent unfestive saturnalia, a civic undoing by the socially subordinate in order to expose the hypocrisies of authority and the irrelevance of social category:

> Matrons, turn incontinent!
> Obedience fail in children! Slaves and fools,
> Pluck the grave wrinkled senate from the bench,
> And minister in their steads! To general filths
> Convert, o'th'instant, green virginity!
> Do't in your parents' eyes! Bankrupts, hold fast;
> Rather than render back, out with your knives,
> And cut your trusters' throats! Bound servants, steal!
> Large-handed robbers your grave masters are,
> And pill by law. Maid to thy master's bed;
> Thy mistress is o'th'brothel! [4.1.3–13]

His emphasis on female sexuality, disobedient children, and thieving servants, moreover, creates a social landscape recognizably akin to what we saw in Plautus and shall see again in Middleton city comedy, with its impatient heirs, adventurous wives, and scheming prostitutes. For Timon, this vision of wholesale social collapse, the second stage in unbuilding the city after the collapse of his household, serves to justify misanthropy and rationalize self-banishment. For us, his negative evocation of the wide range of normative social relationships and ordinary conditions of "domestic awe, night-rest, and neighbourhood" (17) serves as a reminder of more complex social perspectives: scheming wives, servants, and children played no part in the disintegration of Timon's household. The collapse of civic order must return the city to the life of presocial conflict antedating its origins, the future reenacting the past. And Timon's choice of a personal future reenacting the racial past of primitive men in the forest suggests the psychic regression and spiritual death to which he is committing himself.

Thus Timon's cave and the action that takes place before it serve as emblems of the presocial past and apocalyptic future of Athens at the same time that they express his bitter mental isolation. The banquet yields to the cave. Furthermore, this coming together of future and past around the archetypal misanthrope suggests a social cycle of creation and destruction not unlike the creation and destruction of heroes in Shakespeare's Roman plays. Even at his cave, Timon remains an enormous attraction for Athens, so that his encounters in acts 4 and 5 become negative mirrors of earlier stage action in the same way that the second banquet functioned as a mirror image of the first. But, instead of being the object of aggressive appetite, Timon has become the subject, turning his visitors into successive objects of a vengeful misanthropy as cannibalistic in its rage as Athens's greedy parasitism. Brandishing a root, he tells Apemantus, "That the whole life in Athens were in this! / Thus would I eat it" (4.3.283–84).

While Athens's cannibalism destroyed Timon's substance and civic identity, Timon's new power transforms the dramatis personae of acts 4 and 5 into symbolic actors in a new mythology, what Winifred Nowottny has aptly described as a "myth of Prostitution" replacing the orthodox myth of Order.[20] Timon's earlier need to draw men to him with bounty has become a complementary need to draw out hostility that will confirm his new social mythology, his anticivic identity. Indeed, the succession of characters whom Timon meets here is so perfectly suited to his new imaginative needs that their encounters come to resemble a dream in which the subject can reshape intractable reality. Timon gets a chance to reenact in a new and aggressive key earlier exchanges with Apemantus. He re-creates the role of patron for the poet and painter, this time rewarding them with stones: "You are an alchemist, make gold of that!" (5.1.113). And he meets with evident gratification the whores and bandits who validate his misanthropic vision. With audible regret, he must exempt his loyal steward from an otherwise universal hatred: "How fain would I have hated all mankind, / And thou redeem'st thyself" (4.3.503–4). Yet, although Timon initially treats his discovery of gold as a betrayal by the earth to which he had looked for food, gold soon becomes as crucial to his new social vision as it was to the old. Now, however, instead of seeing gold naively as an instrument for forging social ties, he sees it as god-like in its power to obliterate them.[21] It is possible to argue that Timon's display of gold here only serves to expose the social destructiveness of compulsive bounty which had been hidden before. That is, although the spirit in which the gold is offered has changed utterly, the social consequences of the act have not changed at all: Timon's constant message to his visitors is merely to remain as they are, to "whore still" (149), to "rob one another" (448). Only Apemantus remains unmoved by Timon's gold, largely because of a greater emotional turmoil at losing his personal currency of singularity. Yet their ferocity toward each other suggests an emotional currency comparable to gold in feeling and effect: their exchange precipitates a greater aggressiveness, distance, and social isolation.

Shakespeare does not present Timon's misanthropy as indiscriminate. Instead, through the related symbols of gold and whores, Shakespeare reveals the consistency of Timon's vision of universal appetite creating universal thievery.[22] The tragedy for Timon is not that he is indiscriminate—the example of the steward contradicts this—but that he comes to believe that nature, under the aegis of Fortune, is:

> Common mother, thou
> Whose womb unmeasurable and infinite breast
> Teems and feeds all; whose self-same mettle,
> Whereof thy proud child, arrogant man, is puff'd
> Engenders the black toad and adder blue,
> The gilded newt and eyeless venom'd worm,
> With all th'abhorred births below crisp heaven
> Whereon Hyperion's quick'ning fire doth shine:
>
> [4.3.179–86]

Despite the power of this vision of indifferent nature and Timon's rejection of hierarchical correspondence, however, the enduring centrality of gold to Timon's social outlook implies a nihilism as naive as the idealism it replaces. But the words of his despair, powerfully articulated in the fierce valedictory speeches of act 5, hint at their own rebuttal by resonating with echoes of the Christian gospel.[23]

The resolution of Alcibiades' threat to Athens also emphasizes Christian themes of mercy and forgiveness. Nevertheless, although arguments have been offered to make Alcibiades' decision to spare the city into a counterweight to Timon's bitter death, the final moments of the play do not strongly support them. Shakespeare refuses to accord Athens the significance and compensatory value that monumentality and long historical perspective give Rome. Instead, Timon's final encounters with the poet and painter and with the senatorial delegation reiterate the irremediable corruption of Athenian institutions and the Athenian soul. The senators visit Timon not from remorse, but from desperation. Their confessions of a "forgetfulness too general gross" (5.1.143) and promises of "special dignities which vacant lie" (141) sound as hollow and self-interested as their earlier flattery.[24] Even at the brink of disaster, the city remains obdurately materialistic, offering Timon

> a recompense more fruitful
> Than their offence can weigh down by the dram—
> Ay, even such heaps and sums of love and wealth
> As shall to thee blot out what wrongs were theirs,
> [5.1.149–52]

The absoluteness of Timon's misanthropy makes his refusal to help Athens inevitable.[25] But the unattractiveness of the Athenian delegation, presented as the climax of a parade of rogues, also makes the rebuff oddly sympathetic and right. This appeal to our sense of justice cannot help but temper the response to Alcibiades' display of mercy toward this "coward and lascivious town" (5.4.1). The conclusion of the play fails to demonstrate Alcibiades' magnanimity or to celebrate the city's escape. The senators make no promises to reform, but argue on narrower grounds for the innocence and dignity of the city's distant past and the less-than-total guilt of its current inhabitants:

These walls of ours
Were not erected by their hands from whom
You have receiv'd your grief; nor are they such
That these great tow'rs, trophies, and schools should fall
For private faults in them.   [5.4.22–26]

Though rightly spared, Athens remains fallen, with only the barest indi-
cations—compared with *Coriolanus* or even *Titus Andronicus*—of cause
to rejoice. The city remains implicated by the general Elizabethan de-
rogation of Greek culture.[26] Athens's lack of civic nobility is perhaps
best expressed by the ambiguous stature of its redeemer and his two
whores. If Timon's bitter echoes of the gospel serve to remind us of the
mercy he lacks, the senator's pastoral characterization of Alcibiades is
equally inapt:

like a shepherd,
Approach the fold and cull th'infected forth,
But kill not all together.   [5.4.42–44]

Despite Athens's survival, the final attention of the play remains with
Timon's epitaph, his bitter rejection of self and city. Although there can
be little doubt that Shakespeare's portrayal of Timon throughout the play
is designed to prevent us from full identification with his fortunes and
death, Shakespeare also denies Athens the nobility and moral worth that
would ensure our complete disaffection from him. Instead Shakespeare
apportions responsibility for Timon's misanthropy between the deeply
flawed city and Timon himself, the city's noblest product. What is ultimately most unsettling about this play is its insistence upon the chronic
failure of the human community. This time Shakespeare refuses to grant
his audience onstage and off the genuinely cathartic release of grief and
impoverishment subsumed by a larger civic communion.

This residue of self-division in play world and audience also attends the
unfolding action in *Sejanus* and *Catiline*. Jonson's characterization of
Rome, particularly in *Sejanus*, is even more negative finally than Shakespeare's portrait of the customarily derided Athens. Jonson constructs
the plots of both on fairly conventional tragic models, *Sejanus* conforming
to the *de casibus* pattern and *Catiline* to that of the conspiracy play.[27] He

adds the satiric material of sexual intrigue to keep the drive of the satire "against society-at-large rather than against the solitary villain."[28] We have already seen how Shakespeare's nearly complete exclusion from *Timon* of normative female figures suggests the coldness and meanness of Athens and how Alcibiades' entourage of whores serves to blur the moral contrast between his mercy and Timon's obduracy. In *Sejanus* and *Catiline,* Jonson creates an analogous significance for women, who are mostly notable for their duplicity and a sexuality completely controlled by self-promotion. Furthermore, Jonson's interest in society-at-large also goes some way toward justifying the bewilderingly large casts of characters in both plays and explaining his lack of interest in sustained characterization of all but the focal figures.[29] Shakespeare creates a similar effect of unattractive panorama in *Timon* by leaving so many characters unnamed, distinguished only by profession or class.[30] Jonson creates this satiric perspective in *Sejanus* and *Catiline* primarily, however, to illustrate the interconnections among sex, politics, and the rhetorical eloquence so much a part of *romanitas.* That is, Jonson makes his audience share the satirist's obsession with the discrepancies between words and deeds, between ostensible and actual meaning, in order to underscore the power of language as a dangerous, because essentially neutral, political instrument. A comment in *The Discoveries* suggests Jonson's belief in language as a social barometer: "Wheresoever, manners, and fashions are corrupted, language is. It imitates the publicke riot. The excesse of Feasts, and apparell, are the notes of a sick State; and the wantonnesse of language, of a sick mind" (954–58). In *Sejanus* and *Catiline,* Jonson's preoccupation with the moral condition of language and its large social effects is even more pronounced and more acutely targeted. Events not only make sex central to politics but also insist upon language and sex as analogous instruments of political domination and thus as symbolic indicators of social well-being.

The beautiful phrase—"to bruise the name of Romans"—which denounces Tiberius's architectural elevation of Sejanus in act 1 suggests Jonson's attention to the threat against even simple denomination by the perversions of power. The deeper menace in the instrumental analogies between sex and language is clearest, perhaps, in acts 2 and 3 of *Sejanus* when the protagonist undertakes two separate but related courses of action to promote his political ambitions. In the one case, Sejanus seeks to further his political control of the Senate by triumphing over those men whom he and Tiberius have agreed to single out for trial and execution. In the other, he seeks to move closer to the throne by seducing Livia, the wife of Drusus and daughter-in-law of Tiberius—that is, by using his body again for self-promotion. Ironically, however, the post-seduction scene between Sejanus and Livia displays a sexual arrogance in Sejanus that is dangerous and stupid, and it foreshadows a political arrogance even more dangerous and naive in relation to Tiberius.

Like Tiberius in act 1, perverting the honorific terms of Roman political discourse, Sejanus perverts the Neoplatonic idiom of heroic love: "I protest / My selfe through rarefied, and turn'd all flame / In your affection" (2.31–33). He promises Livia that she will "shine / Bright, as the Moone, among the lesser lights, / And share the sov'raigntie of all the world" (35–37). Jonson carefully places the speech, however, in a derisive dramatic context that exposes its incongruities and contradictions. The speech comes just after Sejanus, Livia, and the physician Eudemus have begun to consider the base mechanics of Drusus's poisoning. Jonson satirizes Sejanus's sexuality by having him aroused at the mention of Drusus's cupbearer, a "delicate youth" (23) more easily approached through sex than through gold. Even the promises of political co-sovereignty which Sejanus offers Livia are derided when Sejanus must excuse himself, momentarily, to receive the emperor's messenger and commands. Livia herself seems hardly overwhelmed by Sejanus, accepting his attentions with a cool satisfaction and an unruffled self-absorption that causes her to turn to Eudemus for a reapplication of makeup. The contrast between Eudemus's effusiveness about his new patron and Livia's unimpressed self-absorption reveals the sordid foundations of Sejanus's language and sexual pretensions. He seems unconscious of the final irony in the seduction—that he fits as beautifully into Livia's plans as she fits into his.

His confidence about this seduction prepares ironically for his encounter with the emperor. Livia, although hardly "conquered," is a far more compliant political partner than Tiberius. Their conversation ostensibly concerns legislative tactics in the continuing persecution of the Germanicans. At a deeper level, it manifests rival attempts at linguistic domination in a power struggle that only Tiberius seems to perceive. By asking Sejanus "when the master-prince / Of all the world, SEJANUS, saith, he feares; / Is it not fatall?" (165–67), Tiberius appears to give him the conversational lead and psychological advantage. Tiberius's apparent fearfulness contrasts sharply with Sejanus's blasphemous rejection of fearfulness only moments before: "Tell proud JOVE," he commands his aspiring soul, "Betweene his power, and thine, there is no oddes. / 'Twas onely feare, first, in the world made gods" (2.160–62). It soon becomes clear however that Sejanus is merely Tiberius's catechist, producing the answers the emperor has anticipated:

> We can no longer
> Keepe on our masque to thee, our deare SEJANUS.
> Thy thoughts are ours, in all, and we but proov'd
> Their voice, in our designes, which by assenting
> Hath more confirm'd us, then if heartning Jove
> Had, from his hundred statues, bid us strike,
> And at the stroke clickt all his marble thumb's.
>
> [2.278–84]

Naively, Sejanus accepts this ominously subtle profession of sincerity. He fails here, as he failed with Livia, to perceive danger in Tiberius's possession of political designs which antedate and include his own—"thy thoughts are ours, in all." He fails to foresee the peril in his design to aggravate Tiberius's cruelty by presenting "the shapes / Of dangers, greater then they are" (384–85) even though he realizes that a fearful Tiberius "doth not easily learne to stop, or spare / Where he may doubt" (389–90). Most importantly, he defines as merely real, rather than as real and strategic, Tiberius's confessions of fear and dependency:

> Worke then, my art, on CAESAR's feares, as they
> On those they feare, till all my letts be clear'd:
> And he in ruines of his house, and hate
> Of all his subjects, bury his owne state:
> When, with my peace, and safty, I will rise,
> By making him the publike sacrifice.
>
> [399–404]

His mistake about Tiberius is one the Germanicans never make. If Sejanus imagines he fully comprehends Tiberius, the Germanicans know they do not: "By Jove," says Arruntius, "I am not OEDIPUS inough / To understand this SPHYNX" (3.64–65).

This ironic picture of an exultant Sejanus imagining triumphs over an emperor he so clearly underestimates is given a larger political significance in the Senate scene of act 3 when Tiberius and Sejanus orchestrate an attack upon the Roman ideals of public service and historical recognition embodied in the general Caius Silius and the historian Cremutius Cordus. The Senate scene corroborates the psychological relationship between Tiberius's fears and his need for intimidating display. As Silius points out before stabbing himself, Tiberius resents the dependency that imperial gratitude for public service implies: "The meanes that makes your greatnesse, must not come / In mention of it" (311–12). Tiberius's manipulation of the Senate here closely resembles his treatment of Sejanus earlier, for his attack upon the two Germanicans is prefaced by an ostentatious deference toward the authority of the Senate and by personal confessions of weakness and dependency.

This emphasis upon imperial neurosis further underscores what Sejanus is unable to comprehend: that the greater his insistence upon loyalty and service to the emperor, the more threatening he will appear. His proposal to marry Livia is doomed by the very political triumph it follows so closely upon and by the expressions of devotion with which it is presented. Even more interesting in this second, barbed exchange with Tiberius is how disastrously Sejanus proves to have overestimated sex and underestimated language. Although he himself has always subordinated sexual appetite to political ends, he fails to recognize the same habit in Tiberius:

> Sleepe,
> Voluptuous CAESAR, and securitie
> Seize on thy stupide powers, and leave them dead
> To publique cares, awake but to thy lusts.
> The strength of which makes thy libidinous soule
> Itch to leave *Rome*.   [598–603]

Ironically, Tiberius's preparations for departure have the effect of making security "seize" on Sejanus, while Tiberius himself, the proleptic student of Machiavelli, makes the retreat a superior stratagem in their political chess game. To leave off "would appeare / Doubt: or (what lesse becomes a prince) low feare" (631–32).[31]

Even in the full realization of Sejanus's intentions Tiberius does not resemble Tacitus's picture of a tormented, fearful, highly superstitious psychotic.[32] Rather Jonson presents a tyrant whose recognition of his limitations creates political advantage. Tiberius's controlled couplets and pragmatic vocabulary reveal complete self-command:

> 'Tis then a part of supreme skill, to grace
> No man too much; but hold a certaine space
> Between th'ascenders rise, and thine owne flat,
> Lest, when all rounds be reach'd, his aime be that.
>
> [643–46]

By contrast, Sejanus's bolder rhetorical flights of self-description—of "winged haste," of "this my braine, / This sparkling forge" (590; 593–94)—display a hubristic recklessness that can only threaten and collide with the emperor's determination to survive. Indeed, it is Tiberius's perception of the contrast between his own cautiousness and Sejanus's reckless courage that elevates Macro as a surrogate in the match: "The proofe wee'll give: / That, while two poysons wrastle, we may live" (653–54). As Sejanus's successful political plotting had begun act 3, so Macro's gleeful assumption of Sejanus's functions ends it. The circular structure foreshadows Sejanus's fall at the same time that it symbolizes the nature of historical process in Tiberius's Rome—to replace one archintriguer with another. It is as part of history that Macro sees himself in a sly understatement of ironic homage to the statue imagery with which Tiberius had announced Sejanus's elevation and which now anticipates Sejanus's dismemberment at the end of the play: "It is no uncouth thing / To see fresh buildings from old ruines spring" (748–49).

Jonson's masterful portrait of the tyrannical emperor has led students of the play to wonder why Jonson removes Tiberius from the two final acts. However, by removing the emperor physically, Jonson can dramatize more effectively the contrast between the seemingly invincible power of Tiberius as word or idea and the horrific corporeal vulnerability of his chosen instruments. Tiberius is the idea of Rome, Sejanus the most prominent part of its body. Early in the play, Tiberius made himself a statue in the collective imagination, while the statue of Sejanus was only an artifact in Pompey's theater. Tiberius's power has been entirely rhetorical and psychological, using physical instruments like Sejanus and Macro for direct operations on the body politic. Thus Tiberius can as effectively exercise power by letter, as his famous epistolary abandonment of Sejanus in act 5 attests. Furthermore, Tiberius's habit of concealing himself behind verbal masks, enigmatic gestures, and the protective bodies of his henchmen makes his withdrawal to Capri entirely consistent. He is so given to evasion and indirection that he finally comes to resemble an unambiguously evil version of the disguised duke figure more conventionally represented by Marston's Malevole-Altofronto or Shakespeare's dark duke in *Measure for Measure*. For disguise, Tiberius substitutes absence and a literal surrogate, and he is all the more demonic because of his invisibility. Like the other disguised dukes, Tiberius is at once spectator, actor, and playmaker, an invisible puppeteer whose theater of sexual cruelty on Capri is a symbolic version of the city of Rome.[33] We have seen enough of Tiberius's resentment of dependency to sense the particular gratifications for him of theatrical omnipotence at Capri and, long distance, at Rome. And the mirroring effect of this implied inner play of sexual perversions serves to reiterate the symbolic connections between sex and politics in Rome.

However, it is Sejanus, finally, who expresses most completely the idea of Rome in this grim play. Sejanus is the paradigmatic sycophant and thus—in a play that dramatizes social decline by sexual parody of self-denying service to the state—the paradigmatic Roman. (He has taken over as paradigm from the Germanicans whose choric function expresses the morbidity of their *romanitas*.) The curve of his rise and fall is tracked primarily by references to the condition and use of his body. Sejanus gradually changes from being the "noted pathick" to being a monumental presence after Tiberius bronzes him. Jonson emphasizes Sejanus's powerful, ambiguous sexuality in the seduction of Livia, the encounter with and poisoning of Drusus, and finally in the rescue of Tiberius in the collapse of the cave: by "ore-hanging Caesar" in a "labouring posture" (4.53, 56) he places his body between Tiberius and a certain death. Although the rescue is widely believed to ensure Sejanus's position, we may interpret the rescue as further proof to Tiberius of his own continuing dependency. Throughout the play, the power of Sejanus is most consistently expressed as derived from reliance upon his body and its enormous capacity to suffer (as pathic) and to act:

> I, that did helpe
> To fell the loftie Cedar of the world,
> GERMANICUS; that, at one stroke, cut downe
> DRUSUS, that upright Elme; wither'd his vine;
> Laid SILIUS, and SABINUS, two strong Okes,
> Flat on the earth.   [5.241–46]

Appropriately, the first physical sign of imminent catastrophe is Sejanus's isolation in the Senate as the cowardly senators "shift their places" in an effort to move away from him (5.608 S. D.). Jonson's symbolic use of Sejanus's body also explains why the reported disintegration of Sejanus's statue—that symbol of Tiberius's favor—motivates his dismemberment and even that of his children, the secondary remnants of his physical existence. Given the attention in the play to Sejanus's body, the grisly details of the dismemberment (for which Jonson had only indirect historical warrant) define it ironically as Sejanus's consummate accomplishment as "noted pathick"—a final act of submission to the state. There can be no civic redemption in this dramatic reenactment of the relationship of Sejanus and Tiberius. It achieves full and terrible meaning, instead, as a dark antitype of civic possibility because Sejanus, massive in strength and vulnerability, becomes finally a negative symbol of the civic corpus sacrificed to the survival of its ruling idea—Tiberius.

A similar conjunction of language, sex, and politics in *Catiline* suggests the consistency of Jonson's view as he turns to an earlier chapter in Roman history. In *Catiline*, however, the central opposition is not, as in *Sejanus*, between two essentially evil figures, one of whom holds power that the other aspires to. It is rather between two men, Catiline and Cicero, who are morally unalike yet equally ambitious. We have already noted imagery of incest and monstrous births at the opening, which prepares for the contrast between Catiline's criminal sexuality and the normative parenthood of Cicero. But the chief interest of the play in the relation of sex to politics concerns the role of women in Catiline's conspiracy as "alternative symbols of the body politic."[34]

Of the few women in *Catiline*, Fulvia particularly stands for important characteristics of the Roman body politic. The attention that she pays to her body identifies it as a political symbol, a Roman Dol Common. Her deliberations over an earring, a hairstyle, and a gown make her an obvious demonstration of the political power which wearing "the spoiles of nations, in an eare" requires. Her sexual code of favors bestowed in proportion to goods and services received sounds in context like a vulgar parody of *romanitas*. Her imperiousness of tone throughout much of act 2, moreover, suggests that she sees herself larger than life, inexorable in her material demands, and almost mythic in her longings:

> I'am not taken
> With a cob-swan, or a high-mounting bull,
> As foolish LEDA, and EUROPA were,
> But the bright gold, with DANAE.   [2.179–82]

With the entrance of the aging, jealous Sempronia, the analogies between political struggle and sexual competition become even clearer. By making Fulvia's decision to help the Republic in part an act of sexual revenge against Sempronia to prove her greater influence, Jonson underscores the importance of his sexual theme. Outmaneuvered by Sempronia into admitting a former lover who "do's not yeeld the crop that he was wont" (165), Fulvia decides to reassert her power by making Curius reveal the secrets of the conspiracy. Jonson's addition to his source is significant: Sallust says only that Fulvia "had no thought of concealing such a peril to her country," but the specific sexual motivation of her act here undercuts its patriotism.[35]

There is irony, of course, in the discrepancy here between the pettiness of motive and the nobility of effect. There is even greater irony in the similarity between Fulvia's power over Curius and the power ideally exercised by mother Rome over her more steadfast citizens. More importantly, Curius's final words in the act reiterate the identification of Fulvia as sexual object with the city as political prize. Echoing the Petrarchan association of lovemaking and warfare, Curius prophesies the sack of Rome:

> Ile speake it, in thine armes, let us goe in.
> *Rome* will be sack'd, her wealth will be our prize;
> By publique ruine, private spirits must rise.
> [2.360–62]

By offering herself sexually, Fulvia substitutes for the city and thus saves it; she becomes the body "politic."

Cicero, too, unconsciously underscores the association of Fulvia with Rome in the oddly rather sexual imagery he employs to strengthen Curius's resolve to betray the conspiracy:

> Stand
> Firme for your countrey; and become a man
> Honor'd, and lov'd. It were a noble life,
> To be found dead, embracing her.
>   [3.397–400]

It remains an open question, however, whether Curius would rather be found alive, embracing Fulvia, as his comic response suggests: "Most noble *Consul,* I am yours, and hers; / I mean my countries" (3.407–8).

That these ironic analogies between sexual power and political behavior deflate Roman pretensions on both sides of the conspiracy explains the similarities Jonson takes pains to draw between Catiline and Cicero. There is an uncomfortable similarity between Catiline's rhetorical bravado in act 1 and Cicero's self-congratulation on winning election to the consulship: "New men, before me, none," he boasts. "At my first suite; in my just yeere, preferd / To all competitors" (3.25–27). It is difficult to ignore the inflated quality of Cicero's rhetoric or the pleasure he takes in hearing himself speak, especially since Jonson tends to permit ironic asides from hostile auditors, here Crassus and Caesar. Indeed, the increasingly high sense Cicero has of his merit complements Catiline's exaggerated estimate of his criminality. The two men also share a marked contempt for the people whom they must use as means to their different political ends. In his long apostrophe to the city after receiving word of the conspiracy, Cicero sees the role of the courtesan as proof of the gods' scorn for the city:

> Thinke, thinke, hereafter,
> What thy needes were, when thou must use such meanes:
> And lay it to thy brest, how much the gods
> Upbraid thy foule neglect of them; by making
> So vile a thing, the author of thy safetie.
> They could have wrought by nobler wayes.   [3.452–57]

Three hundred lines later, Catiline echoes the thought and even Cicero's phrase, "such aides, as geese, and harlots" (464), but sees the shame as his own:

> What ministers men must, for practice, use!
> The rash, th'ambitious, needy, desperate,
> Foolish, and wretched, ev'n the dregs of mankind,
> To whores, and women! still, it must be so.
>
> [3.714–17]

Critics have pointed out any number of these verbal and dramatic parallels between Cicero and Catiline. Cicero's smugness has been seen as evidence of Jonson's characteristic inability to dramatize credible and attractive good characters; or as the appropriate self-esteem of an ideal figure; or more persuasively as the symptom of Cicero's crucial naiveté.[36] Jonson errs fatally by letting Cicero speak so often at great length. But Jonson's translation of Cicero's "prodigious rhetoricke" allows us to recognize in Cicero a hubris and ambition virtually equivalent to Catiline's in dimension, although not in moral condition. The puerility of Catiline's assumption that he can obliterate a city with a violence transcending "the boyling of *Charybdis,* the seas wildnesse" (3.653) bears comparison with Cicero's personal mission as the savior of Rome. Both are compounded of large shares of personal vanity. Cicero's claim to have saved Rome from destruction is not just premature, but mistaken. I would argue that Jonson's portrayal of analogous strengths and weaknesses in the two leaders demonstrates that no act in the political arena, however valid on moral grounds, is without important measures of vanity and self-interest which may be fatal to the common good. Cicero expresses part of the same idea when he plans to ensure the cooperation of his fellow consul Antonius by frank bribe: "'Tis well, if some men will doe well, for price: / So few are vertuous, when the reward's away" (3.479–80).

Throughout the play, Jonson assumes enough historical knowledge in his audience about the fates of Cicero, Catiline, Caesar, and Cato to concentrate instead on the political questions raised by their pride and ambition. The breadth of his interest in the effect of ambition on the social order can be gauged by the almost comic variety of ambition evident in the secondary characters. Political ambition is at its most absurd in Lentulus who boasts, "Men marke me more, of late, as I come forth" (1.271) and later complains of the plan to fire the city: "I like not fire: / 'Twill too much wast my citie" (3.617–18). In Cato, by contrast, personal ambition gives way to ferocious verbal advocacy of the Republic. Yet Cato's reiterated self-portrait as the spiritual barometer of Rome gives him an exacerbated sense of self, a high esteem for his dignity clearly akin to the ambition of others, particularly of Cethegus. " 'Twere wrong with *Rome,*" he tells Cethegus, "when CATILINE and thou / Doe threat, if CATO fear'd" (3.218–19). For Caesar, Catiline and the conspirators are merely stalking horses for his own ambition, as the conspirators are for Catiline's.

The rivalry between Caesar and Catiline is given further emphasis by its reflection in Sempronia and Fulvia. The older courtesan is partly ambitious for her sex: "There are of us can be as exquisite traytors, / As ere a male-conspirator of you all" (4.723–24). For her part, Fulvia denies ambition as a motive although she also tells Curius:

> Come, doe you thinke, I'ld walke in any plot,
> Where madame SEMPRONIA should take place of me,
> And FULVIA come i'the *rere,* or o'the *by?*
>
> [3.375–77]

Like Cicero, if less nobly, Fulvia has discovered the rewards of attaching personal ambition to the common weal.

Thus the similarities between the personified mother city and the courtesan, whom Cicero likens to the geese whose cackling saved the Capitol in 390 B.C., are roughly equivalent in thematic importance to the similarities between Cicero and Catiline. Jonson even emphasizes the analogy, and its relation to the theme of ambition, by having Cicero describe the city's celebration of Fulvia as its savior:

> What an honor
> Hath shee atchieved to her selfe! What voices,
> Titles, and loud applauses will pursue her,
> Through every street! What windores will be fill'd
> To shoot eyes at her!
> . . . .
> But dead, her very name will be a statue!

Not wrought for time, but rooted in the minds
Of all posteritie: when brasse, and marble,
I, and the *Capitol* it selfe is dust!

[3.344–48;352–55]

This description of triumphal entry, reminiscent perhaps of Rome's celebration of Volumnia at the end of *Coriolanus,* turns the courtesan into a
city *Tyche,* an emblem of the fate of the city. But Cicero's private irony,
concealed from Fulvia, is present for us: the metaphorical transaction of
city and whore is complete when the whore—like Tiberius in *Sejanus*—
becomes a statue in the historical imagination.

Fulvia's selfish motives do produce social benefit. But they are a parodic reflection of the motives of Catiline and Cicero as well. The basis of
Fulvia's power is sex. Catiline, whose crimes are sexual and political and
whose vanity about sex and politics is monumental, has high ambitions to
destroy the city and mete out huge material rewards for himself and his
followers. He would thus compel the recognition of a mother city whose
official esteem and rewards he cannot seem to gain. He must recognize
the authority of Rome even while rejecting it, however, while Cicero
serves that authority to which he has allied his love of the republic and his
personal ambitions for power. Cicero's reverence for Rome, his long
years of service to the Republic, his rhetorical brilliance, and extensive
writing had made him the Renaissance symbol of Roman citizenship. Jonson counts on this significance in his dramatic portrayal even though he
refuses to idealize Cicero.

Probably one of the reasons that Jonson cannot bring this play to full
dramatic life is that he tries to arouse more interest in the political
institutions than in the individuals who would serve or destroy them.
Some part of this rather satiric contrast between the idea of Rome and
the individual Romans themselves is involved in the surprised reaction of
the Allobrogian ambassadors on seeing senators *"passe by, quaking, and
trembling"* (4.1.S.D.):

Can these men feare? who are not onely ours,
But the worlds masters?
. . . .
Of all that passe, I doe not see a face

> Worthy a man; that dares looke up, and stand
> One thunder out: but downe-ward all, like beasts,
> Running away from every flash is made.
> The falling world could not deserve such basenesse.
>
> [4.1–2;7–11]

The Allobrogians recognize the genuine authority of Cato and Cicero, who "seeme of another race" (4.36). And they come to see the practical wisdom of acquiescing to what Cicero calls the "accustom'd greatnesse" of Rome—its power to exercise an institutional will. A great part of Cicero's political and rhetorical effectiveness in the play comes from the impersonal authority of Rome which resounds in his voice. It is an authority compounded of a long and dignified past, historically sanctioned institutions, the walls that Cicero would put between Catiline and the Roman people—all that is represented by the earthly city to which even Augustine at its demise paid awed tribute. Jonson's insistent personification of the city—itself highly conventional until the elevation of Fulvia—suggests the mixture of nobility and weakness, of virtue and villainy with which he invests the city, her citizens, and her political life. This may partly be attributable to his use of Sallust, who believed that institutions and cities had a life cycle of growth and decay like the physical body of man, that a commonwealth resembled human nature in its characteristic failings.[37] Jonson's characterization of Fulvia, the whore who helped save mother Rome, implies his pragmatic, even wry assessment of the foundations of political behavior, as his exposure of similarities in Catiline and Cicero implies a refusal to attach simple moral labels to men in public life.

In the end, Catiline can only offer his followers a spectacle of destruction and material benefit. Cicero offers a nobler prospect: secular immortality, a creative share in the exalted historical continuum his language repeatedly invokes, loyalty to an imperfect parent who is nevertheless the ultimate source of all rewards and benefits. But Cicero's vigorous examination of Rome's debilitated moral state and his heroic efforts to save the city from the Catilinarian conspirators are only apparently victorious. Cicero cannot save Rome from the danger that he in part exemplifies, the ambition that, by its very tendency to pit self against other, threatens the intrinsically communal nature of civic institutions. Cicero is misled by a naive, self-important belief in his powers to save a city, a belief that Jonson's choice of historiographical source would seem to refute. In the imagery that Cicero employs, he diagnoses the conspiracy headed by Catiline as the disease that infects Rome. The audience knows that Caesar exemplifies the disease of antisocial ambition far more dangerously than Catiline.[38] That Caesar survives at the end of the play—a survival ruefully sanctioned by Cicero himself in the words, "CAESAR, be safe" (5.582)—becomes a clear reminder of the insatiable nature of imperial ambition and of the future civil strife that Caesar and Caesarism will provoke, including eventually of course the execution of Cicero himself.

Jonson refuses to create a spiritually triumphant hero for Rome in his tragedies, thus denying his plays a conventional tragic import. But he also refuses to accept as anything less than tragic the slow death of the ancient city whose institutions and literature he revered. There is unmistakable poignancy in Jonson's translations of Cicero's frequent glorifications of Rome, like this one near the end of the play:

> Lay but the thought of it, before you, *Fathers,*
> Thinke but with me you saw this glorious citie,
> The light of all the earth, tower of all nations,
> Sodainely falling in one flame.   [5.258–61]

Jonson's audience knows what Cicero's did not. The words, translated not invented, are a reminder that the city was always larger in its aspirations and in its idea of itself than any one of its citizens. It was participation in the immortal idea of Rome that Rome always offered to its mortal members and that Jonson offers here. His dramatization of Rome insists, far more emphatically than Shakespeare's, on the disparity between the great idea of commonwealth and the flawed ability of even its best citizens, who are capable of articulating its ideals but incapable finally of preserving them.

The city of tragedy in Shakespeare and Jonson thus reveals its doubleness by containing the forces of fratricide and creativity as the yoked halves of a single nature, as the expression of a single, profoundly ambivalent impulse to create and destroy. In plays like *Titus Andronicus* and *Timon of Athens,* the tragedy of the hero is the tragedy of his city because ongoing civic process requires the destruction of the very men in whom the city is most fully reflected. For Jonson this doubleness in the tragic city is contained in ironic contrasts between individuals or groups of individuals rather than in the tragic interdependence of the city and a gigantic figure like Titus or Coriolanus. Thus Cicero's Rome is also Catiline's Rome, the great mother of nations is saved by a whore, and Caesar will survive Catiline as Catiline survived Sulla. Rome in *Sejanus* is a city more of the dead than the living. *Romanitas* has become memory not continuum, memory of men like Germanicus in whom the monumental past was compounded. His antithesis, Tiberius, inaugurates a new, debased civic ideal—the ideal of his own survival. Monumentality, for Tiberius, means finding himself a strategic place in the minds of his tyrannized Senate, so that they will always operate as extensions of imperial will and not as men in a city.

CHAPTER FIVE

The Commonwealth Fained:
Jonson's Masques
and Middleton's Civic Pageants

By the beginning of the seventeenth century, London had firmly established itself over any other place in England as the dominant location for all forms of dramatic entertainment.[1] One reason for this predominance (aside from the obvious one of the city's size) was the unofficial dramatic rivalry between court and city stimulated by James I's unwillingness to take part in London civic pageantry and by the increasing elaborateness in rhetoric and expenditure of the Twelfth Night masques at court. The emulous response of the city fathers focused effort on the London Lord Mayor's Show, an annual spectacular procession accompanying the installation of a new mayor on October 29. But the rivalry between the two forms of entertainment underscores their common raison d'etre—to mark yearly festival occasions when the communities at court or in the city came together to reiterate common social ideals through praise of the ruling figures who ought to embody those ideals most completely.

The role of London as central dramatic locus, taken together with Jacobean society's preoccupation with central authority, invites us to look in the masque and pageant for expressions of civic self-consciousness and especially to see the task of the masque and pageant writers as analogous to those other poets of urban space, the humanist architects of the Italian Renaissance. For, like the architects with their blueprints of the *ville radieuse*, the masque and pageant writers were commissioned to design an ideal image for the actual communities where they lived and worked. There is no place in these entertainments for the strong ambivalence about the relations of great men to their cities that we have found in the tragic city of Jonson and Shakespeare. There is no doubleness of nature or image in the clear atmosphere of the communities of praise. But, if the tragic city is its own antithesis, the ideal city of masque and pageant functions as antithesis to other, less perfect communities, as we shall see. Instead of being threatened by the protection and example of its greatest individuals, this insistently benign community sees itself as fulfilled in them. It expends its highest energies not to destroy but to praise. Thus the tragic image of a city starved by cannibal feasting on its heroes is replaced by the sublimated self-gratification of official homage, the community feeding on its idealized reflection.

Standing opposed to the tragic city, the community of praise is also opposed to the city of satire in Jacobean city comedy, which is my concern in the chapter to come. Of particular significance for our present purposes is that the two playwrights most closely associated with the entertainments—Jonson with the masque and Thomas Middleton with the civic pageant—are also the two playwrights most influential in the development of city comedy. In their contradictory employments, they occupy ground polarized between *laus* in the entertainments and *vituperatio* in the comedies: people and places celebrated in the one form are held up for ridicule in the other and for similar reasons. The ambivalence about urban life which is perforce missing from the entertainments is to be discovered instead in the writers, for whom urban symbol and urban reality are precisely opposed.[2] The nature of that opposition between London in the entertainments and London in the comedies will become clearer in the next chapter. Here I am more narrowly concerned with the nature of ideal community in masque and pageant and with the parallels that may be drawn between them and the ideal cities we encountered in chapter 1.

For one thing, the civic or courtly poet is no less preoccupied than the architect with the proper relationship between symbolic form and the idea of the city. Both must translate that relationship into works of art that make apprehensible to a community its ideal self. The architect produces a plan for a star-shaped city named for his prince. The masque or pageant poet transforms the commission to praise into a dramatic form that enacts the right relations of subject to subject, subject to sovereign, and of citizen to city. The heroic roles that Jonson and Middleton provide for the participants in their entertainments have much in common with the themes of the ideal city, themes of harmony, civility, uniformity, and reason. Architecture is one of the arts on which court and civic entertainments depend—in Jonson's formulation, the body of the form as poetry is the soul.[3] Architecture and the revels share some of the same social functions, to offer the means for a fuller social experience and strengthen the desire to live in society.[4] Both presuppose a general cultural awareness of the symbolic expressiveness of place.

The long tradition of civic entertainments throughout Europe defined the city as an ever-changing theater. The physical properties of a city were capable of changing to meet the particular demands of a royal entry, ceremonial procession, or religious festival. George Kernodle has noted how conventional the emblematic devices of the medieval and Renaissance street theaters were: similar castles, gates, ships, arbors, and rocks reappear all over Europe, any of them symbolizing the city itself. Eventually, urban design and pageant architecture became reciprocally influential, with actual city gates, towers, and building facades closely resembling their pageant counterparts.[5]

A similar interaction took place between stage design and city planning—the city as theater, the theater as city. The direction of Renaissance urban design toward receding perspectives and uniform profiles seems not to have influenced but to have followed from the scenic backdrops built for the new theaters.[6] Furthermore, there is a significant interrelationship among urban design, dramatic theory, and the social hierarchy, with social divisions being analogous to generic classification. In his architectural treatise, Sebastiano Serlio, for instance, reproduces three stage backdrops—for tragedy, comedy, and pastoral. The scenic contrast between tragedy and comedy is a contrast between two cities. In the comic city, "above all, the scene should have its house of the procuress (*ruffiana*), its tavern, and its church."[7] The house of the procuress does in fact occupy a prominent position downstage, while the church cuts off the receding perspective at the rear. Serlio, moreover, associates comedy with vernacular architecture: the houses of private persons in the comic city contain Gothic arches and the scene as a whole lacks the classicism so prominent in the tragic scene. The tragic city by contrast contains noble residences in a distinctly classical style, a sharply receding perspective open for a great distance, and monumental pyramids and obelisks.

Rounded triumphal arches were the symbol for ancient Rome, and the architects of civic pageants used them to suggest how their cities presented the rebirth of Roman power and magnificence just as stage architects used them to dignify their tragic scene. The growing use of the triumphal arch in Renaissance festivals also testifies to the power of classical nostalgia, because "the arch made a poor stage." Even so, when London commemorated James's coronation procession in March 1604, the seven triumphal arches placed along the traditional route replaced all other kinds of pageant architecture.[8]

Like the city itself, however, pageant architecture reflected its diverse heritage. The typical sixteenth-century arch, decorated with torches, banners, tapestries, heraldic devices and still resembling the medieval city gates, borrowed from medieval and Roman architecture and from most other decorative arts of the time.[9] The arches that Stephen Harrison produced for James's coronation procession display just this kind of decorative exuberance. Decorative conventions in pageant architecture play a part comparable to history in the development of the city. For the city and its occasional celebrations, the present moment is necessarily a compendium of the past.

The circumstances of outdoor entertainments in the Renaissance must also have contributed to a sophisticated awareness of the interaction of city and theater, reality and symbol. Just as there are audiences both onstage and off in the theater, so for the civic entertainments there were audiences within audiences. As the pageant-actor spoke to the king or lord mayor, they were watched by an audience in the street, in facing windows, or on rooftops. Shakespeare's descriptions of the crowds welcoming Pompey, Caesar, and Coriolanus provide evidence of the mood and noise of such occasions more directly than one might otherwise imagine. As Gordon R. Kipling has suggested, Elizabethans regarded their civic entertainments as triumphs in the tradition of the Caesars.[10] Such multiplicity of perspectives not only created a sense of the theatrical dimension of all public action, but also reminded each participant in the pageant's ceremonial of his relationships to other participants and of their common relationship to the historical continuum. This had been true for the Roman triumph since its culmination came at that moment when the hero offered thanks to his patron deity and once again validated that hierarchy that puts heroes over the common people and gods over heroes.[11] At such moments the reciprocity ideally underlying the relation of hero to city became clear since the triumph represented communal recognition of individual action ostensibly undertaken for the common good. The civic pageants of the English Renaissance, particularly the Lord Mayor's Shows, tend to be less personal.[12] The ultimate function of these pageants is less to celebrate an individual than to remind the rulers and population of a town or city about their collective higher purposes.

But the audience perspectives that obtain for these pageant theaters take on even greater significance in the deeply symbolic world of the masque. In Per Palme's account of the building of the new Whitehall Banqueting House, it is clear that the hall was designed for two stages, one being the raised central platform that supported the throne and the other the raised area at the far end of the hall where the masque took place. Since Inigo Jones arranged the receding perspectives of his stage to be seen correctly only from where the king sat, the stage and the places it represented are defined through their relation to the king. Jones also designed the interior of the hall to emphasize orderly movement in depth along lines of receding perspective, making sure that stage and auditorium mirrored each other structurally. King, court, and spectacle were bound together in a network of spatial symbolisms.[13] Thus, the perspectives that Jones created are more sophisticated than, but essentially little different from, the perspectives that the civic pageants sought to create for their multiple audiences. Citizen and courtier alike saw familiar places metamorphosed by theatrical illusion in a way that made each person part of a larger social metaphor and made each consider himself in relation to certain governing abstractions. Like the court assembled for a masque, the city assembled for a pageant could imagine itself as a symbolic social entity. It could find itself mirrored in the ideal by the mediation of civic spectacle as the court was mirrored by the ideal image of the masque. That this idealization required a redisposition of space suggests the affinity of masque and pageant with that social metaphor which I have called the ideal city. Like the architects' plans for the ideal city, the masque and pageant promise to make this city temporarily realizable through the illusions of dramatic form.

The Masque

Strictly speaking, the Jonsonian masque does not present an ideal city, but the ideal image of a royal court. The masque is like the ideal city, however, in its basic function—to express the values of a specific social group in order to enhance its self-cohesion.[14] As idealizing forms, the ideal city and the masque share a common emphasis on geometry, uniformity, regularity, and reason. The masque, like the city, was thought to represent an instance of universal design, especially perhaps in using dance as the masquers' chief means of self-representation.[15] The individuality of each dancer is absorbed by the complex geometry of the dances. In such a context, individual virtuosity must serve conformity because each dancer forms part of a larger pattern which can obtain only through group discipline. Thus Jonson's descriptions of the dances tend to emphasize their intricacy because difficulty here is expressive of a common social effort:

> Then, as all actions of mankind
>   are but a Laborinth, or maze,
>   so let your Daunces be entwin'd,
>   yet not perplex men, unto gaze.
> But measur'd, and so numerous too,
>   as men may read each act you doo.
> [*Pleasure Reconciled to Vertue*, 261–66]

The moving bodies of the dancers take on the absolute clarity and significance of numbers. Their symbolism is very close to the idea we have seen in the architectural treatises that form, particularly architectural form, "is derived from the form and measure of man and from his members"

(Filarete's *Treatise*, bk. 1, fol. 5ʳ, p. 10). Jonson describes the masquers in the last dance of *The Masque of Queenes* in the mathematical idiom of Renaissance aesthetics:

> After which, they daunc'd theyr third *Daunce;* then which a more *numerous* composition could not be seene: *graphically* dispos'd into *letters,* and honoring the Name of the most sweete, and ingenious *Prince, Charles, Duke of Yorke* Wherin, beside that principall grace of perspicuity, the motions were so even, & apt, and theyr expression so just; as if *Mathematicians* had lost *proportion,* they might there have found it. [749–56]

There are even more specific resemblances between the Jonsonian masque and the *ville radieuse* of the humanist architects. The roads of that city, we recall, lead to a central gathering place where the major institutions of the city are located. A similarly strong centripetal tendency is indigenous to the masque because the theatrical arts that work together for the occasion validate themselves through the monarch occupying the central seat in the hall. Recognition of the center is thus implicit in all the masques, but in some of them Jonson explicitly spells out a journey to the center. The daughters of Niger in the 1605 *Masque of Blackness* have traveled westward from Ethiopia looking for a place so central that the sun, instead of rising or setting, *"leaves that* Clymat *of the sky, / To comfort of a greater* Light" (193–94). In *News from the New World*, the masquers have been "rapt above the Moone far in speculation" of the king's virtues (304–5):

> These, by how much higher they have beene carried from earth to contemplate your greatnesse, have now conceiv'd the more haste and hope in this their returne home to approach your goodnesse. [308–12]

One function of perspective scenes is to exaggerate movement toward the center: "DELIGHT / Is seene to come as afarre off" (*Vision of Delight,* 3–4). Masques that draw heavily on the materials of Jonsonian comedy also define the place as central. Characters such as Robin Goodfellow of *Love Restored,* deaf mother Venus in *Christmas His Masque,* or the citizens from London's brewery district in the *Masque of Augurs* turn the antimasque into a description of their difficulties in getting into the hall.

Even masques such as *The Masque of Oberon,* whose initial movement is inward toward its own scenic environment, turn back as the masquers descend to move closer to the presence whose powers they have sought to reflect. The significance of such strongly defined centers is the same for both masque and *ville radieuse*. In such hierarchical societies, recognition of the center aligns the parts of the rest. Once the masquers have recognized the throne, they can choose partners in a larger dance, imposing form on the community in a radiating pattern not unlike that of the *ville radieuse*.

Perhaps the strongest connection between the masque and the ideal city, however, concerns the challenge to time. From the beginning, Jonson creates dramatic situations that identify the court as the center of civilization, as in the journey of the Ethiopian nymphs to Brittania. As early as the *Masque of Blackness,* Jonson betrays frustration with the impermanence of the masque. He justifies printing masque texts to save their occasions "as well from Ignorance, as Envie, two common evills, the one of *censure,* the other of *oblivion*" (*Masque of Blackness,* 13–14). Experimentation with the materials of the antimasque allows Jonson to create masques that act out the diffusion of culture, presenting ideal order as a continuing accomplishment.[16] In doing so he tries to wrest the masque from the control of time even during performance and to give the masque world historical solidity. Poetry takes over for architecture as the essential agent of historical memory. The masque founds its ideal city again and again.

Once Jonson introduces the antimasque as a regular part of the form, the implicitly dialectical structure of the masque becomes explicitly so.[17] However, when he starts to use characters from the belowstairs worlds of court and city, he makes the contrast between masque and antimasque far more socially expressive than a contrast between hags and queens in *Queens* could be. Because the main masque is associated with the great Renaissance values of hierarchy, regularity, harmony, and historical greatness, Jonson characterizes the world of the antimasque as fully mortal—subject to time, to sense, and especially to the physical world of obdurate things. This subjection to time and things affects the antimasquers primarily in two ways—by making their language inexpressive or irregular, and by making them the subjects rather than the rulers of their environments. Yet the fact of such limitations also means that the antimasquers do form individual communities, ones less than ideal but nonetheless genuinely communal in their shared idioms, imperfections, and conditions of existence. The antimasque worlds lack the historicity evident in the masque and crucial to classical *urbanitas,* but in Augustinian terms even the earthly city is a city.

The major feature of the language of antimasques is its particularity. But the idioms subdivide further according to the antimasques' moral and intellectual distance from the center. The witches in *Masque of Queens,* for example, carry on rats, vipers, snakes, and other gruesome properties; listing them is a major function of their verse: "I have bene gathering Wolves hayres," proclaims the second hag, "The mad Doggs foame, and the Adders eares" (159–60). The more rarefied classical nature of *Oberon* provides the satyrs with aesthetic materials for personal adornment—gilding for their feet, perfumed powders for their heads, and shell or flower bracelets for their arms and legs. But their body art is primitive and fully immersed in time. Comus, in *Pleasure Reconciled to Virtue,* stands closer to civilization, since the belly god has been engaged in transforming nature from raw to cooked. But in his opening hymn the god almost disappears beneath the cumulative weight of his inventions:

> Roome, roome, make roome for the bouncing belly,
> first father of Sauce, and deviser of gelly,
> Prime master of arts, and the giver of wit,
> that found out the excellent ingine, the spit,
> the plough, and the flaile, the mill, and the Hoppar,
> the hutch, and the bowlter, the furnace, and coppar.
> [13–18]

The effect of such a mass of kitchen objects is not unlike the swirling primal matter that fills up the stage in *The Alchemist.* Here, the list attempts to inflate the kitchen over which Comus presides into microcosmic importance, a world which, like that of Face and Subtle, advertises itself as complete. But the test of any antimasque's place in the hierarchy is always in the social metamorphosis it proves capable of effecting. Here, the bacchic antimasquers' devotion to the lower senses and animal pleasures reverses the processes of civilization, turning people into objects instead of turning objects into art: "men that drink hard, and serve the belly in any place of quality (as the *Joviall Tinkers*, or a *lusty kindred*) are living measures of drinck: and can transforme themselves, & doe every daie, to *Bottles* or *Tuns* when they please" (72–76).

This downward metamorphosis serves to justify the low place of the antimasquers in the social scheme and to underscore how limited their social contribution must be. The more grotesque or disorderly the anti-masquers are, the more limited, graceless, and concrete their language is. The witches in *Queens* speak in charm and jingles, a repetitive verse that implies mutable, accidental oral traditions. The stichomythic satyrs in *Oberon* seem incapable of protracted utterance or semantic complexity except through collective effort. The verse of the hymn to Comus in *Pleasure Reconciled to Virtue*, as we have seen, combines strong rhythms, an extremely rigid syntactic pattern, and an entirely concrete diction to produce a stratified and monotonous song, symptomatic Jonson would say of the lives of characters enmeshed in the world of sense.[18]

But, after Jonson introduces a prose antimasque with *Love Restored* in 1612, the linguistic contrast between the masque and antimasque does not require weak poetry to stand against the good. The prose of the antimasquers suggests stratification without necessitating antithetical verse forms. Antimasque diction remains relatively concrete, especially when compared with the abstract diction we shall find in the masque lyrics. But the objects themselves have lost the demonic quality of the witches' property. Thus the Children of Father Christmas in the little *Christmas His Masque* describe their clothes, their properties, and their servants in a virtual alphabet of the London citizenry. Robin Goodfellow describes the kind of persons he thought about becoming in order to gain entry to the hall in *Love Restored*. Some of the particularity comes by way of the trades of the antimasquers, as with the printer, chronicler, and factor in *News from the World*, the shepherds and fencers in *Pan's Anniversary*, or the brewers from St. Katherine's in *The Masque of Augurs*. Linguistic irregularity may result from nationality, as with the Welshmen in *For the Honor of Wales* or the Irish footmen in *The Irish Masque*. Jonson even occasionally allows antimasque particularity the dignity of blank verse, as in the cook's colloquy with the poet in *Neptune's Triumph*.

In its tendency toward concrete diction, toward the distortions of dialect and the verbal ephemera of colloquialism, the prose of the antimasque reveals its allegiance to the world of sense. But this language does not normally need to be expunged from the memory as do the witches and their verses in *The Masque of Queens*. Its looser prose discipline and its less shapely forms need only to be placed by means of a contrast with the rarefied lyrics of the main masque.

But the antimasque communities reveal their most crucial limitations when they are set against the keystone of Renaissance aspiration—the desire at the heart of ideal city plans for man to be, as Pico della Mirandola says, the maker and molder of forms.[19] The Bowl-bearer's boast in *Pleasure Reconciled to Virtue* that drinkers can transform themselves when they please appears to be a deliberate comic echo of such Renaissance aspiration. In question, however, is not only the transformation of human form, but the transformation of the human environment. The characters of the antimasque tend to reverse Pico's process: their significance is fixed by the objects of their environment. Instead of exerting control over nature, the antimasquers become tuns and bottles, or imperfect creatures with helms of limbecks on their heads as in *Mercury Vindicated*. And, when they do pretend more seriously to higher ambitions, as does the cook in *Neptune's Triumph* in claiming the universal dominion of the Renaissance architect, their connection to the lower order is exposed. Thus the cook argues that all knowledge is ultimately physical in nature, and language merely a way of pointing out things. He is engaged, like the poet and painter in *Timon of Athens*, in a *paragone* with the poet:[20]

> A *Master-Cooke!* why, he is the man of men,
> For a Professor! He designes, he drawes,
> He paints, he carves, he builds, he fortifies,
> Makes *Citadels* of curious foule, and fish.
>
> [88–89]

The irredeemable physicality of the cook's antimasque finally defeats his claims to artistic merit. At the same time that he inflates metaphor with culinary fortification, he reduces form in the work of art to a question of size. With "persons, to present the meates" of his antimasque, he offers an *olla podrida* in a pot which is not quite large enough to include a camel and an elephant. The cook's reliance on size betrays his indecorum: he would usurp a place belonging to the poet, spokesman for a higher order. Such striving for place is, in fact, generally characteristic of the antimasque. The alchemists promise "a poore *Page* o'the Larder . . . he shalbe *Phisician* for the Houshold" (*Mercury Vindicated*, 72–73). The Irishmen in *The Irish Masque* contend for the privilege of speaking before the king.

Unlike the witches, however, many of these characters drawn from contemporary life do belong in the court world; unlike the satyrs, they may even be regarded as necessary to it. A court can do without satyrs, but it cannot do without cooks, footmen, or suppliers of ale. The characters associated with household service, particularly with the service of food and drink, underscore Jonson's interest in celebrating a social order based on functional accommodation. The world of the court is ideal because, like the city in classical urban panegyric, it gives purpose to the physical world just as it employs and transforms the citizens of the antimasque. Their presence in the hall defines them as the recipients of royal largesse, either in their fictive capacities as London citizens or Irish footmen or in their actual capacities as professional actors hired for the occasion. In fact, many of the entertainments, such as *Love Restored, The Irish Masque,* and *The Golden Age Restored,* used the King's Men, who were technically members of the household anyway. Citizen or servant antimasquers commit the indecorum of taking over center stage not out of malignity or disloyalty. Their behavior more often reflects naive devotion, as the brewer's clerk in *The Masque of Augurs* makes clear: "Our comming was to shew our loves, sir, and to make a little merry with his Majesty to night" (63–64). When the brewers realize that the bears and the artist Vangoose, whom they have brought along in hopes of presenting the masque, are appropriate only for the antimasque, they accede to their place in the entertainment and thus to their place in the world:

> Sir, all our request is, since we are come, we may be admitted, if not for a Masque, for an *Antick-mask*; and as we shall deserve therein, we desire to be returned with credit to the Buttry, from whence we came, for reward, or to the Porters Lodge with discredit, for our Punishment. [148–62]

Here the contrast between the antimasque and the masque expresses the ideal political reciprocity of a class-based social hierarchy. The antimasque exists to place and to celebrate those members of the community who take care of its ongoing physical life and whose earthly reward is epitomized by credit at the buttery.

The antimasques become the physical base of the life of the court—the actual city in service to an earthly social ideal. Jonson must then use the properties of the main masque to assert the masquers' consummate attainment of ideal form. He does this, in part, as I noted earlier, by associating the dancers with mathematics and proportion. Imagery drawn from the arts, but especially from numbers, geometry, music, and Renaissance physics, often dominates the lyrics. The language is also notable for the abstractness of its diction, typified by Cupid's description of the masquers' advent in *Love Restored* to "figure the ten ornaments / That do each courtly presence grace" (256–57). He continues:

> As *musique* them in forme shall put,
> So will they keep their measures true,
> And make still their proportions new,
> Till all become one *harmonie,*
> Of *honor,* and of *courtesie,*
> True *valure,* and *urbanitie,*
> Of *confidence, alacritie,*
> Of *promptnesse,* and of *industrie,*
> *Habilitie, Realitie.* [260–68]

At times Jonson sets the language of the main masque apart from the antimasque not with this kind of abstractness but with insistently metaphoric language that asserts its capacity to transmute the physical world of the antimasque into its immaterial counterpart. The Chorus of *Neptune's Triumph* performs such a function after the cook's departure by speaking of the *"relishes of rime"* and the *"sweets, and salts"* of laughter, the sensations accompanying Prince Charles's return from Spain. The emotions aroused by the celebrations so nearly approach the ineffable that they are *"materials* [that] *scarce have names"* (391). And James, resolver of all contrarieties, can be described only through paradox, here asserting a social ideal of perpetual use and perpetual renewal:

> Nowe turne and view the wonders of the deepe,
> Where *Proteus* heards, & *Neptunes* Orkes doe keep,

> Where all is plough'd, yet still the pasture's greene,
> The wayes are found, and yet no path is seene.
>
> [466–69]

In this urge to leap beyond the world of physical limit lies the central impulse of Jonson's masques. In *The Vision of Delight*, Jonson describes the pleasure of seeing the dance as so intense that it will be always present in the mind's eye and as so edifying that it transmutes its audience:

> Againe, againe; you cannot be
> Of such a true delight too free,
>   Which who once saw would ever see;
> And if they could the object prize,
> Would while it lasts not thinke to rise,
>   But wish their bodies all were eyes.
>
> [217–22]

Jonson presents the advent of the masquers in *Oberon* as an ascension of the elements toward an increasing immateriality symbolized finally by the king:

> Melt earth to sea, sea flow to ayre,
>   And ayre flie into fire,
> Whilst we, in tunes, to ARTHURS chayre
>   Beare OBERONS desire;
>   Then which there nothing can be higher,
> Save JAMES, to whom it flyes:
> But he the wonder is of tongues, of eares, of eyes.
>
> [300–306]

The final significance of such recurrent gestures toward ineffability is to project a world where natural law has been completely understood and brought under human control. The masque radically extends the possibilities of human action: the dead return, man reenters the Golden Age, and moves with ease between heaven and earth.[21] The masque transforms society, as architecture transformed the city, into a work of art. Masquers reenact a ritual acknowledgment of the bonds that link them to the king and to society in a form that emphasizes the rational and artistic faculties of civilized society. In its emphasis on achieved control of the natural order for the improvement of the common life, Jonson's panegyric of the Stuart court ought to remind us of the praises of cities. If the city panegyrists locate the source of that control of nature in the city itself, the Jacobean poet locates it in the king. But the vision of civilized order remains fundamentally similar because the masque, like the ideal city, is a form of the mind set against time. Thus for Jonson the Platonist, as for Socrates, the ideal city can ultimately be realized only in the mind and only by means of the mind's best tool—language. His insistence on immateriality as the final implication of the physical structures of the masque makes this clear: even in the elaborate architectural allegory of *The Masque of Queens*, where the House of Fame depicts classical heroes supported by the "men-making *Poets*" who have celebrated them, architecture must submit to language. The heroes are remembered not because of their deeds or because they are the subjects of numerous statues, but because they did not "scorne the Muse, and dye, forgot" (389). Yet even this assertion pales before the greatest capacity of language, to assert an ideal reality not as *res* but as *verbum:* the architectural House of Fame which Jones created for *The Masque of Queens* betokens the conceptual House of Fame which is created by poetry, a house that is "all of *echo* made, / Where never dies the sound" (725–26). If architectural form enables the city to embody the historical record, the poetry of the masque rescues the court's life in time from oblivion. The masque, like the ideal city, enters the memory and waits for apotheosis.

The Pageant

Like his counterpart at court, the poet commissioned by civic authorities to celebrate a Royal Entry or a Lord Mayor's Show had to satisfy the demands of Madam Expectation, "who is so severe an exactresse of duties; ever a tyrannous mistresse: and most times a pressing enemie" (*Neptune's Triumph*, 55–56). Although the professional writers of the city were delighted enough with pageant commissions to compete eagerly for them, they faced a host of technical difficulties solved at court by designing a Banqueting Hall suited to the performance of masques. With all the visual and acoustical difficulties of an open-air procession, the pageant poet faced severe handicaps. Although Gordon Kipling has recently demonstrated the sophistication and formal integrity of many pageants, there is also no denying that a show unfolding along a processional route can only have been intelligible to the members of the procession, not to the outer audience stationed throughout the city.[22] Furthermore, in the case of the Mayoralty Shows, although the city was as studious of its magnificence as the court, its magnificence was personified by a lord mayor well below the king in symbolic importance. The image of its ideal self must have seemed less available to the city than to the court, particularly in the difficult economic circumstances after 1615 when the merchant princes of the city were "worried merchant princes caught between the discontent of the city poor on one side and the exactions and monopoly grants of a spendthrift court on the other."[23] Furthermore, while the court obviously regarded playing at masques as an efflorescence of its nature, the city seems to have been identified with work—with everyday not holiday. Dekker, for instance, so completely associates the idea of a city with work that he finds London during the 1604 coronation entertainments to be no more a "Citie, (because that during these tryumphes, shee puts off her formall habite of Trade and Commerce, treading even Thrift it selfe under foote,) but now becomes a Reveller and a Courtier."[24] Celebrations of the city, furthermore, do not automatically carry with them the inherent moral importance that the obligation to praise the sovereign bestows on the masque. The court does not have to acknowledge the city as the city has to acknowledge the court. The pageants make clear how much of the traditional importance of London derives from the presence of the king, without whom London would not be the center of the kingdom. Dekker constructs an elaborate conceit describing London's loss of "borrowed Majestie" as James passed out of the city on his processional day:

> And thus have wee (lowely and aloofe) followed our Soveraigne through the seaven Triumphal gates of this his Court Royall, which name, as *London* received at the rysing of the *Sunne;* so now at his going from her (even in a moment) She lost that honour: And being (like an Actor on a Stage) stript out of her borrowed Majestie, she resignes her former shape

and title of Citie; nor is it quite lost, considering it went along with him, to whom it is due. For such Vertue is begotten in Princes, that their verie presence hath power to turn a Village to a Citie, and to make a Citie appeare great as a Kingdome. [*The Magnificent Entertainment,* 1534–44]

Yet the pageant poet tried to insist on the symbolic centrality of his community. References to London's ancient title of *camera regis* remind the city that its centrality derived from the king and remind the king of the power and protection that only London could offer. This kind of reciprocity underlies Dekker's simile in the 1604 *Entertainment* of the city as royal court: each stop at a city landmark represented a different part of the royal palace, the Little Conduit for example becoming the Privy Chamber, the device at St. Mildred's in the Poultry signifying the Presence Chamber, and so forth. In his 1613 mayoral show, *The Triumphs of Truth*, Middleton emphasizes the religious implications of London as *camera regis*. A "reverend mother" personifying the city reminds the newly installed mayor:

> This place is the king's chamber; all pollution,
> Sin, and uncleanness, must be lock'd out here,
> And be kept sweet with sanctity, faith and fear;
> [p. 238]

The Recorder of the City welcomed James at the coronation entertainment with a similar trope, drawn from Revelation, inviting him to "come, therefore, O worthiest of Kings, as a glorious bridegroome through your Royall chamber."[25]

In the 1626 *Triumphs of Health and Prosperity,* the first Lord Mayor's Show after the accession of Charles, Middleton uses a figure personifying government to redefine the proper relations of city and king and of city and kingdom. The Platonic correspondence between the human body and the body politic becomes proof of the centrality of London:

> With just propriety does this city stand,
> As fix'd by fate, i' the middle of the land;
> It has, as in the body, the heart's place,
> Fit for her works of piety and grace,
>
> . . . .
> And as the heart, in its meridian seat,

Is styl'd the fountain of the body's heat,
The first thing receives life, the last that dies,
Those properties experience well applies
To this most loyal city, that hath been
In former ages, as in these times, seen
The fountain of affection, duty, zeal,
And taught all cities through the commonweal;
The first that receives quickening life and spirit
From the king's grace, which still she strives t'inherit,
And, like the heart, will be the last that dies
In any duty toward good supplies.   [pp. 408–9]

The speech is a particularly good example of the recurrent tension in descriptions of London's centrality between acknowledging how much London owes to the king and how much the king owes to the city. In its emphasis on loyalty, the speech may well have been intended to reassure Charles of the loyalty of the city despite its refusal earlier of his request for borrowed funds.[26] But against the assertions of loyalty stand reminders of the city's critical importance to the state, reminders that may have been thought particularly appropriate for a king whose dislike of the city had prompted him to disallow any coronation entry at all. The idea of the *camera regis* works both ways. If the king and his court occupy that still point at absolute center, London surrounds them. At the same time, without the chamber of his sweet security, Middleton implies, the king's order would not (and did not) survive.

Another impulse seems to run throughout the pageants to present the greatness and magnificence of the city apart from, if not precisely equal to, the magnificence of Whitehall. Nowhere is this impulse more fully attested to than in Jonson's design and accompanying text for the first coronation arch at Fenchurch. The occasion was one in which the presence of the sovereign would matter most of all. Yet the effect of the arch, particularly as represented in Jonson's text, is less to welcome the king than to impress him with the power and antiquity of the city he was privileged to rule over. Of course the words running across the front of the arch—"Par domus haec coelo sed minor est domino"—assured the king that the city was "farre inferior to the master thereof" (22). But even the need for such self-deprecation may suggest how laudatory the rest of the Fenchurch text is about a city that might "(by *Hyperbole*) be said to touch the starres, and reach up to heaven" (20–21). The city's sort of greatness, furthermore, differs substantially from that of kings or masquers. Time, which threatens masquers, verifies the greatness of cities, which exist in and through time. Thus Jonson's numerous classical allusions function not only, as Dekker noted scornfully "to shew how nimbly we can carve up the whole messe of the Poets" (*Magnificent Entertainment*, 58), but also to underscore duration of London as a city and thus as the chief source of Britain's historical continuity with the classical past. Even in 61 A.D., Jonson's reference to an incident from Tacitus suggests London was "a busy centre, chiefly through its crowd of merchants and stores" (*Annals*, 14.33). To longevity Jonson adds suggestions of the power of the city—both actual and symbolic. If Britain is "a world divided from the world" (46), London is the nation's epitome, the seat of empire. It is also tempting to find a description of the power of the city contained in the motto Jonson attaches to the figure of Wisdom, "per me reges regnant" (62). If the moralist wants to emphasize the need of a sovereign to rule through wisdom, the poet of the city might well want to remind the king that he needs to rule through London as well. This suggestion is further reinforced by the figures supporting Theosophia— the "rich, reverend, and antique" Genius of the City and the figures flanking him—symbolic representations of the city fathers and the military might of the city. "With those armes of councel and strength," Jonson notes, "the *Genius* was able to extinguish the kings enemies, and preserve his citizens" (94–95). In such assertions of the power of the city lies the essential function of the arch to express not only "the state and magnificence (as proper to a triumphall Arch) but the very site, fabricke, strength, policie, dignitie, and affections of the Citie" (244–46). There is a sense too that London best expresses itself. All the allegorical figures and iconographic motifs on the facade of the arch were designed to support and lead the eye up to a model of the London skyline, "houses, towres, and steeples, set off in prospective" (3–4). Genius's first words to the king emphasize the freedom of the response of London, this point of time producing what "the Roman, Saxon, Dane, and Norman yoke" (275) did not—the will to obey. Furthermore, the Genius goes on to glorify the beauty of an urban welcome before he even mentions the king directly:

> Now London reare
> Thy forehead high, and on it strive to weare
> Thy choisest gems; teach thy steepe Towres to rise
> Higher with people: set with sparkling eyes
> Thy spacious windowes; and in every street,
> Let thronging joy, love, and amazement meet.
> [276–81]

While James is undeniably the center of this historical moment, the moment itself is defined as the product of the city's long duration in time—a duration that has also served to produce the present magnificence of the city.

This idealized city history takes on particular significance once we realize the extent to which the civic entertainments identify London's past with that of the nation as a whole. This is particularly noticeable with James's coronation entertainments since they did not commemorate the accession of the king (which had occurred nearly eight months earlier) but merely his ceremonial entry into London. Even so, the *flamen martialis* that greeted James just before he left the city contrasted the present March 15 with Caesar's disastrous Ides of March. And since James's passage through the city could take place only after the plague had fallen off, Jonson introduces the figure Electra, who tells her listeners she has ceased mourning—both for the fall of Troy and for the sickness in London. James's procession through London, freeing "thy *Chamber* from the noyse / Of warre and tumult" (732–33), is the beginning of a *pax Augusta*. Strained though such conceits may be, Jonson's efforts to bring the Roman past to bear on a present moment are clearly crucial to London's sense of self-importance. As James succeeds Elizabeth, so London succeeds Rome as the embodiment of the idea of historical record.

For Middleton, the presence of mythological figures in civic entertainments and the comparison of civic officials to their ancient Roman counterparts are ways of magnifying the men and the entertainments. A mounted Pallas met the Lord Mayor and his retinue in 1620, on a day set aside for the "generall Training," telling them:

> Why here the Ancient Romane Honor dwels,
> A Praetor, Generall; Senators, Colonels;
> Captaines, grave Citizens; so richly inspir'd,

> They can assist in Councell, if requir'd,
> And set Court-Causes in as fayre a Forme,
> As they doe Men, here, without Rage or Storme:
> [*Honourable Entertainments*, 4.30–35]

Such mythologizing cannot extend the range of action available to civic officials as radically as it does that of the masquers, but even in a lesser celebration the classical past helps to magnify the occasion. The social value that noble birth and place in court accords the masquers, the history of the city gives to the men that civic entertainments are designed to honor. Just as Jonson seeks to impress James with the antiquity of the greatness of London, so Middleton emphasizes again and again the continuity of civic traditions and their place in the historical record. Even on minor occasions, he scrupulously records when a celebration has been discontinued or if there has been an unusual interval between celebrations. When Pallas was to meet the group riding out for the General Training, Middleton had her complain "of nothing but Neglect, / That such a noble Cities Arm'd Defence / Should be so seldome seene" (*Entertainments*, 4.39–41). More importantly, Middleton provides the civic entertainments with the same ethical justification used for the lavish court entertainments, obliging the city to display the Aristotelian liberality of princes. In a preface to the 1613 *Triumphs of Truth*, which he thought important enough to reprint elsewhere, Middleton explains:

> There is no subject upon earth received into the place of his government with the like state and magnificence as is the Lord Mayor of the city of London. This being then, infallible—like the mistress of our triumphs [London, presumably]—and not to be denied of any, how careful ought those gentlemen to be, to whose discretion and judgment the weight and charge of such a business is entirely referred and committed by the whole Society, to have all things correspondent to that generous and noble freeness of cost and liberality. [p. 233]

Most of Middleton's Lord Mayor's Shows involve an explicit recognition of the past. In *The Triumphs of Love and Antiquity* (1619), figures personifying Example and Antiquity praised worthy former mayors from the Skinners' Company. Antiquity insisted upon the importance of the historical record for the proper functioning of the community:

No year, month, day or hour, that brings in place
Good works and noble, for the city's grace,
But I record, that after-times may see
What former were, and how they ought to be
Fruitful and thankful, in fair actions flowing,
To meet heaven's blessings, to which much is owing.

[p. 323]

The texts of almost every one of Middleton's Lord Mayor's Shows include the names, dates, and important accomplishments of past mayors
from the company to which the present Lord Mayor belonged, "as an
example and encouragement to all virtuous and industrious deservers in
time to come" (p. 302). Banners with such worthy names would be hung
from pageant castles and occasionally the figures representing past Lord
Mayors would actually ride on the pageant cars.[27]

This insistence on time and exemplary historical figures indicates how
the pageants could be used to draw connections between a city's traditions and the preservation of civic order. As a yearly celebration, the
Lord Mayor's Show recalls the past and augurs the future. Although the
person of the magistrate changes yearly, the tradition of the shows themselves and the historical record of "fair actions flowing" which they represent demonstrate that the order of the city is self-perpetuating. Unlike
the masque, which tries to place its ideal community in a poetic structure
outside the world bound by sense and time, the pageant makes the weight
of history a central part of its meaning because time is the essential
medium for expressing the identity and greatness of a city.

Like the masque, then, the pageant seeks to define exemplary figures
whom spectators can admire and imitate. Both forms offer the same
secular reward—fame—to the people they celebrate. In the masque,
however, the masquers need demonstrate neither ability nor qualifications
for their roles: they merely have to belong to the courtly society the
masque celebrates. Once they have presented themselves, danced, and
inaugurated the revels, they have fulfilled the requirements of the masque
for virtue and for heroic stature. The pageant on the other hand insists
on the open-endedness of its traditions in order to suggest to the Lord
Mayor that his significance at the investiture is mostly potential. His
fame will depend, like that of former Lord Mayors, on hard work and

self-sacrifice, as Middleton suggests in comparing the self-made citizen with complacent nobility:

> And 'tis the noblest splendour upon earth
> For a man to add a glory to his birth,
> All his life's race with honour'd acts commix'd,
> Than to be nobly born and there stand fix'd,
> As if 'twere competent virtue for whole life
> To be begot a lord.
>
> [*Triumphs of Integrity*, p. 387]

The pageants draw on several conventional tropes to indicate the difficulties of the magistrate's year in office. The morality tradition provides a conception of the magistrate as Christian pilgrim, undertaking his duties in part for the promise of salvation. A speech in *The Triumphs of Health and Prosperity* calls the mayor's year "a time given / To treasure up good actions fit for heaven" (p. 410). The year can also be described as a sort of chivalric test of strength and commitment:

> A whole year's reverend care in righting wrongs,
> And guarding innocence from malicious tongues,
> Must be employ'd in virtue's sacred right
> Before this place be fill'd.
>
> [*Triumphs of Honour and Industry*, p. 303]

The Angel of Truth in *The Triumphs of Truth* describes the year as a series of temptations, making the magistrate's office a test of the soul to perceive illusion and deception:

> Wake on, the victory is not half yet won;
> Thou wilt still be assaulted, thou shalt meet
> With many dangers that in voice seem sweet,
> And ways most pleasant to a worldling's eye;
> My mistress has but one, but that leads high.
>
> [p. 240]

The emphasis of the pageants on Christian good works also blends imperceptibly with the classical idea of heroic labours. The 1623 *Triumphs of Integrity* for the Drapers featured Tamburlaine among "great commanders . . . that were originally sprung from shepherds and humble beginnings" (p. 386). The 1619 *Triumphs of Love and Antiquity* for the Skinners presented Orpheus who compared a commonwealth to a wilderness needing to be dressed and pruned. In *The Triumphs of Health and Prosperity*, a speech from a pageant car representing Drake's *Golden Hind* used the trope of the sea of state to bring together heroic labor, mercantile adventurousness, and the difficulties of the magistrate's office:

> The world's a sea, and every magistrate
> Takes a year's voyage when he takes this state;
> Nor on these seas are there less dangers found
> Than those on which the bold adventurer's bound.
> [pp. 406–7]

This identification of the adventurous commercial spirit with the heroic tradition turns the getting of wealth into a demonstration of heroic accomplishment. It is a flattery particularly appropriate for mayors elected from companies involved in high-stake overseas ventures. Thus, each of the shows which Middleton provided for the Grocers displays pageant islands with Indian youths among spice trees. India herself, the Queen of Merchandise, was seated in a pageant car accompanied by Industry who with "her associate Traffic or Merchandise, who holds a globe in her hand, knits love and peace amongst all nations" (p. 298). We ought to note that merchandise and the traffic of getting and spending are particularly singled out in the city comedies as reasons for the absence of love and peace within the city itself, let alone among all nations. Here, Middleton makes the splendor of Indian pageant spectacles symbolic of heroic effort to use wealth in the service of the commonwealth. Middleton tries to use the evidence of wealth as panegyrists of Rome had done—as justification for a growing national sense of imperial destiny centered in London. But it should also be noted that Middleton always ties these celebrations of the commercial spirit to a rather medieval notion of Christian service and to his understanding of the needs of the commonwealth. In *The Triumphs of Honour and Industry*, Industry describes herself as "the life-blood of praise" whose mighty power "gets both wealth and love" (pp. 298, 299). And, although wealth is a constant theme in the pageants, it is usually made subservient to an ethic of utility and transformed into the expression of bounty. Middleton describes that bounty, moreover, much as Italian civic

[147]

humanists had described the manifold blessings of city life. In *The Triumphs of Truth,* a reverend mother personifying London makes the development of the individual completely dependent on the benefits of a city, whose careful nurturing of her sons "set wholesome and religious laws before / The footsteps of thy youth" (p. 237). She goes on to say:

> The duty of a mother I have shown,
> Through all the rites of pure affection,
> In care, in government, in wealth, in honour,
> Brought thee to what thou art, thou'st all from me.
>
> [p. 237]

Her bounty extends even to those neglectful sons who "willfully retire / Themselves from doing grace and service to me, / When they've got all they can, or hope for from me" (p. 238). With a mercy resembling the divine, London would bless all her sons so that any unkindness reveals "no defect in me" (p. 238). Such civic bountifulness has much in common, of course, with the royal bounty that Jonson images in *The Gypsies Metamorphosed* as "a hand not greiv'd, but when it ceases" (14). The circle of reciprocity which bounty ideally initiates, in eliciting and repaying services, is also echoed in the pageants, which constantly remind the mayor that liberality in office is a measure of greatness. Thus in the *Triumphs of Honour and Industry,* the mayor's honor is his bounty:

> Nothing deads honour more than to behold
> Plenty coop'd up, and bounty faint and cold,
> Which ought to be the free life of the year;
> For bounty 'twas ordain'd to make that clear,
> Which is the light of goodness and of fame,
> And puts by honour from the cloud of shame.
>
> [p. 306]

In part the lines remind us of the hospitality and feast-giving which were so much a part of the mayor's duties and which required a willingness to spend—with royal alacrity if not royal sums. A sense underlies the obligatory flattery of all Middleton's civic entertainments of how important generosity of spirit is as a civic ideal. That Middleton—as we shall see—never discovers such generosity of spirit in the city portrayed in the comedies may well explain his invoking it here, *laudando praecipere.*

As Margot Heinemann suggests, there is "no attack on the rebellious poor" anywhere in Middleton's work, while his rival Anthony Munday had used Lord Mayor Walworth's suppression of the fourteenth-century Wat Tyler rebellion in his 1616 pageant.[28] For Middleton, the idea of reciprocity is central to urban life. He suggests that the splendor of these shows attests to a fellowship within the sponsoring company that ought to be imitated in the community at large and ought to be exemplified above all in the Mayor. In *The Triumphs of Love and Antiquity*, for example, he likens the robes with which the Skinners supply royalty to the Lord Mayors elected from their company; as the robes adorn the king, so the Mayor adorns the city. Their Shows are like robes, too, "adorning their adorners with their love" (p. 324). "Be careful, then, great Lord," Antiquity tells the Mayor, "to bring forth deeds / To match that honour that from hence proceeds" (p. 324). *The Triumphs of Health and Prosperity* ends on a similar note, telling the Lord Mayor that if his year brings noble works "then is thy brotherhood for their love and cost / Requited amply" (p. 410).

The emphasis in these pageants on service and responsibility, on the labors of the magistrate's office, is clearly very different from the masque's usual presentation of its ideal figures as symbols who need only dance perfectly in order to fulfill the symbolism of their roles. The ease of the masques gives way to earnestness in the pageants. Yet Middleton's purpose is not very different from that of Jonson's as masque writer. Middleton's elevation of worthy Lord Mayors past and present to heroic stature really serves to glorify the city for whom such labors are undertaken, to make the city's sense of self as satisfying as the court's. Of course the virtues of the city are much less abstract than the court's, as the greater emphasis of the pageants on service, good works, and prosperity suggests. But the corollary insistence of the pageants on the city's ability to produce, nurture, and finally celebrate its worthiest citizens also betrays the extent to which the pageants ministered to the city's self-esteem by challenging aristocratic assumptions that birth, courtly grace, and royal favor matter most of all. In the succession of Lord Mayors, the city presents its community of the elect and reaffirms its worth in them. The city affirms its order as essentially self-perpetuating and a greatness that is the product of its own life in time.

CHAPTER SIX

Parasites and Sub-parasites: The City as Predator in Jonson and Middleton

Our *Scene* is *London*, 'cause we would make knowne,
 No countries mirth is better then our owne,
No clime breeds better matter, for your whore,
 Bawd, squire, impostor, many persons more,
Whose manners, now call'd humors, feed the stage.
[*The Alchemist*, prologue 5–9]

In Jonson's wry joke about the excellent badness of London, the self-congratulation of masque and pageant reappears in a new, ironic light. London becomes an ideal commonwealth only for satirists feeding the stage. The abundance and prosperity attributed in the entertainments to exemplary government has here bred better matter for whores and rogues; the social behavior held up for civic emulation has now become the source of comic spleen. Jonson's mocking boast about London as exemplary comic subject represents the other side of the coin: instead of a society "joyfully contemplating its well-being," we have a society ironically contemplating its viciousness.[1] Ideal reciprocity has given way to obsessive striving for place.

Of the many playwrights who contributed to the rapid emergence of city comedy early in the seventeenth century, Jonson and Middleton, heavily involved with the city comedies and with court or civic entertainments, represent most clearly the polarized attitudes toward the city which is my continuing focus. Middleton's career as a pageant writer begins in earnest in 1613, the same year his finest city comedy, *A Chaste Maid in Cheapside*, appeared at the Swan.[2] At the same time that Jonson was undertaking commissions to portray the court as classical or Arthurian heroes, the usurer had become the type of contemporary villain because he symbolized "forces of aggression, ruthless materialism, aspiration and anarchy in Jacobean society."[3] Part of the discrepancy between the city as it appears in the playwrights' entertainments and the city as it appears in their plays may be attributed to the usual differences between a city as it ought to be and a city as it is. The problem with this inference is that it requires not only a simplistic dismissal of the idealization in the entertainments but a simplistic acceptance of the satire in the comedies as well. In fact, exaggeration in both directions links the genres, *laus* lining up quite specifically against *vituperatio* for antithetical literary treatment. Thus the festival celebration of the present moment is echoed negatively in the insistence of the comedies that times have never been worse. "Every part of the world shoots up daily into more subtlety," laments the courtesan's mother in Middleton's *A Mad World, My Masters* (1.1.140). She would prefer less competition. In *The Devil Is An Ass*, Satan mocks Pug for underestimating London vice: "We must therefore ayme / At extraordinary subtill ones, now" (1.1.115–16). If the entertainments require dressing up topography and people in heroic or allegorical trappings, the city comedies require the reverse—a symbolic dressing down, an apparent removal of artifice. In the Induction to *Michaelmas Term*, personifications of the four London law-terms enter dressed in "civil black"—the color belonging both to the gowns of city officials and to the devil. Serious moral intent and artful selection are quickly denied, however, in Michaelmas Term's offhand comment: "He that expects any great quarrels in law to be handled here will be fondly deceived; this only presents those familiar accidents which happen'd in town in the circumference of those six weeks whereof Michaelmas Term is lord" (Induction, 69–73).[4]

A similar disclaimer against artifice is presented more elaborately in the induction to *Bartholomew Fair*. As part of his contract with the spectators, Jonson asks his audience to expect no better than a fair will afford;

what is probable in a fair is absolutely essential in a play about a fair by an author "loth to make Nature afraid in his *Playes*" (129). Jonson also insists on the social realism of *The Alchemist* by setting the play "here, in the friers" (1.1.17), which is a reference to the place of the play and to the place of the playhouse as well.[5] Such insistence on creative self-limitation, on treating only what the "familiar accidents" of the city have provided, functions like the symbolic decoration of the entertainments. Both assert that the city, rather than the playwright, is ultimately responsible for its praise or blame.

This assertion is essential to urban portraiture in the city comedies precisely because that portrait is so negative. If the masques present a benign world where natural law has been brought under human control, the comedies offer a polar image of urban society in the sway of natural law as predatory appetite. In such a city, the idea of community means that each character defines place only in terms of his self-interest. The members of this community have ties not to each other, but only a direct tie of self-interest and survival to the city itself. The participation and unity so central to masque and pageant turn out here to be the main-springs of intrigue. Civic order in such a city is as fixed and as self-perpetuating as the order of masque and pageant. Instead of the benevolent circle of reciprocities, however, the satiric city regulates the lives of its citizens through a ruthless and competitive predatory cycle that gives every rogue his gull, dooms every guller to be gulled himself, values intellectual cunning over moral integrity, and rewards no one.[6] Patterns of predatory behavior underlie the action of all these comedies in varying degrees and turn the comic convention of "the biter bit" into a summary judgment of urban society. The predatory order comes to take on the universal validity of natural law.

Jonson and Middleton make the impersonal operations of the predatory cycle believable by creating an urban atmosphere in which aggressive individualism has become an accepted behavioral norm and reductive conceptions about human nature hold sway. Such an atmosphere becomes an implicit counterstatement to the pageants' praise of mercantile adventurism as the source of so much civic benefit. Community in the city comedies does have a common world-view, like the communities of masque and pageant. This community, however, because it is degenerate, simply accepts ruthless self-interest as governing human behavior. It assumes what in fact usually turns out to be true—that each man is like his neighbor in being his neighbor's enemy.

A good index to the moral temper of these comedies is their general depiction of women, because the idealization of women which we found to be so conventional in praises of cities is here turned around. London is a reverend mother in the entertainments; the mothers in city comedy may well be bawds. Female sensuality, a given in most city comedy, is particularly common in Middleton. The unmarried woman is often a courtesan, the virtuous virgin is almost an anomaly. But the most common female type is the wife whose leisure feeds sensuality and makes time for adultery. Examples abound, from Fallace in *Every Man Out,* to Mrs. Harebrain in *A Mad World, My Masters.* Female sensuality is most often expressed as cliché in city comedy, the inevitable complement to the endless cuckoldry jokes. Andrew Lethe, for instance, assumes that Thomasine Quomodo's objections to him as prospective son-in-law concern her designs to have him "as a private friend to her own pleasures" (*Michaelmas Term,* 1.1.210–11). But she is outraged at the suggestion because "tis for his betters to have opportunity of me" (2.3.7–8). The gallants Rearage and Salewood make casual conversation comparing a "little venturing cousin" to a "virgin of five bastards wedded" (1.1.9,15). *A Chaste Maid in Cheapside* is supposed to sound oxymoronic, like Dekker's *Honest Whore.*[7] In *Bartholomew Fair,* Mrs. Littlewit accepts Knockem's argument that "it is the vapour of spirit in the wife, to cuckold, now adaies; as it is the vapour of fashion, in the husband, not to suspect" (4.5.50–51). The sensuality of city wives is such, according to Ramping Alice, the punk of Turnbull, that "the poore common whores can ha' no traffique, for the privy rich ones" (4.5.69–70). Touchwood Senior keeps a stable of gullible young men around to marry the wenches he has ruined, and Middleton often makes the trick of his plots the marriage of an unknowing man to a whore.

The significance of female sensuality for the city is that sexual stereotypes finally become expressive of pervasive cynicism. Middleton's citizens assume gallants to be lecherous—and are usually right. If merchants like Quomodo seem not to be particularly interested in sex, it is because they have traded sexual prowess for financial gain and value women at a lesser rate than "that which she often treads on, yet commands her: / Land, fair neat land" (*Michaelmas Term*, 1.1.100–101).[8]

The corollary to treating people like property is to treat property like people. In *A Trick to Catch the Old One*, Witgood apostrophizes to his newly recovered mortgage in the diction of a lover: "Thou soul of my estate I kiss thee, / I miss life's comfort when I miss thee" (4.2.87–88). Old Hoard waxes as rhapsodic about the lands he thinks his rich widow owns: "When I wake, I think of her lands—that revives me" (4.4.6–7). Perhaps it is this habit of humanizing property while dehumanizing people which makes credible the casualness G. J. Watson has noticed in *A Trick to Catch the Old One* with which characters accept vicious sharking as the way of the world.[9] After Lucre and Hoard quarrel over the right to cozen a young heir, Lucre appeals to the way of the world in his defense: "I got the purchase, true: was't not any man's case? Yes. Will a wise man stand as a bawd whilst another wipes his nose of the bargain? No, I answer no in that case" (1.3.11–14). Dick Follywit, the most sympathetic character in *A Mad World, My Masters*, lightheartedly describes the downfall of his own higher nature: "I was wont yet to pity the simple, and leave 'em some money; 'slid, now I gull 'em without conscience" (1.1.19–21).

This acceptance of human baseness as predictable and thus natural is reinforced by the evident physicality of human nature: the community becomes merely a collection of appetites. This low assessment of human nature is particularly apparent, perhaps, in *A Chaste Maid in Cheapside*. Middleton fixes the mental focus of all Cheapside well below the navel: his characters are preternaturally alert to obscene innuendo, which they find everywhere. Characterization in the play is almost exclusively a matter of sexual capacity and proclivity, which serves to lower our mental focus as well in what R. B. Parker has called the mood of a soiled saturnalia.[10] Jonson's depiction of the human animal tends to be less exclusively sexual than Middleton's, but it is not more exalted. Pig-woman Ursula, the life-force of *Bartholomew Fair*, "is all fire, and fat, . . . I doe water the ground in knots, as I goe" (2.2.50–52). The urge to relieve themselves brings Mrs. Overdo and Win Littlewit to Ursula's booth, where Knockem persuades them to become "birds o'the game." Jonas Barish has noted the frustration of physical function in *Epicoene* epitomized by La-Foole's captivity with a full bladder in a locked closet.[11]

Even apart from scatology, Jonson customarily associates his characters with unattractive physical images that almost turn the urban landscape into an Elizabethan junkyard. In *Bartholomew Fair*, there is Joan Trash's gingerbread, "stale bread, rotten egges, musty ginger, and dead honey" (2.2.9–10), or Bartholomew Cokes's brain, "hung with cockelshels, pebbles, fine wheat-strawes, and here and there a chicken's feather" (1.5.95–97). All this is as nothing compared to *The Alchemist* with its whelps, black and melancholic worms, powdercorns, dunghills, moldy slippers, rats, stills, glasses, spiders, brooms, and dust.[12] Perhaps the urban landscape is less finely enumerated in *Volpone* not only because it is set in Venice, but also because humanity there has already turned animal. For both writers, however, the point of emphasizing physiological function and of creating such a dense material substratum is to belie any claim that urban man controls either himself or his environment. The city is not the home of the life of reason, as it was for the ancients; nor is it proof of man's spiritual aspirations and capacities, as it was for the Italian humanists. The unattractive solidity of the city and the animal-like behavior of its people fix human nature in the city firmly in the bottom half of the chain of being.

The predominance of predation in city comedy makes the nature of human association not only ruthless but interdependent and involuntary as well. The material resources of these cities are so limited that the rogue is completely dependent on rich conies or foolish benefactors; they are his food. And he must always conduct his affairs under the threat of ferocious competition. Middleton's Quomodo, who habitually rationalizes his activities as the normative response to class conflict, seems thoroughly imbued with the competitive spirit, praising the man who "never walks but thinks, / Ne rides but plots" (*Michaelmas Term*, 1.1.96–97). Competition makes class solidarity a mere illusion. Quomodo's man Shortyard has no compunction about cheating Quomodo's foolish son Sim, and the gallants Rearage and Cockstone wait cynically for the naive newcomer Easy to get the "city powd'ring" (1.1.56). In *Bartholomew Fair*, although Leatherhead calls Joan Trash sister, he quarrels fiercely over territory: "hinder not the prospect of my shop," he tells the gingerbread seller, "or I'll ha'it proclaim'd i'the *Fayre*, what stuffe they are made on" (2.2.4–6). The economic scramble not only divides members of a class, but also members of a family as well.[13] Theodorus Witgood in *A Trick to Catch the Old One* wants to recoup what his uncle has taken from him, just as Dauphine Eugenie wants to make sure of Morose's legacy. Dick Follywit explains what has turned him to cony-catching in general and to grandfather-catching in particular: "I shall have all when he has nothing; but now he has all, I shall have nothing" (*A Mad World, My Masters,* 1.1.41–42). Family ties are so attenuated by the competitive struggle that Middleton's young men sound just like Plautus's wishing for the deaths of their elders. Fitsgrave asks the young gallants of *Your Five Gallants,* "Are your fathers dead, gentlemen, you're so merry?" (4.8.288–89).[14] Follywit explains filial coldness as a natural response to paternal closefistedness: "they cannot abide to see us merry all the while they're above ground, and that makes so many laugh at their fathers' funerals" (1.1.45–47). And his attitude is confirmed by Lucre's denial of the nephew by whom he has profited: "If he riot, 'tis he must want it; if he surfeit, 'tis he must feel it; if he drab it, 'tis he must lie by't; what's this to me?" (*A Trick to Catch the Old One,* 1.3.30–32).

Ironically, the consequence of denying familial or communal bonds is to reassert them in the parodic form of inverted community. Involuntary fellowship becomes the order of the day, as when Pursenet complains that "a man cannot have a quean to himself! let him but turn his back, the best of her is chipt away like a court loaf" (*Your Five Gallants,* 3.2.97–98). However, he achieves self-command by realizing the impossibility of keeping anything to oneself in the city. Sharing finally represents a cyclical order by which all live:

> Does my boy pick and I steal to enrich myself, to keep her, to maintain him? why, this is right the sequence of the world. A lord maintains her, she maintains a knight, he maintains a whore, she maintains a captain. So in like manner the pocket keeps my boy, he keeps me, I keep her, she keeps him; it runs like quicksilver from one to another. [3.2.100–07]

The age-old hierarchies remain, but reciprocity here ironically opposes the bountiful order of masque and pageant. The emblem of cyclical order in the play is a chain of pearl which travels around the circle of gallants by gift and theft. The crucial recognition occurs when, tracing the ownership of the jewels, the gallants learn they are all parasites and thus form a community of interests. " 'Sfoot," declares Goldstone, "I perceive we are all natural brothers" (4.7.213).

In most of the plays, this recognition of ironic fellowship is less conscious. But because such sharing is always involuntary, it seems to result inevitably from the discrepancy between the limited resources of the city and the limitless appetites of its citizens. Over and over action reinforces the fact of limit. In all Bartholomew Fair, there is apparently one chamber pot, while Ursula's fear that she and Knockem will be "undone for want of fowle" (4.5.14) persuades Knockem to turn to Mrs. Overdo and Win Littlewit. Jonson's alchemical rogues pretend to transform men and matter, but all they really do is broker money and goods. A similar illusion about the meaning of gold deceives Volpone, Mosca, and the suitors, for Volpone elevates gold into a symbol of aspiration beyond the fact of limit or, more importantly, need of community, surpassing "all sublunary joys in children, parents, friends" (1.1.17). Volpone declares himself outside the common exchange of gold for labor, since he lives by "no trade, no venter" (1.1.33). For their part, the suitors regard him as the city merchants regarded the fabled Indies—as an investment repaying tenfold the worth of ventured goods. But the predatory cycle of city comedy is at its barest in Volpone, where the sequence of visits probably represents the order in which birds descend on carrion.[15] Abundance in Venice is so illusory that even souls seem to be in short supply. Androgyno admits having shared his with Pythagoras, Crates the Cynic, and Euphorbus killed at Troy. In such a world, Volpone at best could only get what his clients give and ends up getting exactly what they do—nothing.

Reciprocity, it would appear, governs the predatory city no less than the ideal commonwealth of masque and pageant. The urban communities here live not off land, but off each other. As Edward Partridge comments about Volpone, "the final food is man."[16] This recognition propels Mosca's self-delighted soliloquy, when he understands that he epitomizes the rest of the world; what everyone else does by nature and without knowing, he knows and does best of all: "almost / All the wise world is little else, in nature, / But Parasites or Sub-parasites" (3.1.11–13). The sub-parasites in A Trick to Catch the Old One are Hoard's two friends

Lamprey and Spitchcock, voracious eel-like fish. In *Michaelmas Term*, Dick Hellgill describes the town gallants as "gilded flies" upon the flesh of the Country Wench (1.2.48). Characters' amusement at the follies of their neighbors becomes the appetite of the intellect, predation sublimated.

The only resource of the city is its people, actors in the urban comedy. The purchase of any other resource is as illusory as Volpone's gold or the alchemical promise. Unfortunately, like other city dwellers, these comic citizens had regarded their mother city as truly bountiful, if only for them. Thus Michaelmas Term sees his law term as a version of the natural cycle, this "autumnian blessing" of a "silver harvest" (1.1.6,10). When he wonders if gulls come up "thick enough," he is told, "like hops and harlots, sir" (14–15). The outcome of all the city comedies, however, reinforces the fact of limit by closing the circle of reciprocity—the biter, no matter how clever or sympathetic he may be, is always bit. The ironic severity of urban limit makes Follywit's bride his grandfather's whore or Hoard's wife Witgood's whore; it explains why Lovewit will return to town to end the venture tripartite and why Overdo will find no enormities at the fair; or it makes Morose's hopes for a silent woman absurd. Comic convention operates as natural law, the ruthless circularity of the urban game.

This figure of the circle, although it may symbolize perfection as in masque or pageant, can also symbolize empty, meaningless movement.[17] The circularity of action in urban comedies, seen as a function of the predatory cycle, ironically produces the illusion of bewildering change without effecting any real change at all.[18] Characters come up to the city in the hope of self-transformation, a hope that also motivates such natives as Dapper and Drugger in *The Alchemist*. One of the first apparent changes the city works on the newcomer is to separate him from his roots, resulting in loss of identity for Lethe and the Country Wench in *Michaelmas Term*. Loss of identity in Lethe is loss of memory, since he cannot remember his acquaintance of the night before. Both he and the Country Wench are unrecognizable to their parents, and the Country Wench confesses, "I scarce know myself" (3.1.30–31).[19] For such characters, new clothes are the most obvious symptom of illusory change. Clothes have the power to prevent parents from recognizing children, as in *Michaelmas Term*, or to swallow up land, as when Carlo tells Sordido to become a gentleman by turning "foure or five hundred acres of your best land into two or three trunks of apparel" (*Every Man Out*, 1.2.41–42). For the pander Dick Hellgill, clothes have more substantiality than people: "What base birth does not raiment make glorious? And what glorious births do not rags make infamous? Why should not a woman confess what she is now, since the finest are but deluding shadows, begot between tirewomen and tailors?" (*Michaelmas Term*, 3.1.1–5).

The dramatists want us to recognize that the change effected by costume is only outward, and thus illusory. So also, however, are the transformations effected or merely promised by the transfer of lands, goods, or gold, primarily because possession in such predatory cities is only temporary. Although the predatory cycle guarantees change as instability, it precludes change as gradual amelioration for the individual or society. Predation also precludes the historical process always associated with cities: there can be no change in the closed circle of the predatory system, merely recycling. Though each of the city intriguers thinks himself capable of effecting change for himself by standing at the end of the predatory chain to receive all the spoils, he proves to be a member of the commonwealth offering as nourishment to the next man what he had taken from the last. There are bitter moments when, at the height of success, the schemer may realize the circularity of urban activity and the purposelessness of his behavior. Quomodo, although imagining himself immune, anticipates that his son will be gulled: "our posterity commonly foil'd at the same weapon at which we play'd rarely" (4.1.84–85). Instead of releasing Quomodo from the predatory cycle, however, this recognition only affixes him more closely to it by prompting his catastrophic decision to counterfeit death. The decision allows Shortyard to gull Sim Quomodo and returns Quomodo's newly acquired lands to their rightful owner, Easy. For urban game-players, there is no way out or up. The city exacts a brutal justice in the self-perpetuating order of the predatory cycle. Volpone's gold ends up bequeathed to the city's incurables, a condition bitterly descriptive of nearly the whole city. In such comedies, the city awards itself the only victories.

One reason that predation is so frightening an image for civic life in city comedy is that there is really no other place to go. "Alas, poor birds," laments Shortyard's boy about the incoming countryfolk, "that cannot keep the sweet country, where they fly at pleasure, but must needs come to the city to have their wings clip'd" (3.2.19–21). Masque and pageant make a similar assumption about their own centrality, as we have seen. In the comedies, however, the centrality of the city is less an attribution of supreme value than a recognition of the limited capacity and unlimited appetite of social man. Rome is central in Juvenal's satires, we recall, because he cannot finally escape its magnetic pull, caught as he is between hatred and fascination. Both Jonson and Middleton find an analogous inevitability in urban settings: no one escapes being drawn into the predatory chain of events.

Much of this suggested centrality in Jonson's comic city results from his skill at deploying the classical unity of place, particularly in the four great comedies from *Volpone* to *Bartholomew Fair*. Each setting in those plays has a magnetic attraction of its own, which functions as an intensification of the attraction which the city as a whole seems to have for country. It is a crucial part of the opening business of each play to demonstrate the attraction of the setting (as in *Volpone* and *The Alchemist*) or to orchestrate a movement into it (as in *Epicoene* and *Bartholomew Fair*).

Each setting, furthermore, becomes progressively more inclusive and seemingly more compelling than its predecessor. The bedchamber that draws predatory birds in *Volpone* is succeeded by Morose's house in *Epicoene*, invaded by a college of ladies and their followers. The alchemical rogues would like to draw into their house in the Friars whoever has not left the plague-ridden city.[20] But the Smithfield fairground does attract everyone, and Jonson strains the limits of coherent dramatic plotting to prove it.[21] More important, Jonson gives his settings a civic dimension, making them expressive not only of the characters but also of an idea of the city as well.

Volpone for instance is structured neatly around a contrast between private and public space. More precisely, the contrast between Volpone's house and the Venetian courtroom is mediated by the neutral, communal space of the piazza, where Volpone is free to erect his mountebank's platform. Each of these settings becomes a theater within the theater, containing scenes from different dramatic, or quasidramatic, genres— the deathbed scene, the seduction scene, the mountebank's spiel, the judgment scenes. For Volpone, other places are secondary to the prime space of his bedchamber, which is as essential to his security as London, *camera regis,* was to the king's. His claim to physical centrality is supported by the behavior of the suitors, who identify their deepest self-interest with the outcome of events in the Magnifico's chamber. Private space stimulates private interest and the reverse; anyone who acts in Volpone's bedchamber has entered a competition that opposes his own interests to the community's. Jonson even suggests that Volpone's bedchamber is itself a kind of city. Alberti argued that a "city, according to the Opinion of Philosophers, be no more than a great House, and . . . a House be a little City" (*De re aed.,* bk. 1, chap. 9, p. 13). The members of Volpone's household—Nano, Androgyno, Castrone—represent a spectrum of deficiencies, a parody of urban variety. They also provide this city's version of civilization, offering parodies of history and culture in their little entertainment. And, as Alvin Kernan has pointed out, Volpone's initial act of worshipping his gold attempts to redefine Renaissance cosmology and religious belief.[22] Volpone's house, moreover, redefines the nature of human bonding. By persuading Corbaccio to disinherit his son and Corvino to prostitute his wife, Volpone attempts to destroy the two bonds in which a city has most at stake. He would reduce all bonds, social and familial, to the single, material bond implied in a legacy.

Volpone's claim of physical centrality is thus also a claim of supreme civic authority which goes essentially undisputed until act 5. Our awareness of Mosca's greater power in the role of hypocritical servant helps to prepare for Corvino's flogging of Volpone in the piazza and, more importantly, for Volpone's defeat in the courtroom. Until the final judgment scene, Volpone suffers only partial and temporary setbacks, yet he does so because he has ventured outside his secure chamber. Even Volpone's performance on the mountebank's stage, usually regarded as an expression of the genuine, dangerous individuality of the Renaissance actor, brings Volpone an unaccustomed vulnerability.[23] So does his involuntary introduction to the courtroom in act 4, as he says:

> I ne're was in dislike with my disguise
> Till this fled moment; here, 'twas good, in private,
> But in your publike, *Cave,* whil'st I breathe.
>
> [5.1.2–4]

In one sense, then, the courtroom of the Scrutineo demonstrates the triumph of public over private, the triumph of the city over the dangerously outsize house within it. Yet this earthly city is no ideal, for there is a large discrepancy between the operations of ideal justice and the accidental justice that reveals these rogues. Venice has institutions that are supposed to govern civic life. But the ideal operation of those institutions requires a moral integrity which is lacking in the corrupt and greedy Venetian justices and which is ineffectual in Celia and Bonario. The moral denouement here results from a falling-out among the rogues, which Jonson presents as inevitable: "Mischiefes feed / Like beasts, till they be fat, and then they bleed" (5.12.150–51). Only the self-limiting nature of the urban law of universal appetite saves Venice from the two rogues whose vitality, wit, and greed epitomize its worse and its best self. The Scrutino merely pronounces judgment on an intrigue that has already run its course.

In *Epicoene*, Morose's house provides a setting comparable to Volpone's bedchamber. Once Jonson has defined the relationships among the members of the other households in the play, the crucial action is to move the city to Morose since he will not go to it. Like nature, the city abhors a vacuum. It seeks to open up and fill urban space that Morose would keep completely private, filled only with the sound of his voice. Descriptions of Morose's house suggest that, like Volpone, he is trying to create a theater within the theater, a city within a city. He claims that he does not "neglect those things, that make for the dignitie of the commonwealth" (5.3.56–57), but his actions contradict all that commonwealth customarily means. He is a city planner in reverse; instead of valuing easy movement among parts of the city, "hee hath chosen a street to lie in, so narrow at both ends, that it will receive no coaches, nor carts, nor any of these common noises" (1.1.167–69). He is also a master of fortifications, rather like the cook in *Neptune's Triumph*, double-walling his rooms and caulking his windows. But for Jonson as for the Romans a city of one is a contradiction. Morose is even more solipsistic than Catiline or Tiberius, Jonson's other spectacular city destroyers. He is a spider, spinning from his innards the web of words that is his home. And like the spider, he becomes a version of the bad artist—the bad architect as well as the bad poet—thinking wrongly with a later, Miltonic version of the bad architect and poet that the mind can be its own place. The city begins for Morose as it began for presocial man when he discovers that he does not suffice for his own needs—the need being Morose's desire to disinherit Dauphine. Once Morose has committed himself to marriage, the building block of a community, he cannot prevent as much community as exists here from moving in to share his space, merging the city outside with the city inside. Jonson does not present community victory over this antisocial individual as an unambiguously happy event. The community takes too much pleasure in the torment of its major victim, dehumanizing him as he attempted to dehumanize them until he is forced to confess, "I am no man, ladies" (5.4.44).[24] Morose is not the only would-be domestic tyrant in the play. Mrs. Otter, who "would bee Princesse, and raigne in mine owne house" (3.1.33–34), finds her power restored finally with the submission of her husband. Perhaps justice lies in the fact that Morose, who does not really want a wife, does not in the end have one. But the familial bond he has sought to deny is finally the one he cannot avoid: Dauphine, the source of his torment, is also the source of his release. The success of this community's invasion of the city of one does demonstrate explicitly what other city plays leave implicit—that the city can neither be denied, silenced, nor evaded. It is the nature of the city and the houses and playhouses within it to be as inclusive as possible, even if the urban community is far from ideal.

Jonson changes ground in *Bartholomew Fair,* from a city inside a city to a city outside the walls. By using a familiar spatial symbol like the fairgrounds, Jonson can also draw upon the spatial symbolism of the medieval stage. Placed at stage-left, Ursula's barbeque pit would represent hell-mouth; the puppet booth, at stage-right, would signify the play's "heaven," where the final orderings take place. The stocks at down-center become a fitting emblem for the trials of this life.[25] Such a staging allows the fair to represent not just holiday but everyday as well. This suggestion is reinforced at the opening of act 2 when Adam Overdo presents the fair as a civic proving-ground while Leatherhead and Joan Trash set up their booths onstage behind him. His presence as authority-in-disguise, his ostentatious allusions to the classical past, and his refrain—"Well, in Justice name, and the Kings; and for the commonwealth" (2.1.1–2;48–49)—prepare us to regard action at the fair as a genuine test case of "the nature of our people, / Our city's institutions, and the terms / For common justice" (*Measure for Measure*, 1.1.9–11). That Overdo is himself undone by the fair affects the validity of the social test no more than the similar exposure of the duke in *Measure for Measure*.[26] Jonson's aesthetic contract with his audience yields to a more complex presentation of the social contract which underlies the fair itself and the idea of the city which it expresses. For all their disparateness before and during the fair, the fairgoers do function as a minimal community simply because each has identified a reason to collect in the same space. The parallel with citizenship is clear. Whether opposed to the fair or not, the fairgoers share a status that for the occasion highlights and limits other differences among them. In its concentration, the fair is even more a city than the city itself, its notion of reciprocity simpler but no less fundamental since everyone at the fair expects to get or lose something in its course. That Jonson intends us to accept the fair world as a manic version of everyday rather than as an alternative to it is clearest in the experience of Overdo himself. His expectation of finding enormities ignores Jonson's warning against those who would expect servant monsters or "better ware then a *Fayre* will affoord" (115–16). Furthermore, like the city itself, the fair is only apparently chaotic. While it may intensify normal social and comic processes, Jonson has insisted at the beginning that it will not deviate from them. And if the fair breaks down preexisting relationships, it serves its own best interest in creating new ones—the two marriages in prospect at the end.[27]

But none of Jonson's plays, not even *Bartholomew Fair*, exceeds *The Alchemist* in a significant interpretation of the city through extreme adherence to unity of time and place. By setting the play in the Blackfriars neighborhood in 1610 and making the fictive time coterminous with performance, Jonson attempts to make the stage an extension of everyday reality.[28] The effect is not only to imply that the audience is capable of being gulled like Dapper or Drugger; it is also to make the audience into Blackfriars neighbors doing exactly what the trio is always worrying about—listening in. Edward Partridge has noticed the martial and political references that join the alchemical imagery that pervades the play, references that John Mebane has recently argued constitute Jonson's attack on the radical millenary and utopian movements of his day.[29] But the gulls, too, have civic pretensions. Epicure Mammon wants, among other things, to eradicate disease, age, poverty, and other social ills. Like the merchant princes of the pageants, he would disperse his fortune in pious works and public service. That solutions to such problems should come as pallid afterthoughts to elaborate sensual fantasies suggests a disproportion between self-interest and public service in the amassing of great speculative fortunes which the pageants overlook. The temporal ambitions of the Anabaptists are more explicit, although their willingness to use bribery satirizes the corrupt "civill *Magistrate*" (3.1.42) no less than the religious enthusiast.

Here, as in *Volpone*, Jonson uses the city within a city to imply inevitable defeat for all who dream of turning the age to gold. The gulls imagine the one prosaic city house in the play as the home of the Queen of Faery, Novo Orbe, the seat of necromancy, an alchemical laboratory, a school for quarreling, and a matchmaker's data bank. Yet even its fictive reality is an illusion. What Jonson makes especially absurd about his gulls' illusions is their expectation that actuality can ever be more than actuality, that a city can be other than the sum of everyday. Our recognition of this absurdity becomes inescapable when Jonson turns the focus of the play inside out with the arrival of Lovewit and the neighbors, preparing the audience for the moment when he will turn them out, too, into the actual world of the Blackfriars. Transformation will occur only in the least ambitious character of all; Dame Pliant becomes Mistress Lovewit. The commonwealth promises once again to renew itself, but the promise in so cynical a union is ironic.

Thus *The Alchemist* represents an intensification of the dramatic strategy which Jonson uses to good effect in the other three great comedies. His urban settings take on a suggestion not simply of probability, but of inevitability in an emphatic use of the metaphoric dimensions of the Elizabethan stage. Jonson demonstrates the symbolic centrality of his urban settings by offering no alternative. Most Jonsonian characters live physically constricted lives. Morose never leaves his house. Volpone, who seems to have spent three years entertaining suitors in his chamber, encounters disaster each time he leaves it. Face makes forays into plague-ridden London, but we only see their results. Only Bartholomew Fair-goers represent an apparent exception, since they are not trapped in one place and the fair is temporary. Yet the fair, man-made like Jonson's other environments, cannot escape the implication that man—not nature—is responsible for what goes on within it.[30] Such a recognition explains the poverty of nature imagery in Jonson's plays, a lack directly attributable to the characters.[31] There is much more nature imagery in the masques. The satiric meaning these dramatic characters attribute to their settings is a function not of their importance but of their dramatic creator's skill and ethos. In all four of the comedies, for instance, there is an evident, highly charged tension between the narrow physical scope of the scene and the complexity of the action and atmosphere it contains. Jonson evokes the urban world by filling up his stage with diverse people, an often immense range of physical reference, and a tangle of linguistic accents. The contrast with the ordered materiality of the masque world is conspicuous. Part of the action of any masque is one of selection— excluding or transforming certain environments, extolling uniformity in the masquers. Unacceptable landscapes vanish, while characters from the city act their parts in the antimasque and either leave or step aside for the advent of their social superiors. The ideal community is thoroughly at one with a benevolent, pristine natural world that it understands and in some measure controls. The operating principle of the ideal common-wealth, like all the ideal cities of the Renaissance, is one of controlled inclusiveness. But inclusiveness in the comic communities represents di-versity without distinction, the antithesis of hierarchy.[32] Jonson's comic societies include one fox, one fruitfly, one crow, one vulture, two parrots, and a hawk; or three rogues of differently disreputable backgrounds who assume different roles while gulling one tobacconist, one lawyer, one quarrelsome rustic, two Anabaptists, one knighted voluptary; or one near idiot, his tutor, one lunatic, one disguised justice, and so forth.[33] The degree and uniformity of the masque has yielded to disorderly hetero-geneity, to the sensation of uncontrolled inclusiveness—a city planner's nightmare. Even so, these communities are communities because they are packed into the same dense urban space.[34] Morose cannot prevent the city from moving in on him any more than he can prevent his wife from talking. The fair takes its own course despite the attempts of Overdo, Busy, and Wasp to control it. And the biggest problem for the alchemical trio—where they are going to put everyone—is a miniature version of the basic urban dilemma. Furthermore, the density of verbal texture in these plays ties the Jonsonian characters even more firmly to their settings and gives their heterogeneity correspondences throughout the microcosm. Like the characters in the antimasque, these are characters tied to and expressed by the objects in their worlds.

Thus, if the sense of centrality which the masques and pageants create for the places they celebrate confirms a sense of spaciousness in order and decorum, the kind of centrality to which the comic city aspires produces an imitation of chaos. This is the negative side of the pageants' glorification of urban abundance. The city is so crowded, so complex, so full, and so dramatically sufficient to the action that its inhabitants are almost inevitably deluded into thinking that it and they are complete and essential.

Of course Jonson delights in the imaginative power of his comic cities and of the real city they imitate. But the juxtaposed visions of the communities in the comedies and the communities in the masques—a rough juxtaposition of real and ideal—suggest an imaginative division in Jonson comparable to the division we found in Juvenal.[35] He cannot reject the disorderly city that so fascinates him any more than Juvenal can leave Rome. And, although it is true that the approximate justice of Jonson's denouements may imply recognition of a more perfect city, that justice is far more rigorous in *Volpone* and *Epicoene* than it is in the two later comedies where the city is most disorderly. Order as a social phenomenon within the plays yields to order as an aesthetic phenomenon achieved by the playwright alone. He is the urban alchemist, transforming the materials of actuality into art. The regularity, uniformity, and unanimity so essential to the masque give way to a comic celebration of the urban particular, even if the place *is* as dirty as Smithfield and as stinking every whit.

Perhaps Jonson did see the image of an ideal city reflected in the splendor of the court on masquing nights. But the ideal city itself can only have existed for him as it did for the Platonic Socrates—in heaven. In order to celebrate ideal community on earth, he had to bring in the antimasque.

Instead of concentrating narrowly on a specific place and group of characters, Middleton focuses interest on a generalized scene or action, as titles like *A Mad World, My Masters* or *Michaelmas Term* or even *A Chaste Maid in Cheapside* suggest. Middleton is less interested in outsize personalities than in the pervasive qualities of a scene. The symbolic household in Jonson yields to a symbolic region, like Cheapside, or a symbolic season, like Michaelmas Term. Jonson uses the city as a place in which giant predators lure victims into their restricted spaces, analogues for the city. But, although Middleton does invest Quomodo's darkly lit shop with infernal implications, it is less important than Jonson's important interiors.[36] In general, Middleton allows a sense of the entire city to control mood and to provide the chief thematic unity of a play. Furthermore, instead of Jonsonian constriction Middleton presents the first effects of the city as a sense of liberating opportunity and unrestricted freedom of action that will prove to be a trap only at the end. His characters are far freer than Jonson's to move around, within, and beyond the confines of the city; they have the illusion of psychologically free space. And, in at least two of the city plays—*Michaelmas Term* and *A Mad World, My Masters*—Middleton opens the action on street scenes and rapidly introduces characters from each of the several groups that make up the multiple plot.

These public scenes enable Middleton to make his characters part of a much larger, seemingly openended community that stretches out beyond the confines of the stage and defines the city as a treasure house of financial and social opportunity. Encounters on the street set various subplots in motion. In *A Trick to Catch the Old One*, Theodorus Witgood regards London as the only place to recoup his bankrupt fortunes. And, sure enough, the first person the theater of the city presents is his designated prey, Uncle Lucre the usurer, locked with his adversary Hoard in the very attitude of combat that will ensure Witgood's success. In *Michaelmas Term*, right after Quomodo describes the land he intends to possess in Essex, he spots the owner of the land, Master Easy, whom the city seems to have offered to his hand. "That's he, that's he!" (1.1.115), rings out from the merchant with the exultation of the hunter spotting long-sought-after game. Easy himself, who has had to wait until his father's death to come up to the city, is welcomed with the assurance that "here's gallants of all sizes, of all lasts" (1.1.44). He responds with a declaration of new-found independence from rustic confinement: "You have easily possess'd me, I am free; / Let those live hinds that know not liberty" (1.1.47–48). His attitude is quite specifically antipastoral, probably meant to remind us ironically of those, like Rosalind and Touchstone, who flee court or city for the sensation of liberty in Arden.[37]

Something more is going on here than comic economy of predictable coincidence. Middleton uses coincidence to suggest urban opportunity, the heady sense of possibility experienced most strongly by the newcomer but clearly available to a seasoned native like Quomodo. As we shall see, Shakespeare achieves much the same effect, with an even more manic intensity, in *The Comedy of Errors*, where the wandering twins walk the streets of Ephesus only to be presented with a ready-made dinner, wife, household, girlfriend, chain of gold, and set of acquaintances. And, rather like *The Comedy of Errors* again, this bustle of activity on Middleton's streets provides more community and generates more relationships than individual city dwellers may desire or comprehend. His introductory scenes demonstrate a large network of relationships tying his characters together, but the same expansiveness prevents those characters from fully appreciating it. For Middleton, the city creates community and makes it ironic or perverse at the same time. Dick Follywit and Frank Gullman, the courtesan, are part of the same community in *A Mad World, My Masters* not simply because both can walk out onto the same stage at different moments of the opening scene, but also because they share without knowing it a close relationship with the same man: Follywit's grandfather, old Sir Bounteous, is Gullman's lover. This relationship will be superseded by an even closer one when Follywit marries Gullman. Gullman herself is a common bond between Penitent Brothel and Master Harebrain, since by making her his wife's best friend Harebrain enables Gullman to function as Penitent Brothel's bawd.

The irony of unconscious relationships permeates the atmosphere and defines the nature of community in Middleton's other plays, too. In *Michaelmas Term*, Master Rearage withdraws from the stage to avoid being seen by Quomodo, who does not want him as his daughter's suitor. At almost the same time Quomodo singles out Easy, planning a relationship of which Easy is as yet unaware, but winding up with a relationship he did not plan: Easy, at least temporarily, marries Quomodo's wife. The street provides the upstart Andrew Lethe with an old mother he can refuse to acknowledge because she does not recognize his new appearance. His old mother will become his new servant. In *A Chaste Maid in Cheapside,* the Welsh woman whom Sir Walter Whorehound presents as his niece is actually his mistress, while Mistress Allwit's baby whom he acknowledges as his godchild is actually his bastard. Yellowhammer, taking an order for a ring from Touchwood Junior, sees him only as a customer and not a future son-in-law.

For Middleton, this loose web of multiple relationships creates more ironic possibilities and a more effective sense of urban life than the intensifying technique of Jonson's crowded interiors and narrowly compressed actions. His characters, unlike Jonson's, have relationships and connections extending beyond the play. A recent editor of *A Trick to Catch the Old One* points out the number of nameless people we hear about, but never see: the widow hunters Witgood mentions in 3.1.253–58; the widows hunting Witgood whom Lucre imagines in 2.1.310–19; or the matches that Lucre boasts of having made in 2.1.333–35.[38] The effect of this extension is to imply that what Middleton dramatizes has been selected almost at random from an urban abundance of comic material— like the humors crowding the stage which Jonson mentions in the prologue to *The Alchemist.* The potential of the city for comic opportunity is most obvious in *A Chaste Maid,* perhaps because the multiple relationships among the characters make the cast appear larger than it is. Richard Levin has counted four separate main actions in the play affecting four households—the Yellowhammers, the Allwits, the Kixes, and the Touchwoods. The resulting subplots are comparable in complexity to those in *Bartholomew Fair.*[39] Here, however, Middleton makes the multiple plot expressive of a complex urban community that stands for a larger, more complex community implied in the Allwit christening or the young lovers' mock funeral.

Middleton's interest in establishing the representativeness of his characters is particularly important in *A Chaste Maid in Cheapside* because of the extremes of sexual license which it depicts. This is a community that has so thoroughly lost normative social control of basic biological function that it makes Vienna in *Measure for Measure* look well run by comparison. At the beginning of act 2, for example, Touchwood Senior com-

ments ironically on a new Lenten severity as evidence for civic order, in a
speech that takes away in the last three lines what it had granted before:

> There has been more religious wholesome laws
> In the half circle of a year erected
> For common good, than memory ever knew of,
> Setting apart corruption of promoters,
> And other poisonous officers that infect
> And with a venomous breath taint every goodness.
>
> [2.1.112–17]

The speech contains a deeper irony, prompted by our awareness of sexual
profligacy and the other varieties of sexual irregularity in the play completely untouched by "religious wholesome laws." Touchwood himself
will have good reason to be grateful for civic corruption since the prospect of obtaining a salable loin of mutton prompts the two Lenten promoters to keep the basket in which the Country Wench has deposited her
baby—adulterously fathered by Touchwood himself. The praiser of civic
order also tells us he hinders every haymaking by the pregnancies he
causes, and by the end of the play he will have impregnated Lady Kix with
an illegitimate heir to the fortune Sir Walter Whorehound expects to
inherit. By insisting on the Kixes's own satisfaction in the matter and on
Sir Walter's unworthiness as heir, Middleton prevents us from making
simple moral judgments.[40] What is clear is the ineffectuality of law to
adjudicate Lenten behavior or legitimate succession in Cheapside.

Allwit, too, exemplifies the disparity between public order and private
misrule. His status as wittol has not made him immune to social concern:
he too exclaims against promoters and appears shocked by Sir Walter's
intention to stand as godfather to his own bastard. And, although his own
behavior attests to a remarkable combination of shamelessness, laziness,
and greed, he is as disgusted by the incontinent gluttony of the Puritan
gossips as he is by their professions of humility and struggles for prece-
dence at the christening. Throughout the play, such formal social structures as those personified in the promoters or represented by the christening prove not only corrupt but also powerless either to express or to
regulate actual behavior.

[171]

A more effective method of social control seems to exist in the informal pressure of the community on the Yellowhammers when they try to prevent Moll from marrying Touchwood Junior. The activities of the promoters, and the reactions of other characters to them, have already hinted that few actions in Cheapside go unobserved. This is one negative aspect of the group solidarity celebrated in the civic pageants or the masques. But, if the nameless promoters represent official forms of surveillance, equally anonymous watermen and Cheapside neighbors condemn the Yellowhammers for their cruelty to Moll. Fear of the neighborhood motivates Yellowhammer's decision to stay away from Moll's funeral:

> All the whole street will hate us, and the world
> Point me out cruel: it is our best course, wife,
> After we have given order for the funeral,
> To absent ourselves till she be laid in ground.
>
> [5.2.92–95]

Sir Oliver declares he "would not have my cruelty so talk'd on / To any child of mine for a monopoly" (5.3.27–28). The funeral itself draws "such running, / Such rumours, and such throngs" (5.3.20–21) that the Yellowhammers' behavior seems prudent. And the community becomes partially responsible for the lovers' wedding when they arise from their coffins.

There is also a suggestion, however, that the emotional outpouring of the community here is prompted by the self-indulgence so evident at the Allwit christening. The Puritan gossips are sloppily demonstrative to the Allwit baby and to Tim Yellowhammer, while Lady Kix spends much of the play in tears. Emotional indulgence thus becomes part of the general lack of self-restraint throughout Cheapside. If social control first requires self-control, Cheapside seems virtually ungovernable. Allwit's question to the promoters—"What cares colon here for Lent?" (2.2.79)—could stand as motto for the play. The Kixes's offer to house the Touchwoods will not curb Touchwood's ungovernable potency; the play is not even sure that it should.[41] But Sir Oliver will provide Touchwood with a sexual outlet that may lessen the social damage he has heretofore created. And Sir Oliver will take Allwit's place as the contented cuckold of Cheapside. The best that the mind can do in Cheapside is exemplified in Tim Yellowhammer's syllogistic attempt to prove his newly married whore an honest woman.

This sense of social panorama in Middleton's comedy eventually creates a symbolic centrality for his cities no less powerful than it is for Jonson's. The magnetism of the city appears strongest, perhaps, in *Michaelmas Term* where the seasonal influx of visitors and returning natives demonstrates the city's "contentious fathom" (Inductio, 7). The city reaches out to grasp all that the country has to offer. The city harvests the crop the country plants:

> And what by sweat from the rough earth they draw
> Is to enrich this silver harvest, Law;
> And so through wealthy variance and fat brawl,
> The barn is made but steward to the hall.
> Come they up thick enough?
>
> [Inductio, 9–13]

Michaelmas Term makes much use of the familiar city-country contrast, in part to underscore the comic contrast between Easy's desire to leave his country estates and Quomodo's desire to possess them. But, although Michaelmas Term regards conscience as a garment to be discarded in London, Middleton himself blurs any distinction between country virtue and city vice in the characters who actually come up.[42] The Country Wench is only too eager for a taste of city life. Her transformation by fashionable clothes repeats that of Andrew Lethe, which predates the play. Their metamorphoses demonstrate that shape-shifting is not a device restricted only to the citizenry. And their marriage at the end of the play, which Lethe regards as an unjustifiable humiliation, actually unites two country characters of comparable social backgrounds.

Michaelmas Term is also the play in which Middleton most strongly emphasizes the city's sense of itself as a world apart, with its natural law and internal dynamic. Another symptom here of the predatory relation of the city to the countryside is the urban characters' appropriation of nature imagery to rationalize a hunter-victim relationship that they regard as universal. Gulls are lambs to be fleeced, bucks to be struck, and trouts to be caught. Michaelmas Term describes writs as "wild fowl" that return with "clients, like dried straws, between their bills" to use for nest building (Inductio, 57, 60). Characters' frequent use of such urban adages establishes the predominance of class consciousness among citizens and gentry. Even the characters in this play regard the warfare between the two classes—"our deadly enmity, which thus stands: / They're busy 'bout our wives, we 'bout their lands" (1.1.106–7)—as a social truth almost too tired to be worth repeating. Quomodo is as aware as we are of the utter conventionality of his social aspirations to own land, to educate his son and to marry his daughter to a gentleman. His confidence about gulling Easy stems less from Shortyard's skill than from the victim's predictability:

> Keep foot by foot with him, out-dare his expenses,
> Flatter, dice, and brothel to him;
> Give him a sweet taste of sensuality;
> Train him to every wasteful sin, that he
> May quickly need health, but especially money.
>
> [1.1.120–24]

The fascination that the city holds for newcomer Easy is complemented by the equal appeal that the country holds for Quomodo, the quintessential citizen. The country is not, however, any more real an alternative to London in *Michaelmas Term* than it is in Jonsonian comedy. Quomodo's descriptions of the natural landscape have the tone as well as the essential unreality of vision:

> Oh, that sweet, neat, comely, proper, delicate parcel of land, like a fine gentlewoman i'th' waist, not so great as pretty, pretty; the trees in summer whistling, the silver waters by the banks harmoniously gliding. [2.3.82–86]

Quomodo laughs to think "how the very thought of green fields puts a man into sweet inventions" (4.1.79–80), which in this case are apparently unfamiliar sexual daydreams. But Quomodo never really imagines himself as anything other than a citizen of London. The city provides the essential context for his most rapt dreams of landowning, the mirror for his self-admiration. Thinking he will now be "divulg'd a landed man / Throughout the Livery," (3.4.5–6), Quomodo turns himself into the subject of an imaginary London conversation:

> —Whither is the worshipful Master Quomodo and his fair bedfellow rid forth?—To his land in Essex!—Whence comes those goodly load of

logs?—From his land in Essex!—Where grows this pleasant fruit? says
one citizen's wife in the Row.—At Master Quomodo's orchard in Essex.
[3.4.13–17]

Even for a citizen like Quomodo, however, the city is no less a trap than it is
for the gulls he fleeces. His acquisitiveness so alienates his family that they
rejoice in his death. And Quomodo listens, ashamed, while his fellow
liverymen disparage both him and his fortune: "Merely enrich'd by
shifts / And coz'nages" (4.4.16–17). Because Quomodo cannot prevent
Sim from losing his patrimony as the other prodigal sons of the play lose
theirs, Quomodo himself ends up behaving prodigally. Like Easy he has
foolishly set his hand to a deed that takes all his property away and that
cannot be remanded by the profession of ignorance: "I did I knew not
what" (5.3.72).

Having the "freedom of the city" in this play becomes an increasingly
ironic phrase. Formally it designates those who belong to one of the livery
companies in the city; informally, it connotes insider status, as when Dick
Hellgill tells the Country Wench, "Virginity is no city trade, / You're out
o'th' freedom, when you're a maid" (1.2.43–44). Michaelmas Term describes his hand as free from restraint or scruple. Easy is repeatedly
described as free and fresh, free-breasted, meaning free from suspicion,
free to spend, and vulnerable. Easy is free in a different way after losing his
lands to Quomodo. "Y'are a free man," Quomodo tells him, ironically,
"you may deal in what you please and go whither you will" (4.1.49–50).
Freedom here is just another word for nothing left to lose.[43] But the idea of
freedom rebounds ironically on Quomodo since Easy is also free to marry
Thomasine Quomodo, just as she imagines herself free to marry him. In
the end the freedom of this city exists for no one. Quomodo ends up being
his "own affliction" (5.3.164), free neither from himself nor from his
awareness of having been cuckolded. But the play is especially grim in its
denial of distinction between gulls and rogues and natives and newcomers
in the successive stages of the "city powdering." The veteran gallants
regard newcomers like Lethe and Easy with some condescension. But they
too have been deceived by Shortyard's impersonation of Master Blastfield
and are just about to turn on him when he assumes a new identity. The
country parents who travel to the city in the course of the action have

difficulty recognizing their offspring, but Quomodo also has been deceived by Lethe's transformation from Andrew Gruel to fashionable gallant. The Country Wench's father has not learned enough from a youthful experience as urban victim to detect his daughter under her new clothes. The most he manages is to realize that he serves no gentlewoman, but a bawd. What unites the country people is not a common commitment to simple virtue, but a common identity as past, present, or future victims of the city powdering. Lethe's mother and the Country Wench's father almost immediately lose their freedom since necessity turns them into servants. Middleton refuses, however, to idealize any of his countryfolk, sharply undercutting the country father's status as spokesman for rural virtue and giving Mother Gruel a sexual appetite for young courtiers comparable to—if more grotesque than—Thomasine Quomodo's.

The entrapping magnetism of the city thus becomes part of a patterned temporal sequence which—like the predatory cycle with which it is aligned—effectively negates the possibility of positive urban change. The city alone benefits from this pattern, since it serves to perpetuate the city's imaginative appeal. In this sequence, gentry like Easy come up to town and lose their money by gambling or whoring and their patrimony in a commodity swindle. Debt- and disease-ridden, they may remain in the city like Rearage and Salewood and think of the country only for rent collections. They may, like the country father, finally reject "this man-devouring city" entirely and return to rural poverty.

This Juvenalian rejection of the city counts for very little in the moral vision of the play. More significant is the circularity within which the merchant class is trapped. Turning their profits into the means to purchase gentlemanly status means becoming prey to sharpers like themselves. Recognition of this irony is so widespread in city comedy that Jonson rings a final change on it in *The Devil Is an Ass,* when Plutarchus begs his father not to make him a gentleman:

> In a descent, or two, wee come to be
> Just i' their state, fit to be coozend, like 'hem.
> And I had rather ha' tarryed i' your trade.
> [3.1.28–30]

But the importance of this pattern for the satiric thrust of city comedy is to suggest at least one way that the city ensures its survival as the ultimate predator. If every swindling citizen is either a potential gull or the producer of gulls, there will always be prey for the predatory city. It is the one commodity that transcends the fact of limit. For Middleton, the contentious fathom of the city is so powerful that it allures the countryman and traps the citizen. The city's power is a product of the greediness of the city's embrace, because the city is a version of the Renaissance overreacher, unwilling to let anyone or anything go.

CHAPTER SEVEN

The Nature of Our People:
Shakespeare's City Comedies

Shakespeare's evident disinclination to place comic action in contemporary London sets him apart from other major comic dramatists of his time. For Jonson, the Ciceronian axiom that comedy present "deedes, and language such as men doe use" (*Every Man In*, 1) seems to contain an implicit corollary—in the city we inhabit.[1] Plays like *The Alchemist* or *Bartholomew Fair* do not simply assume their relation to actuality; in various ways, as we have seen, they insist upon it. But, for Shakespeare, the Jonsonian connections between comic convention and the contemporary London scene do not apply. Moreover, Shakespeare also tends to ruralize his comic cities: the Messina of *Much Ado,* the Padua of *Taming of the Shrew,* and the Athens of *Midsummer Night's Dream* lack almost all nitty-gritty traces of urban habitation but the name.[2] There are, however, distinct exceptions to this general rule in three Shakespearean comedies not ordinarily linked together—*The Comedy of Errors, The Merchant of Venice,* and *Measure for Measure.* The urban milieu in each is far more important than a vague backdrop like Messina. In each play, the city experiences a crisis of its own being which grows out of and is parallel to the experiences of its characters. The comic crisis that the characters must resolve interlocks with the crisis of an entire social order.

In arguing for the social distinctiveness of these three plays as a group, I do not mean to wish away the major differences among them of tonality, action, theme, and achievement. For me, however, *The Comedy of Errors, The Merchant of Venice,* and *Measure for Measure* come together by presenting urban environments faced with fundamental dilemmas, paradoxical situations whose implications call the idea of any normative urban community into severe question. In each, the city is confronted with the self-imposed necessity of enforcing a law whose consequences are so clearly inhuman that they can only make mockery of a city's reason for being. The particular logic of the comic action appears to require the city to dismantle itself, either by enforcing a monstrous law or by refusing to. Although the procedure for resolving the comic impasse differs from play to play, the end result is always to reconstitute the city for a greater inclusiveness largely achieved by means of redefinition and conversion.

The importance of the idea of the city to these plays may come into better focus after a brief contrast with *Midsummer Night's Dream* and its ruralized milieu. There, the Athenian law that compels Hermia to the impossible choice of enforced marriage, cloistered chastity, or ritual death functions almost exclusively to provide motive for escape to the forest. The subsequent tangles and transformations there so completely dominate the middle three acts of the play that only the most nervous playgoer will remember the law that sent the lovers to the forest in the first place. The consequences for the social order of the violence and emotional automatism of young lovers or of the imaginative deficiencies of the lower orders are also beside the point. Although Athens can provide colorful evidence of its urban self in the form of the rude mechanicals, the city is not at the forefront of concern.

In the three comedies that are the subject of this chapter, however, the social implications of individual behavior and circumstance are everywhere to be found, even in *The Comedy of Errors*. One of the first issues to be broached in all three plays is the noticeable tension between social identity and individual experience. Particularly apparent in *Errors* is the potential conflict between two different, separately valued kinds of identity. The first of them is clearly historical and public: a captive man is led onstage by his enemies to receive his sentence.[3] The unnamed Syracusan merchant seems to be a political victim, forfeit for belonging to the wrong group. The relentless symmetry of this twin-filled play starts here, where the Syracusan citizen finds an enemy duke bent on using him to complete a pattern begun by "the rancorous outrage of your Duke / To merchants, our well-dealing countrymen" (1.1.6–7).[4] No other identity but the citizenship that dooms him (as it would doom his mirror-image, the Ephesian caught by a duke in Syracuse) would seem relevant here. Yet the duke's curiosity about a man who would trade life at home for death abroad allows the merchant to construct a powerful personal identity that so commands sympathy and pity that the desire to kill the stranger is transformed into the desire to save a fellow man. Egeon's implausible romantic story of shipwreck and separation serves not only structurally as exposition but also thematically as the creation of a personal identity that throws the predominance of his civic identity into question. The two identities could hardly be more distinct, the one betokening anonymity, hostility, and death and the other individuality, sympathy, and life.

Not only is the emotional disparity of the two identities troubling in this context; so also is the duke's obligation to divorce sympathy from judgment and see citizenship as identity. Egeon will not return to the stage until well into act 5, but we do not forget his situation as we do Hermia's, because his brief ambivalent experience of the two faces of Ephesus is played out in full by his twin sons. One finds himself an outcast in his own city, the relationships comprising his identity in collapse, and the other finds a mysteriously rich civic identity where none exists.

This initial distinction between public and private identities carries over in different ways to *The Merchant of Venice* and *Measure for Measure*. The relationship between identity and milieu is far more complex in both plays than in *Errors*, where Ephesus is initially characterized only by its enmity to Syracusans. The exchanges between Antonio and Solanio, Salerio, and Gratiano at the opening of *The Merchant of Venice* suggest a more significant disproportion between self and environment which reverberates throughout the entire play. The chatter of Solanio and Salerio quickly establishes Antonio as a representative of the great trading empire which symbolized Venice for the Elizabethan audience. But Antonio's melancholia sets him apart from the city in a way that reveals himself and it.

Although Solanio and Salerio clearly express deference to Antonio in their beautiful images of the "petty traffickers" giving way before the "signiors and rich burghers" that are his ships, their explanations for his melancholy have a satiric quality that tries to reduce him to categorizable selfhood. Were I you, says Salerio,

> My wind cooling my broth,
> Would blow me to an ague when I thought
> What harm a wind too great might do at sea.
>
> [1.1.22-24]

Antonio's refusal to accept their identification of him with his ventures—
"my merchandise makes me not sad" (1.1.45)—is especially significant
because of his eventual willingness to become himself an object of barter
and means for Bassanio. His aloofness here suggests a selfhood un-
changeable from without and inaccessible to conventional social knowledge or description, thus reducing his companions to tautology: "let us
say you are sad / Because you are not merry" (47-48).

Clearly Shakespeare uses Antonio's apparent ability to live in, yet
apart from, the city in order to foreshadow its distortion in Shylock's
relations with the city. The discrepancy between how Antonio is regarded
by others and how he regards himself seems all the more significant in
view of the contrast it presents with Bassanio, whose "swelling port" has
bankrupted his material worth yet who remains so confident about inner
worth that he will stake everything in Belmont. Leonard Tennenhouse
finds in their relationship a powerful contemporary fantasy that needy
aristocrats might find their way to wealthy wives as the beloved protegés
of merchant patrons; but this works only if we agree that Shakespeare
has idealized Bassanio.[5] I think the scene tilts decisively in favor of Antonio, who reproaches Bassanio not for the loan itself but for the manner
of requesting it:

> You know me well, and herein spend but time
> To wind about my love with circumstance,
> And out of doubt you do me now more wrong
> In making question of my uttermost
> Than if you had made waste of all I have.
>
> [1.1.153-57]

In Antonio's criticism style and morality converge. Bassanio is faulted
not for needing cash, but for using rhetoric.[6] He assumed Antonio
needed persuading.

In outline, this scene of the bankrupt aristocrat seeking credit from
the wealthy city merchant is often replayed in Jacobean city comedy. And,
from Bassanio's aristocratic point of view, the social order of Venice

could hardly be more ideal since his needs for capital seem to be satisfied with only his honor—that is, Antonio's regard for him—as collateral. If the plan to get out of debt, says Antonio,

> stand as you yourself still do,
> Within the eye of honour, be assur'd
> My purse, my person, my extremest means
> Lie all unlock'd to your occasions.
>
> [1.1.136–39]

Even more astonishing from the perspective of city comedy is that Antonio agrees with the assumption underlying Bassanio's request. Since Bassanio owes Antonio "the most in money and in love" (131), a further request for money is additional proof of love. By using a rhetorical indirection that implies a lack of trust in the ideal relationship, Bassanio provokes Antonio's reproof.[7]

The complexities of feeling finally set this scene quite apart from the satirical clarity of its analogue in city comedy. The usual irony there begins when a greedy merchant like Quomodo in Middleton's *Michaelmas Term* extends apparently easy credit out of pretended concern for the gallant's reputation but overplays his hand and loses more than he had stood to gain by gulling the desperate man. With that part in the action taken by Shylock, Shakespeare is free to let a subtler irony play over the relationship of Bassanio and Antonio. Each becomes for a time the victim of the other's idealization of the part he plays in the social order. Antonio extends his extremest means in a generosity based not only on a deep affection for Bassanio but also on a sense of self defined apart from fortune and men's eyes. Bassanio's self-definition appears in this context far more problematic, not only because his request for means will rack Antonio's credit "even to the uttermost" (1.1.181), but also because he intends to approach Belmont with even more elaborate rhetoric of clothes and followers than he had used with Antonio. Although he may retain our sympathy by his genuine feeling for Antonio and by the romance of his venture, we are also aware that the lesson he must learn—to hazard for lead, to stand upon inner worth—is one that Antonio represents and acts upon already.

The full range and complexity of values associated with Venice do not manifest themselves until the delayed appearance in 1.3 of Shylock. The delay underscores the causal relationship between prodigal demands for credit like Bassanio's and the urban existence of a creditor of last resort who, far from being the epitome of generosity, is a reverse image—the gracious lender become demonic cannibal. Even in this first scene, however, Shakespeare is careful to establish a significant tension, largely communicated by Antonio's exchanges with a series of interlocutors culminating in Bassanio, between essential self-worth and external estimation—the critical tension of being in this society.

Shakespeare frames this question of social identity and function in terms of theatrical self-consciousness at the opening of *Measure for Measure*, by presenting a duke setting up a dramatic action that begins not *in media res* but *ex nihilo*. There is nothing *overheard* about the duke's manner here in presenting information. His speech is formal, his syntax frequently inverted to deliberate effect, his vocabulary noticeably abstract, his tone remote and authoritative.[8] The two named characters in this scene exist only at his behest: "Escalus." "My lord" (1–2). He is an unmoved mover, a figure for the dramatic poet, empowering Escalus and particularly Angelo with knowledge, qualities, and roles. He tells Escalus what he says Escalus already knows and informs Angelo that "there is a kind of character in thy life / That to th'observer doth thy history fully unfold" (27–29). Angelo takes on dramatic existence only gradually, first as a name—"Bid come before us Angelo" (15) and then platonically as an idea, a theatrical Adam, a creation of the duke in the duke's own image:

> What figure of us, think you, he will bear?
> For you must know, we have with special soul
> Elected him our absence to supply:
> Lent him our terror, drest him with our love,
> And given his deputation all the organs
> Of our own power.   [1.1.16–21]

The duke's divestiture occasions Angelo's investiture. Angelo owes his very existence in dramatic terms to the prior exigencies of a deputy's role, which is itself secondhand. In a sense he exists because there is someone who wants to watch him act; there is an observer before whom his history will unfold. This is true of course for any dramatic character, but by making it explicit here Shakespeare calls our attention to the play as a play shaping itself onstage. For Angelo this explicitness also highlights his importance as the primary test case in the play: "If any in Vienna be of worth / To undergo such grace and honor / It is Lord Angelo" (1.1.22–24). Just as Angelo cannot be said to exist before he appears onstage, so his virtues cannot be said to exist until they are bodied forth in action: "for if our virtues / Did not go forth of us" the duke tells him, " 'twere all alike / As if we had them not" (33–35). However questionable as doctrine, the duke's definition of virtue in theatrical terms is very nearly axiomatic, especially for a character like Angelo who is introduced as pure agent.[9]

By conventional theatrical standards, this exposition scene is not informative. Instead of offering us people with histories, Shakespeare makes us attend to the gradual construction of the dramatic agent which symbolizes as it initiates the larger processes of playmaking. Instead of presenting us with a particularized dramatic world, the duke's generalized diction makes us consider the dramatic city first as an idea—of "the nature of our people, / Our city's institutions, and the terms / For common justice" (9–11). Shakespeare's refusal here to tell before he has shown is part of what A. P. Rossiter has called the empirical quality of the play.[10] Such a generalized diction prevents us from harboring any firm presuppositions. We are not even given motivation for the duke's Lear-like withdrawal from power, except for his strange and eventually revealing discomfiture with the theatrical necessities of his role: "I'll privily away. I love the people, / But do not like to stage me to their eyes" (1.1.67–68). Within the play, the lack of dramatic preparation finds expression in Angelo's poignant sense of himself as new, naked and formless. His sense of unpreparedness matches our own about the shape of dramatic action in this yet unknown dramatic world.

This arrest of usual exposition has the effect of reminding an audience of its dramatic appetites and of connecting that appetite to the duke's announcement of theme.[11] Here, perhaps in part because of the allusion to judgment in the title of the play, the audience becomes conscious of its critical capacity even as the duke's mention of "the nature of our people" implies a potential identification with the characters onstage. The question of identity assumes a specifically theatrical quality missing in *Errors* or *The Merchant of Venice.* Shakespeare prepares us to see connections among government, self-government, and dramatic illusion. As so often in Jonson, the idea of a city becomes an idea of theater.

Each of these opening scenes alerts us to the characters' social relationships with their cities. This is clearest in *The Comedy of Errors* because of the strongly ambivalent reaction Ephesus has to the merchant Egeon. It is clear in *Measure for Measure* when the Duke tells Angelo he will not be virtuous unless he can translate virtue into action. This is the proviso from which Angelo shrinks, as Isabella will later. *The Merchant of Venice* is perhaps a subtler case since the opening scene is not nearly so self-contained as the other two and focuses inward on complex emotional ties. Yet, throughout the scene, as many critics have noticed, Shakespeare implicates questions of feeling with monetary language. Antonio must deny his ships make him melancholy. The lady richly left in Belmont is "nothing undervalued / To Cato's daughter, Brutus' Portia" (1.1.165–66). The closeness of Bassanio and Antonio is expressed as debt—as owing most. Antonio's complete willingness to put his money where his love is raises him in our estimation, but it also throws the delicate balance of his psychic independence from Venetian commerce into a jeopardy whose grotesqueness soon becomes apparent. That loving is nearly as dangerous for Antonio as hating is for Shylock is ultimately attributable to an aristocratic self-indulgence the more ambiguous for its overpowering attractiveness in Bassanio.

By complicating social identity so early in all three plays, Shakespeare highlights the relation of the individual to a specific social environment. More important, perhaps, the environment in each case seems to contain a hazard—as yet unclear—from which the characters will not escape. Thus the wandering Antipholus no sooner steps onstage in Ephesus than he is warned to conceal his citizenship. In *The Merchant of Venice,* imagery of risk and jeopardy is all the more ominous because of Antonio and Bassanio's expressions of confidence in self and Fortune. The duke in *Measure for Measure* withdraws from his city in a haste so precipitate that it "leaves unquestion'd / Matters of needful value" (1.1.54–55). In each case, characters register a marked degree of interest either in the nature of the urban environment they are about to experience or in the power that they feel able to exercise over it. When Antonio makes no question of his power to raise money for Bassanio, we expect danger.

Admittedly, interest in their environment is not unusual in dramatic characters. What is unusual in Shakespeare is that these environments are so distinctly urban. Shakespeare insists upon the mercantile atmosphere of Ephesus and Venice; he locates the critical hazard initially in aspects of trade. A law barring traffic between trading towns like Ephesus and Syracuse is cruel and unnatural to ongoing civic life, especially when the trade war interrupts a private need as compelling as that of Egeon and the traveling Antipholus to locate their family.[12] The irony of Antonio's mercantilism in *The Merchant of Venice* is that it prevents him from lending to Bassanio directly (with his fortunes all at sea, Antonio has a liquidity problem) but enables him to stand security. Antonio's combination of strength and vulnerability expresses the nature of money and love. It also underscores how central Antonio's character as loving merchant is to the dynamic of Venice. And it is his opposite, Shylock (another combination of strength and vulnerability), who understands this in his ironic wordplay with Bassanio over the nature of Antonio's goodness: "my meaning in saying he is a good man, is to have you understand me that he is sufficient" (1.3.13–15). *Measure for Measure,* as we have seen, replaces the localizing detail of the other two plays with a definition of the city as idea first, rather than as place. But the play also sharply limits the individuality as presented in the first scene to that which is demanded by society—defined as "the nature of our people, / Our city's institutions"—and its need to be governed. In this play, the essential relation between self and city comes before there is any dramatically presented inner life in self or city to make that relation problematical. The valid test of Angelo's mettle can only come, as the duke knows, with direct experience of power. For us, as for Angelo, this transfer of power makes possible a direct experience of the city in 1.2.

In each play, then, the city becomes not just a resonant context for the central comic experience of the characters onstage, but an essential agent and object of change in that experience. Only by attending to the nature of the urban environment in *The Comedy of Errors* can the play's deep concern with the ambiguities of personal and civic identity become fully revealed. The "restless, schizoid condition" of the play's characters is first a feature of their environment.[13] Thus, in seeing two Egeons where only one exists, Ephesus betrays its profound dualism, a communal dualism given literal, individual embodiment when the wandering twins step onstage.[14]

The wandering Antipholus's first moments onstage also suggest the potential doubleness of Ephesus, for even as he is told of its dangerousness for him, he accepts a bag of gold—the gesture emblematic of the commercial exchanges at the heart of urban life. More importantly, by characterizing Ephesus as alternately welcoming and hostile, as home and alien city, Shakespeare associates the city with the closely related archetypal motifs of the pursuing double and of fraternal rivalry. Our awareness of the solution waiting at the denouement helps to distance us from the violence in the play and to see it as farce, but it should not prevent us from recognizing in the action sophisticated literary expression of primitive fears about shadows, reflections, resemblances, and name sharing which Otto Rank has given classic psychoanalytic treatment in *The Double*.[15] Certainly the well-known Pauline associations of Ephesus with witchcraft suggests the potential of the action for terror. The relevance of such archetypes—particularly the fraternal rivalry that we have already come to connect with the idea of the city—allows us to see how Shakespeare uses the farcical action of the doubled twins not only as a paradigm of personal self-fulfillment in family reunion, but also as a paradigm of the radical connectedness of social experience, an ideal relation of self and city which gets tested in the two later plays.

In complementary ways, both Antipholuses have incomplete relationships with the outside world here represented so ambivalently by Ephesus. In the wandering twin, melancholy subjectivity is so overpowering that it displaces social identity, causing him to perceive himself as invisible in Ephesus. The quintessential tourist, he anticipates a unilateral experience of Ephesus because he cannot imagine himself an object of Ephesian experience:

> I'll view the manners of the town,
> Peruse the traders, gaze upon the buildings,
> And then return and sleep within mine inn.
> . . . .
> I will go lose myself,
> And wander up and down to view the city.
> [1.2.12–14;30–31]

His presumption of invisibility is particularly comic given the experience of his father. Antipholus is even more visible than Egeon, although not as the alien he feels himself to be. It is ironic that Ephesus will claim to know him at a time when he fears to have confounded himself. And it is even more ironic—virtually the comic expression of a kind of social revenge—that Ephesus's great gift of mother, brother, and father can come to him only after the city compels him to experience a complex of inexplicable social relationships. Significantly, the order of those imposed relationships moves outward from the domestic world to the world of commerce, so that the wandering Antipholus's experience has the effect of reconstructing from inside out a coherent yet persistently mysterious social self. At first the city threatens his one firm relationship with his servant—when the other Dromio calls him home to dinner. His experience of Ephesus begins, far more than our own, *in medias res:* "The capon burns," he is told, "the pig falls from the spit; / The clock hath strucken twelve upon the bell" (1.2.44–45.)[16] His intended view of public Ephesus—manners, traders, buildings—becomes a concrete view of private Ephesus; he changes from spectator to participant. His melancholy egotism receives its first real jolt when he encounters Adriana, claiming him as her husband. The weakness of his cognitive foundations and his sense of formlessness or invisibility cause the wandering Antipholus to accede to the domestic identity being thrust upon him. His civic identity as a Syracusan provides no advantage in Ephesus. And his personal formlessness can provide no protection from a city whose undeniable solidity inheres in the homely picture of burnt capons and cold meat, the powerful conviction of the outraged wife, and her uncanny recognition of that emblem of personal form—his name. As invisibility gives way to visibility, his sense of firm reality recedes: "To me she speaks, she moves me for her theme; / What, was I married to her in my dream?" (2.2.181–82).

The resemblance of this scene to that first encounter in *Twelfth Night* between Sebastian and Olivia should clarify Shakespeare's greater interest in social nuance here. Social identity matters deeply in Ephesus, as Egeon finds out in discovering the consequences of being a stranger. His son begins to discover the consequences of being a citizen. He could not remain the invisible onlooker in Ephesus because he looks like an Ephesian; he is a twin. But being a twin in Ephesus is virtually a symbolic shorthand for existence in the city of man. Being in Ephesus not only means having a brother, but—such are this city's powers of bounty and intimacy—having his home, his wife, his community, and his dinner too. In this city one cannot take a brother's place without displacing him and those who, like the other Dromio and the two merchants, move in his company. The immediate effect of bringing the wandering Antipholus home to dinner is to lock out the resident Antipholus and to begin the gradual destruction of civic identity in him.

The comic power of the scene at the locked door derives not only from the ancient joke of cuckoldry—as is the case with the parallel scene in the *Amphitruo*—but from its flirtation with incest. The picture of a man locked out of his house and ready to break the doors down is an emblem of domestic civil war. The picture of a man ready to break down his doors because his place within has been usurped by his brother is an emblem of civic self-annihilation, the city-as-family symbolically dismantling itself with the twin disloyalties of wife and brother. The scene presents an image of archetypal fraternal rivalry as clear in its broadly comic way as the opening scene of *Titus Andronicus* where the imperial brothers challenge each other outside the gates of Rome for the right to rule within. Here, although the house certainly contains the possibility of incestuous usurpation, it also contains Luciana who stands for sexual inhibition, the peaceful resolution of conflict, and the continuing maturation of the family.

Furthermore, Shakespeare does not bring the two brothers together until their separate experiences approach equivalent portions of gain, loss, and ensuing disorientation. Although the alien Antipholus has lost a community in the search for a brother, the resident Antipholus has constructed a civic identity without firm familial foundations, without knowing he is a brother. For him, citizenship through marriage in Ephesus must always threaten incest. Thus it is significant that the persuasion the merchant Balthasar uses on the Ephesian Antipholus not to break in should so explicitly make use of the powerful social weapon of shame— the withdrawal of community approval even into the afterlife:

> A vulgar comment will be made of it;
> And that supposed by the common rout
> Against your yet ungalled estimation,

That may with foul intrusion enter in,
And dwell upon your grave when you are dead.
[3.1.100–04]

The resident Antipholus is sensitive to the twin threats of slander and scandal as his twin, having no stake in the regard of this society, would not be. The humiliation of the resident Antipholus, moreover, has been both sexual and social: being barred from his own door has not only revealed him semipublicly as a possible cuckold, but it also has made a mockery of his expansive gestures of warm hospitality to the two merchants. Psychologically, his decision to entertain his guests at the Porpentine is both understandable and realistic, as is his bravado gesture of turning over to the courtesan there the gold chain promised to his wife. His masculine self-image, in some question due to his need to invent stories to defuse her shrewishness, requires compensation for the rebuff it has suffered.

From this point of view, the courtesan plays a key role. The two sisters within the house of Antipholus represent two potential unions for his twin—an ideal one with Luciana and an archetypally destructive one with Adriana. The courtesan completes the pattern by providing the resident Antipholus with an unlawful sexual partner and an alternative, illicit household. The interconnectedness of social life in Ephesus is confirmed: locked out of his house, Antipholus occupies another. Refused by his wife, he turns to a whore—a contrast emblematic of rival cities.

It becomes increasingly evident that the presence of twins has consequences not only for the twins themselves but for the meaning of experience in the interdependent social system in which they move. The economy of structure in the play, in other words, is dramatic and social at the same time since the language and actions of everyone in Ephesus undergo divergent subjective interpretations whose coherence is known only to us. And, even for us, at times, the mirror experiences of the twins reveal an uncanny convergence of action and interpretation: thus the attraction of the wandering twin to the unmarried Luciana reflects a providential loyalty to his brother but she reproaches him for a domestic disloyalty of which his brother is in fact guilty. Luciana attempts to persuade the wanderer of the shame of open disaffection and the wisdom of duplicity:

'Tis double wrong to truant with your bed,
And let her read it in thy looks at board;
Shame hath a bastard fame, well managed;
Ill deeds is doubled with an evil word.

[3.2.17–20]

The stranger cannot be shamed as the husband could. There is broad humor and social irony in this recommendation to incest, especially since the real cause of coldness to one sister is warmth of feeling to the other. The love of the stranger is thus an act of involuntary social beneficence, a removal of the threat of incest that can only appear like madness to Luciana: "What, are you mad that you do reason so?" (3.2.53).

Thus the escalating social effects of the phenomenon of twins are first felt within the household of sisters and servants. But the ongoing life of the city quickly becomes involved in what is, in effect, a social emergency as well as a personal one. One aspect of this social emergency is, of course, factitious: differentiating the twins will point up the perversity of separating Ephesians from Syracusans; the self-protection of Ephesus will turn out to be self-denial. In a more immediate and practical sense, however, differentiating the twins is critical because civic relationships, like marital ones, depend upon the congruence of appearance and reality, upon the possibility of taking one's neighbors at face value. The multiplication of selves which threatens incest and fraternal rivalry within the family threatens the destruction of credit and the collapse of trade in the city. What the twins experience as metamorphosis, the merchants in Ephesus understand as the betrayal of trust. Indeed the two themes of metamorphosis and betrayal begin to come together at the end of act 3, when the Syracusan master and servant articulate for each other their sense of transformation at the hands of women and plan to escape or be "guilty of self-wrong" (3.2.162). The promise of dangerous enchantment which Antipholus associates with Ephesus in general and with Luciana in particular becomes tangible in the mysterious offer by Angelo the jeweler of a chain for which he refuses to accept payment. The moment is one of high comedy not only because of the consequences that we can foresee but also because it so blithely contradicts the probabilities of urban existence—the defensive stratagems that the wandering Antipholus, like other city dwellers, had accepted as axiomatic:

What I should think of this I cannot tell;
But this I think, there's no man is so vain
That would refuse so fair an offer'd chain.
I see a man here needs not live by shifts
When in the streets he meets such golden gifts.
[3.2.178–82]

Another source of comedy is the contrast between the traveling twin's growing bewilderment about this city and our own increasingly firm sense of the ordinariness of life in Ephesus—a sense that the growing disorder of acts 4 and 5 does nothing, really, to disturb. The interconnectedness and intimacy of the city does harbor a potential for destructive fraternal rivalry. And the underside of its apparent generosity to the alien twin may be a form of possessiveness: Adriana will not let him go. But we have already seen a rather idealized version of bourgeois fraternity in the exchange of courtesies between the resident Antipholus and other merchants in act 3.[17] Concern for Antipholus's reputation prompts the merchant Balthasar's advice that he return home in the quiet of evening to find out why a wife of "her wisdom, / Her sober virtue, years and modesty" (3.1.89–90) locked him out. Antipholus attributes the jeweler Angelo's failure to meet him at the Porpentine with the chain to concern for his marriage: "Belike you thought our love would last too long / If it were chain'd together, and therefore came not" (4.1.25–26). Social experience in Ephesus also exhibits an almost perfect paradigm of trade, a bourgeois tidiness about debt, credit, and reputation which we do not find in Venice, for instance, and which only the extraordinary duplication of Antipholuses can disrupt. Angelo owes to the second merchant "even just the sum" (4.1.7) he expects to receive from Antipholus. The second merchant has refrained from importuning his debtor, "nor now I had not, but that I am bound / To Persia, and want guilders for my voyage" (4.1.3–4). The intensity of the quarrel that erupts between Antipholus and the jeweler is a measure of the sense of personal betrayal on both sides and of the authority of the mercantile code which both believe the other to have violated. They too did not need to live by shifts in Ephesus.[18]

Ironically the civic importance and prestige of the resident Antipholus and the normality of Ephesus are clearest when the fortunes of the brothers are completely transposed and they themselves are disoriented. Just after the resident brother has been hauled off to the prison that the Syracusan twin is legally forfeit to, the wandering Antipholus attests with wonder to the fullness of his Ephesian brother's civic life:

> There's not a man I meet but doth salute me
> As if I were their well-acquainted friend,
> And everyone doth call me by my name:
> Some tender money to me, some invite me,
> Some other give me thanks for kindnesses,
> Some offer me commodities to buy.
>
> [4.3.1–6]

His Dromio's punning description of the arresting officer—"not that Adam that kept the paradise, but that Adam that keeps the prison" (16–17)—is more appropriate to the antithetical experiences of the two brothers who seem to be moving about in two different cities. One city arrests you for reasons unknown, another keeps giving you something for nothing. This is the largest symmetry of the play: one city has become two, two brothers have become one. All differences between the twins—that one is a Syracusan, the other an Ephesian; that one is a melancholy loner, the other an eminent, sociable, married, and impatient Rotarian—collapse in the face of the inability of the community to distinguish them. In the course of the action, however, the effect of the identity of the brothers is paradoxically to intensify their sense of personal distinctiveness—even to the point of paranoia.[19] The Syracusan twin, imagining himself the victim of a supernatural conspiracy, perceives the courtesan as the devil: "Satan avoid, I charge thee tempt me not" (4.3.46). His brother rages at his wife: "Dissembling harlot, thou art false in all, / And art confederate with a damned pack / To make a loathsome abject scorn of me" (4.4.99–101). For both twins now, the treachery of the city seems to be symbolized by the falseness of its women, strumpets all.

Shakespeare's point here is partly, of course, to suggest the fragility of normative social life and the essential cooperation of the community at large in objectifying individual self-perception with coherent civic identity. Also, the image of two brothers perceived as one in one city experienced as two expresses, as an idea of the city, the different kinds of self embodied in the two brothers—the one brother feeling incomplete without his twin and losing, in him, a whole city; the other feeling complete, not "twinned," thanks to the customary esteem of Ephesus yet in truth crucially deprived in a way that brings disorder to the whole community. Their antithetical experiences—of inexplicable bounty and recognition on the one hand and inexplicable shame and persecution on the other— bring both to the point of warfare against the city. The crisis between the individual and the city necessitates appeal to higher authorities represented for the stranger twin by the universal maternal sanctuary of the Abbey, for the resident twin by the duke to whom he owes his Ephesian citizenship. It is only partly true to say, as R. A. Foakes has argued, that the final scene before the Abbey reveals the participants all engaged in a private ordering of experience.[20] What so defeats the characters and the duke as well is that they have all sought corroboration from the community for their experiences and have partly found it. Subjectivity and objectivity cannot achieve a reconciliation because the ordinary source of confirmation in comedy—the sense of the comic community—has broken down. And this has happened not because the community has been excluded from the experience of the central protagonists, but because it has been so involved.

The play finally reveals the inevitable participation of community in the most private of searches, when the only thing sought is the specific mirror of self in a twin. Here the self finds a fuller mirror in the city at large and twinship becomes not a destructive aberration that threatens all Ephesus but an intensified image of the new communal norm—a civic fraternity in which even Syracusans belong. There is no more geography at the play's close, no more Corinth or Epidamnum, no more Syracuse and Ephesus. In its enemy city, Ephesus has recognized a twin. And the twins, by finding a family, turn the whole city of Ephesus into a feast of gossips. Ephesus, the city of man, becomes a secular image of the promise which St. Paul makes to the Corinthians: "now I know in part; but then shall I know even as also I am known" (1 Cor. 13:12).

By alternating between Belmont and Venice at the opening of *The Merchant of Venice*, Shakespeare not only draws contrasts between the two settings but also presents Venice discontinuously, with such a sharp disjunction of styles that the city of the first scene seems distorted by its reflection in the third.[21] There is an obvious causal connection between the end of 1.1, when Antonio bids Bassanio "try what my credit can in Venice do" (180), and the opening of 1.3 when Bassanio returns with the Jewish moneylender. The narrative continuity of the action, however, only serves to throw the abrupt shift in dramatic style into sharper relief—a shift obviously caused by Shylock. This second Venetian scene restates the events and themes of the opening in such a severely deromanticized idiom that the male intimacy and deliberate courtliness of the earlier Venice seem, in retrospect, almost a mirage.

The second scene in Venice reminds us of the first by repeating it in a simplified, reverse outline form: Bassanio enters, hearing Shylock's answer to his request for a loan; Antonio's nature, reputation, and fortunes become, as before, the focus of conversation; Antonio enters to offer up his credit to the dangers represented not by the incidental malice of bad weather and rough seas but by the calculated malice of a man hoping for bad weather and rough seas. But this unannounced appearance of Shylock cuts through the earlier mythopoesis to which all the Venetians had tended. The scene, especially at its beginning and end, looks like a proleptic 1590s version of city comedy. Talking not to a sympathetic listener who idealizes his nature and needs, but to one who cares nothing about the use to which the money will be put, Bassanio sounds like an impatient Middleton gallant: "Will you pleasure me? Shall I know your answer?" (6–7). We ought to notice that Portia has disappeared from the request. In her place is the cost of a one-way ticket to Belmont, in Shylock's painstaking enumeration of time, sum, and security: "Three thousand ducats for three months, and Antonio bound" (1.3.8–9). Shylock takes away Antonio's glamor too by replacing the romantic language of maritime hierarchy with a reductive, Iago-like materialism: "But ships are but boards, sailors but men, there be land rats, and water-rats, water-thieves, and land thieves, (I mean pirates) and then there is the peril of waters, winds, and rocks" (19–23).

In the first scene, Antonio had used Bassanio's request for funds as a personal justification of Venetian financial power—his wealth rescuing Bassanio's honor and Bassanio's honor giving purpose to Antonio's use of credit. Here Shylock moves from denying that earlier ethos to a sudden revelation, prompted ironically by Antonio, of a social purpose for himself in the possession of wealth. Shylock first denies the Venetian code by refusing to interpret the loan as even potentially a social act: "I will buy with you, sell with you, talk with you, walk with you, and so following: but I will not eat with you, drink with you, nor pray with you" (1.3.30–33). Shylock perceives social overtures as a process leading to conversion.[22] What is striking here is the contrast between the casual, automatic quality of Bassanio's courtesy—"If it please you to dine with us" (28)—and the ferocity of Shylock's response. For Shylock, there appears to be no possibility of using this transaction to construct any larger social order between them. In this, Shylock shows how different he is from a city comedy villain like Middleton's Quomodo, who appears to be eager to extend credit to those above him in rank as an act of exaggerated social deference but who actually wants to take possession of the land that confers social prestige. Shylock, far more candid, seems to want nothing that Bassanio has to offer; he seems instead to be constructing a city within a city, a city apart. He thereby resembles Jonson's Morose, who would construct a city of one insulated from the noisy London outside his house. Any sympathy for Shylock here will require interpreting Bassanio's invitation to dinner as intensely hypocritical. Shylock can then be understood to reject false sociability bred out of financial need. But to recognize Shylock's specific denial of the Venetian ethos as initially presented is not necessarily to idealize that ethos; we can withhold sympathy from Shylock here without offering it to Bassanio. Shylock would have neither power nor dramatic existence without Venetians like Bassanio whose needs cannot be met within the ideal context of male friendship and social generosity represented by Antonio.

The ambiguity surrounding Bassanio's intended voyage to Belmont is most apparent in being brought about equally by Antonio's complete altruism and Shylock's desire for revenge. Antonio's generosity is powerless to "stead" Bassanio without Shylock's malevolence just as Shylock's malevolence is given opportunity by Antonio's generosity. That this malevolence and generosity are precisely interdependent suggests a dualism in Venice analogous to the dualism of Ephesus but far more expressive because here the destructive dualism is born out of the drive of a youthful protagonist to marriage and fortune—goals that the social order of comedy usually endorses without reservation. The great irony of the scene is that Bassanio's request brings about a revelation and conversion in Shylock which move him beyond the calculating materialism of his initial appearance. Bassanio causes Shylock, as he has caused Antonio, to discover *telos* in the possession of wealth. We watch Shylock slowly give up the temptation to refuse Bassanio and thwart Antonio outright, the temptation to exercise a negative power based on his expressed concern for monetary risk. He realizes instead the pleasures—for him certainly new and perhaps paradoxical—of giving money, even of losing it. He can mock Antonio's generosity with a generosity of his own, by creating a nightmare replacement for it, a negative mirror. Generosity becomes the instrument of a cannibalism which hides behind self-sacrifice. Shylock will "feed fat the ancient grudge I bear him" (1.3.42).

The gradual change in Shylock first manifests itself as interest in Antonio's motives and attitudes, even in his understanding of Scripture. Shylock draws out the scene, until he and Antonio seem to exchange roles. Antonio refuses to see any potential social significance in the bargain just as Shylock is beginning to discover some, telling Shylock to lend as "to thine enemy" (1.3.130). Antonio, empowering Bassanio to Belmont, also reveals for Shylock the limits of materialism, reveals a new interpretation of the erstwhile Christian paradox of the gain in loss. Shylock, inspired by the revelation of the "merry sport," convinced of their conviction of his base materialism, can express what is now self-parody:

> If he should break his day what should I gain
> By the exaction of the forfeiture?
> A pound of man's flesh taken from a man,
> Is not so estimable, profitable neither
> As flesh of muttons, beefs, or goats.
>
> [1.3.159–63]

Shylock's conversion is, of course, both limited and ironic: it extends only to Antonio. He is no more interested than he ever was in establishing social relations with the Gentiles. He has not been converted to generosity. He lets Launcelot go "to one that I would have him help to waste / His borrowed purse" (2.5.49–50), and looks forward to dinner with Bassanio "to feed upon / The prodigal Christian" (2.5.14–15). His famous response to Jessica's desertion, "My daughter! O my ducats! O my daughter!" (2.8.15) confirms that Shylock has not given up materialism. But he has, for once, seen beyond it by discovering unwonted spiritual possibilities, a figurative enlargement of self in a new sort of financial transaction—losing something tangible, money, to gain something intangible, revenge. It is true that Shylock hopes to gain materially by Antonio's death: he tells Tubal "were he out of Venice I can make what merchandise I will" (3.1.117–18). But he also tells the Venetians in court that his "humour" to have Antonio's flesh springs not from a rational cause but from a powerful antipathy; he neither can nor will give reason "more than a lodged hate and a certain loathing" (3.1.60) why he hates Antonio. This answer cannot please the Venetians any more than Shylock's hopes to profit by the death of his opponent, and thus cannot represent a concealment of the economic motive. Rather the two motives—tangible and intangible gain—coexist in Shylock and account for much of his dramatic power in these middle sections of the play. Shakespeare does not allow us to speculate on what Shylock actually expects to happen when he first conceives of the merry bond; giving away money in hope of its loss can only make revenge against Antonio a possibility. The most important effect of Shylock's conversion to a distorted reflection of the Venetian code is to reveal Antonio and Shylock in complementary roles, antithetically mirroring one another to form a central symbol for paradoxical Venice, its peculiar interdependence of generosity and malevolence, of selflessness and selfishness. The compound nature of Venice—like that of Ephesus—means that the protagonists must experience their social context as painfully contradictory and that we cannot ignore its troubling ambivalence. As professed enemies, Antonio and Shylock insist upon their differences—that one is a Christian, the other a Jew; that one eschews interest-taking while the other makes a living from it; that one unlocks his person and his purse to give his friend up to a rival affection, while the other would forever lock up daughter and ducats so that the escape of either counts as betrayal: "O my Christian ducats" (2.8.16).[23] But Shakespeare also gives the two opponents a significant structural resemblance as the two older males out of step with prevailing moods and motives. They are most alike in experiencing the pain of what they must give up to Belmont. Shakespeare emphasizes the parallel by having Solanio and Salerio report Shylock's response to Jessica's elopement and Antonio's bittersweet parting from Bassanio. Bassanio and Jessica arrive in Belmont with some of Shylock's money, or what is left of it after the bon voyage parties in Venice and Jessica's spending spree in Genoa.

The progressive emptying out of Shylock's house and purse and of Venice as a whole as the young characters exchange a lower state for one materially and spiritually higher suggests the interest of the play in demonstrating what everything costs. That one young Venetian leaves a master, one leaves a father, and one leaves a beloved friend who is both parent and patron hints at the deep concern of the play with who and what are left behind.[24] Launcelot's low comic internal debate between a conscience that counsels staying with Shylock and a fiend that would have him run expresses as mock casuistry, a mock moral paradox, the far more serious ambivalences of Jessica's transfer of loyalties.

Jessica's exchange of Jewish father for Christian husband, for all its echoes of blithe elopement in more monochromatic romantic comedies, does not completely escape the critical cost accounting of the play. Jessica complicates and lowers the tone of the elopement scene, assuring Lorenzo that the casket she throws down "is worth the pains" (2.6.33) and burdening herself with an additional store of money and shame (gilt/guilt): "I will make fast the doors and gild myself / With some moe ducats, and be with you straight" (49–50). No more than we wish Portia to remain "a living daughter curb'd by the will of a dead father" (1.2.24–25) can we wish Jessica to remain locked up in her father's house. But we do have reason to wish that she had presented herself more delicately in leaving it.[25] Similarly, Shakespeare allows Shylock to reveal a ridiculous egocentrism in reacting to Jessica's departure—"the curse never fell upon our nation till now, I never felt it till now" (3.1.77–79)—and allows him to jerk like a puppet in response to Tubal's applications of painful and pleasurable stimuli. But the farce does not eradicate our sense, however distanced, of the pain when he cries: "thou torturest me Tubal" (110).

In different ways, Antonio's melancholy and Shylock's rage, like Bassanio's final merrymaking and Jessica's stealthy gilding, make us attend to the social cost of normal youthful drives which Shakespeare here tinges with a due coloration of youthful selfishness. It is a cost epitomized by the helplessness of the city to save Antonio from Shylock and thus use law to ratify the social good of generosity rather than involuntarily to reward the social expression of vindictiveness. However different Bassanio may be from Portia's other suitors in style and suitability, he is like them in possessing a fatal drawback that threatens to prevent him, as guessing wrong has prevented them, from enjoying a prosperous marriage. He guesses right in Belmont, but being a Venetian means that he has not come there financially or emotionally free:

> —when I told you
> My state was nothing, I should then have told you
> That I was worse than nothing; for indeed
> I have engag'd myself to a dear friend,
> Engag'd my friend to his mere enemy
> To feed my means.   [3.2.257–62]

The extreme nature of his debt means that it cannot be erased simply by money. The very point of the casket test—to disregard a favorable exterior by staking one's faith on true worth within—implies that Antonio's life, like his affection, cannot be purchased. Thus the entanglement in Venice of love and debt is reiterated in the relationship between Venice and Belmont: just as Bassanio has had to assume an additional debt of money and love in order to pay for the voyage to Portia, so Portia must pay in something besides money for the human treasure of Venice.

In this interdependence of lives and money in Belmont and Venice the other complementary differences between the two environments hit rock bottom. Even the mercantile risk-taking so highly valued in Venice becomes institutionalized as domestic risk in Belmont: "swear before you choose, if you choose wrong / Never to speak to lady afterward / In way of marriage" (2.1.40–42). Although each environment contains something the other lacks—the men of Venice balanced by the wealth of Belmont—each environment has something to teach the other. What that may be is foreshadowed early on by Nerissa's reaction to Portia's boredom: "they are as sick that surfeit with too much, as they that starve with nothing" (1.2.5–6). Portia is both surfeited and starved—blessed with money but denied putting it to any social use for lack of a husband. Her response to Nerissa's wisdom—"If to do were as easy as to know what were good to do, chapels had been churches" (12–13)—looks forward to the casket test and to the courtroom scene and its sequel, the ring test. By choosing right, Bassanio proves he knows "what were good to do"; his choice is not doing but knowing. Portia's state is similar: she knows what is in the casket, but is powerless to act upon that knowledge by telling her suitor. For both of them, the trial scene and the attempted payment for legal services afterward provide the opportunity for translating knowing into doing and redeeming Venice from its death in Antonio's.

Everyone in this play is called upon to risk something and is called upon to pay, either actually or potentially. Even borrowing and lending, which seem to be the quintessential Venetian acts, are but species of the larger action. Morocco and Aragon command more admiration than the suitors who leave before choosing, but they fail to follow risk-taking to its logical extreme. Bassanio, although he hazards for lead, discovers a hidden cost and an additional hazard: not the interdiction against marrying that the other suitors face, but the more ironic possibility of being mocked with a marriage in name only that gains him the lady richly left in Belmont forever *in potentia*. Bassanio must risk for Antonio what Antonio has risked for him—purse, person, extremest means. Portia, vowing "never shall you lie by Portia's side / With an unquiet soul" (3.2.304–5), stakes her marriage on the resolution of the crisis in Venice. In marrying Bassanio on such terms, she too hazards for lead.[26]

That Shakespeare, just this once, places marriage midway through his comic action suggests how deeply concerned he is with the enormous cost to the city of Bassanio's courtship and marriage.[27] Although it may well be true that we must accept Bassanio's prodigality in Elizabethan terms as the necessary cost of rank, the courtroom crisis in act 4 reveals that Bassanio's initial request for funds has brought into jeopardy not only Antonio's life but the social order of the entire city of Venice as well. If Bassanio has brought out the best in Venice, Antonio's supremely Christian generosity, he has also brought out and given power to the worst, Shylock's malevolence. The union of best and worst in the bond brings the city to a critical impasse—forced to choose between abrogating Antonio's bond and thus the whole structure of law, or allowing the payment of the bond and thus legalizing murder. The renewal of the social order in comedy ordinarily depends on the fulfillment of youthful desires; here, since the marriages have already taken place, it depends on the removal of threat from one who describes himself as "a tainted wether of the flock, / Meetest for death" (4.1.114–15).

Shakespeare delays the arrival of the disguised Portia and Nerissa in the courtroom scene to display the full helplessness of the assembled Venetians, particularly Bassanio. The situation resembles the mythic scene to which Portia alluded in the casket scene when she compared herself to Hesione, "the virgin tribute, paid by howling Troy" (3.2.56) to the sea monster. Here Antonio becomes the sacrificial object. To make the parallel clearer, Shylock twice echoes Portia's phrase, "I stand for sacrifice" (3.2.57), with his own variation: "I stand for judgment"; "I stand here for law" (4.1.103,142). Even the physical dynamics of the scene, with everything hanging upon the arrival of the proper stranger, resembles the casket test. Portia assumes the Herculean role, after Bassanio and Gratiano prove about as effectual as the weeping Dardanian wives. Bassanio's hearty encouragement to Antonio—"The Jew shall have my flesh, blood, bones and all, / Ere thou shalt lose for me one drop of blood" (112–13)—sounds especially fatuous given Shylock's acknowledged right to his bond and his clear uninterest in any flesh but Antonio's. Bassanio misses the clue to Antonio's release in his own words. Furthermore, given Antonio's expressed willingness to die, the most disturbing thing about this scene is not only the idea of Antonio's death but also what happens afterward to Bassanio and Venice. If the courtroom scene reveals the full implications of Shylock's vengefulness, it also underscores Bassanio's increasing sense of guilt and humiliation. We come to see how much easier it is to be the sacrificial object who will "pay instantly with all my heart" (4.1.277) than to be the cause of the sacrifice. And the cause in the fullest sense is not only Bassanio's need for funds but also Venice's need for law, a need even greater than its need for generosity.[28]

We do not, of course, expect the action to culminate in Antonio's onstage butchering. The duke has already expressed our sense that

Shylock probably intends no more than a symbolic demonstration of his power:

> Shylock, the world thinks, and I think so too,
> That thou but leadest this fashion of thy malice
> To the last hour of act.   [4.1.17-19]

But even this expression of the unreality of the crisis acknowledges Shylock's complete control over its resolution and thus over the social order of the city. "If you deny me, fie upon your law! / There is no force in the decrees of Venice" (101-2). Thus Portia's first task as the young lawyer from Rome is to make the city and Bassanio recognize the reliance that they must share with Shylock upon the course of law. Her beautiful speech celebrates the effects of mercy on an undeserving world, but as Lawrence Danson has pointed out, it also demonstrates the irrelevance of mercy to the situation at hand.[29] Mercy is like credit in this play: better to give than to receive, safest not to need at all. Since the sacrifice of Christ, the city of man has prayed for mercy but has also constructed laws to govern in its absence. Thus Bassanio's plea to Balthasar to "wrest once the law to your authority, / To do a great right, do a little wrong" (211-12) exemplifies his failure to recognize that his honor, like the laws of Venice, can survive neither Antonio's death nor the abrogation of the bond.

However cruel Portia's brinksmanship may seem, it has the advantage of testing Shylock's actual inability either to know good or to do it. Only by bringing Shylock to the point of murder can Portia reveal to Venice the full implications of its helplessness and the source of its ultimate strength. And she also makes Bassanio recognize his unworthiness and the consequences of his actions: "But life itself, my wife, and all the world, / Are not with me esteem'd above thy life" (4.1.280-81), he tells Antonio. The casket test provides the most effective clue to understanding Portia's methods here.[30] The nature of the bond, like the appearance of the caskets, depends upon the mentality of those who need to know what it means. Like the leaden casket, it looks forbidding to everyone except Shylock who hopes to gain from it and Portia who has known to look within. Thus it will not do to describe Antonio's release from

Shylock's claim as "the merest technicality," as Barbara Lewalski has done, unless we want to devalue the casket test and the overall emphasis of the play on the social value of interpretive skill.[31] It would have been better for Shylock to have shown mercy in time, but it is better for Venice not to have needed it: only the city of God can afford to run on mercy; Shylock may have flesh but not blood. On its own, Venice must have given itself over to Shylock, becoming forever his bondsman "to make what merchandise I will." But with Portia as secular teacher, Venice can learn the continuing power of its laws to do great right without doing a little wrong. Indeed the details of Shylock's subsequent financial losses and forced conversion—as uncomfortable as they may make us and as unfair as they may seem—represent a surge of renewed authority in the structure of Venetian law to limit and control the power of Shylock and to augment that of Antonio—to subordinate the worse self of the city, its alien part, to the use of its better. Antonio's future ventures, with Shylock's capital and without the burden of Bassanio's needs, can again represent, as they did at the beginning of the play, the mercantile power from which the identity of the city comes.

The ring test that follows allows Portia an opportunity to make Bassanio aware—as the trial scene has made Venice aware—of his vulnerability and of the source of his strength. Once again in Venice, Bassanio becomes a supplicant, although this time to repay a debt not to create one: "grant me two things I pray you,— / Not to deny me, and to pardon me" (4.1.422–23). The moral economy of this play, however, has continually revealed the unforeseen cost or call for sacrifice in every obligation. As Antonio was willing to give his flesh up for Bassanio, so Bassanio must be willing to give up the equivalent of his flesh in return. To refuse the ring was to know good but not to do it; to refuse to turn the mental act represented by the choice of the lead casket into a physical one. It would also represent a specific devaluation of the suffering which Antonio and Bassanio have experienced during the trial—letting Bassanio off free. But for Bassanio to experience the nature of cost in an environment like Belmont, Portia must make him pay in a rarer, non-renewable commodity—her sexual chastity, the pound of flesh nearest his heart. Thus, if giving up the ring becomes a symbol of Bassanio's taking responsibility for his actions, having it returned becomes a symbol of his responsibility for Portia's actions as well. His experience of shame in Venice finds a correspondence in Belmont in the prospect of his own cuckolding. Portia, by being the doctor with whom she lay, is able to keep her betrayal of Bassanio hypothetical, a matter of wordplay only. Yet she thereby makes him recognize the equal weight and interdependence of his obligations to herself and Antonio for not betraying him. The prospect of sexual anxiety for the loss of what cannot be reclaimed mirrors the prospect of awesome guilt at Antonio's death which faced Bassanio in Venice. And he is, in both cases, responsible for his shame in the putative violations of friend and wife. Only after Antonio expresses his untarnished faith in Bassanio, daring to be bound for him again, does Portia ask Antonio to give Bassanio the ring with which she will reclaim and redeem him: "Then you shall be his surety: give him this, / And bid him keep it better than the other" (5.1.254–55).

Daring to be bound again becomes—for Portia, Antonio, and Bassanio—the critical test in Venice and Belmont of the strength of the social fabric, whether the bonds are manifested in money or love. As the trial in Venice has interrupted the marriages in Belmont, so the possibility of infidelity has preceded but not disrupted consummation. In this play, there are no actions without cost to someone, no bonds without some anxiety. Thus even Gratiano's final posy—"Well, while I live, I'll fear no other thing / So sore, as keeping safe Nerissa's ring" (5.1.306–7)—expresses at the level of sexual vulgarity Shakespeare's insistence throughout on the nature of personal and social responsibility: the ring worn by one binds two; the bond between two involves all.

In *The Merchant of Venice*, the threat to an entire social order in the conventional comic appetites of its younger members is adumbrated in Bassanio's need to woo with borrowed funds: to be a Venetian is to owe something to someone; to be a Venetian is to come from a city whose essential dialectic is personified in Antonio and Shylock, reverse images of the urban ethos. The threat to the social order of Vienna in *Measure for Measure* arises from the withdrawal of the duke at the end of the first scene. But the transition from the formality of the blank-verse opening, with the conspicuous generality of its diction and setting, to the apparently informal prose on the public street in 1.2 reveals a more general source of crisis than the duke's withdrawal alone might generate.

If the opening scene seems to function as prologue, the arrival of the city proper in 1.2 seems to begin the action of the play itself. Despite apparent continuity, reinforced by Lucio's initial references to the duke's absence, the scene begins so much *in medias res* that we only learn gradually how much time must have elapsed for the duke's absence to be felt so powerfully. That is, although the opening scene defines itself as before the fact, the action of succeeding scenes seems peculiarly *ex post facto* and narrative continuity seems peculiarly reversed. Angelo does not know the strength and nature of his power at the end of 1.1, although by 1.2 he has arrested Claudio and issued proclamations to pull down houses of resort. But it is not until the opening of the second act, after Lucio has gone to the convent to ask for Isabella's intercession, that we begin to discover the political philosophy that explains and necessarily precedes Angelo's prosecution of Viennese law. Mrs. Overdone is no sooner introduced as a bawd than she worries about being a bawd no longer: "But shall all our houses in the suburbs be pulled down?" (1.2.93). The information of Claudio's arrest "for getting Madam Julietta with child" (66–67) precedes Claudio onstage, and Claudio presents himself in general terms as an object-lesson on the consequences of liberty before he tells the particulars of how and why he "got possession of Julietta's bed" (135). But perhaps the most striking instance of this narrative discontinuity involves the duke himself: Shakespeare presents the consequences of the duke's decision and their consequences—that is, the appointment of Angelo and its effects—while postponing any information about the inner workings of that decision until the duke's conversation with the friar in 1.3.

Such discontinuities represent more than dramatic economy on Shakespeare's part. This separation of behavior from the sources of behavior constitutes the structural equivalent of a social perspective—a dramatic form that reveals consequence before intention, action before motivation. Or, as Lucio remarks, reversing the order of events, "Thy bones are hollow; impiety has made a feast of thee" (1.3.52–53). This is partly a structural working out of the implications of the duke's assertion to Angelo that "if our virtues / Did not go forth of us, 'twere all alike / As if we had them not" (1.1.33–35). More importantly, it is a structural introduction to the essential concern of the play with the discontinuous nature of social life in a city inhabited not by a community but by an aggregate of selves: "Here's a change indeed in the commonwealth!" wails Mrs. Overdone, "What shall become of me?" (1.2.96–97). The essential monism of Vienna manifests itself in the unusual and almost complete absence of family and of the ordinary domestic life so noticeable in Shakespeare's other bourgeois comedies. Even the two communal settings of the play—the prison and the public street—suggest a city of extremes where the essential dialectic, in Lucio's words, between the foppery of freedom and the morality of imprisonment presupposes the attenuation of a richly diverse common life. Thus the stylistic changes in language, action, and tone after the opening scene imply little continuity between the duke's initial vague theorizing about a people he says he loves but intends to hide from and the actualities of urban life summed up in Lucio's sanctimonious pirate who went to sea with only nine commandments, having razed "Thou shalt not steal."

Overall, the consequence of this early dramatic discontinuity is to introduce an environment strongly marked by the alienated sensibility which Arnold Hauser regards as symptomatic of early seventeenth-century culture and which, in the individual, takes the form of narcissism.[32] The psychic procedure by which the antisocial individual withdraws his love from the external world and concentrates it on himself can be discerned in nearly all the major characters of the play. For each, the action of the play precipitates a crisis of the sense of reality which Hauser describes as the eventual psychic crisis for the narcissist and the cultural crisis for an environment. The narcissist, inevitably hating a self he is committed to loving exclusively and unable to test his self-image against external reality, must finally choose between self-love and losing the whole external world. In *Measure for Measure*, the duke's experiment with Angelo proceeds from self-love, seeks to test it in another, and generates a much wider crisis finally involving everyone in the city. Even the absence in the play's environment of any green world, which James Trombetta has explained as Shakespeare's interest in using the city as an image of the whole world, is also relevant here: unable to look to a green world as a reference point for reality, or as a source of psychic healing, this city must look for both within its own space.[33]

Shakespeare discovers the city's primary source of universality in the concentration of its appetites on sexuality in its alienated form—narcissistic self-regard. The material self-concerns of the simpler characters in the play are far easier to document than the subtler but more consequential self-love of characters as complex as Angelo, Isabella, and a duke who is sometimes compared to Divine Providence.[34] Shakespeare uses his major characters so irregularly as to suggest that they are not, in fact, his primary concern in the play.[35] Nevertheless, both the play's essential plot device—substitution—and its principal idea—vicariousness—are expressions of narcissism at one remove—manipulating and observing the experience of another as one's own.[36] The first substitution, of course, is that of Angelo for the duke. But a closer look at the duke's explanations for the substitution reveals a profound alienation from the responsibility to exercise power which is the essence of his function. His acknowledgment to Friar Thomas that he has "ever lov'd the life remov'd" (1.3.8) makes his judicial laxity seem as much the consequence of antisocial inclination as of benevolence. At the same time, he is so awed by the potential consequences of using that power in his own person that he would rather have it appear less dreadful in Angelo.[37] His discomfort about his power implies the strength of its fascination for him and thus the psychological appeal of observing it from a distance. The probability of such a motive is further buttressed by the fact that the duke's two-fold explanation of his behavior does not withstand critical scrutiny, either. He may be interested in tightening up moral standards in Venice or in testing Angelo's nature, but it is hard to see how he can mean to do both—unless, of course, his attitude toward Angelo reflects the ambivalence he feels toward himself.[38] If Angelo succeeds in turning Venice around, the duke can claim to have delegated his power well. If Angelo fails as governor and individual, he will thereby reinforce the duke's justification of his own customary diffidence. Furthermore, the sexual suggestion at the beginning of the duke's conversation with Friar Thomas, which he takes pains to deny, coupled with the duke's skepticism about Angelo's asceticism, provides another hint that the duke's interest in seeing "if power change purpose" (54) is directed as much toward the powerful, enigmatic self that Angelo has replaced as it is toward Angelo on his own.

The duke's self-involvement would be easier to disregard were it not so much of a piece with that of the other characters, most of whom tend to observe themselves primarily through the eyes of others or to project their own motivations on to the behavior of others. Thus the captive Claudio expresses first his shame at being shown to the world, while the Provost, duke-like, withdraws his own complicity from the act: "I do it not in evil disposition, / But from Lord Angelo by special charge" (1.2.110–11). I have already mentioned Claudio's self-portrait as object-lesson of Authority; Isabella responds in analogous fashion to Lucio's description of her as a "thing enskied and sainted" (1.4.34) when she says, "You do blaspheme the good, in mocking me" (38). Urged by Lucio to "assay the power you have" (76) by interceding for Claudio, Isabella's arguments to Angelo reach their rhetorical climax with generic self-observation from a sublime perspective:[39]

> But man, proud man,
> Dress'd in a little brief authority,
> Most ignorant of what he's most assur'd—
> His glassy essence—like an angry ape
> Plays such fantastic tricks before high heaven
> As makes the angels weep; who, with our spleens,
> Would all themselves laugh mortal.
>
> [2.2.118–24]

Even the manifest preoccupation of the play with slander is related to the more inclusive theme of narcissism, since slander and narcissism involve distorted reflections, negative and positive, of the self. The connections between the slanderer and the narcissist are particularly apparent in the relationship of Lucio and the duke, for Lucio's portrait of the duke transforms him into a version of Lucio himself: the duke "had some feeling of the sport; / he knew the service" (3.2.115–16). By making the duke a self-portrait, Lucio can legitimately assert, "I know him and I love him" (145). But the duke's disclaimer requires self-praise:

Let him be but testimonied in his own bringings-forth, and he shall appear to the envious a scholar, a statesman, and a soldier. Therefore you speak unskilfully: or, if your knowledge be more, it is much darkened in your malice. [3.2.140–44]

The duke's own habit of withdrawal, symbolized by the clerical disguise he wears, has created Lucio's malicious opportunity here. It also provides the duke an opportunity for self-admiration. And it supports the truth of Lucio's claim that the duke would have dark deeds darkly answered.

In the play the duke's self-alienation is reflected in Isabella and Angelo. All three imagine themselves to have withdrawn from the sexual arena of Vienna. All three profess diffidence about assaying power even as they take up the reins and discover the nature of tyranny. The introduction of Isabella and Angelo to tyranny—Angelo as perpetrator and Isabella as victim—demonstrates the reasons for both to fear their own effectuality as eloquent woman or public magistrate. In a play that continually identifies sexuality and politics, Isabella and Angelo are novices at both, unable in the one case to anticipate sexual affect and in the other to control it. But their resemblance is clearest, perhaps, in the meaning and power that Isabella's chastity has for them both.[40] From her shrill response to Claudio's hope that she will yield her chastity to save his life, she obviously expects her brother to place as high a value on her virginity as she does. It is, however, symptomatic of her narcissism and Angelo's that Isabella has centered self-love in chastity and identifies sexuality with death. She tells Angelo:

> . . . were I under the terms of death
> Th'impression of keen whips I'd wear as rubies,
> And strip myself to death as to a bed
> That longing have been sick for, ere I'd yield
> My body up to shame.   [3.4.100–104]

She cannot recognize in her words, as critics have done, that her longing for a chaste death is the sublimated expression of sexual deprivation.[41] For us to recognize it, however, is essential to seeing the emotional clash between Claudio and Isabella not as a debate between the relative values of monastic chastity or brotherly love but rather as an example of the extreme collisions of distorted self-interest characteristic of Vienna. In its outlines, the situation resembles the central crisis of *The Merchant of Venice* in that the prospect of Bassanio's dishonor at surviving the sacrifice of Antonio is formally parallel to the prospect of Claudio's in surviving the sacrifice of Isabella's chastity. But, although Antonio's attempts to console Bassanio heighten our sympathy for them both, the very different behavior of brother and sister jeopardizes it because it is Isabella not Claudio who is most sensitive to Claudio's shame. First Isabella shames Claudio by doubting his courage in the face of death. Then, when he does quail, she reminds him of the hatefulness of a "shamed life" (3.1.116) and even accuses him of "a kind of incest, to take life / From thine own sister's shame" (3.1.138–39). His willingness to let her be sexually shamed for him is matched by her unwillingness to have it happen, so that her expressed willingness to lay down her life is completely beside the point.

Thus it is altogether fitting in a city full of separate selves that Angelo should manifest his common humanity by desiring sexual possession of that self which most closely mirrors his and that the image of their sexual union should transform them both into likenesses of their environment. Angelo's response to Isabella makes his sense of their resemblance apparent: his honor needs to be saved from her virtue; her modesty has betrayed his sense; what makes her good makes him desire her foully. Even more interestingly, Angelo compares his new experience of sharp sexual desire with an experience we associate with the retiring duke. Angelo feels breathless:

> So play the foolish throngs with one that swounds,
> Come all to help him, and so stop the air
> By which he should revive.   [2.4.24–26]

Only a woman who has set herself apart from the city as Isabella has done could appeal to a character as withdrawn into narcissism as Angelo, which is why his attempt to possess her is so narrowly sexual. He is concerned only in having her fit her consent to his sharp appetite, rather than arousing some affection in her, because he is interested in secret gratification, not response. In fact, his passion for her requires her abhorrence, since his desire is directed ultimately not at her but at himself.[42] Her hatred for him reinforces his ambivalence about himself as love could not, since her reasons to hate him mirror his own reasons to hate himself. In seducing her, he will destroy the foundations of their common self-love—the social distinction of virginity in a city of stews and prisons.

It is Angelo's disinterest in Isabella except as self-reflective sexual object that brings his behavior most strikingly into line with the rest of Vienna. Not even Claudio and Juliet are genuine exceptions, although Shakespeare allows them both opportunity to assert the mutuality of their "most offenceful act" (2.3.26).[43] He implies something more fundamental than mutuality, however, by providing them little time together onstage, all of it in public, and no words for one another. They are, like everyone else in this city, separate selves. If Claudio is preoccupied with his death, Juliet assures the disguised duke she loves Claudio "as I love the woman that wrong'd him" (2.3.25). She responds to the news of his execution on the morrow by thinking of herself not of him: "O injurious love, / That respites me a life, whose very comfort / Is still a dying horror" (2.3.40–42). Shakespeare refuses to romanticize this or any other sexual relationship in the play: Claudio is "condemned for untrussing," "for filling a bottle with a tundish" (3.2.173,166). From this point of view, the law that condemns a man to death for fornication merely objectifies the tendency of sexuality in this play to focus interest away from sexual object toward sexual subject. In Lucio, an extreme example, sexual appetite proceeds solely from within. He decides to prolong his life by fasting: "I dare not for my head fill my belly: one fruitful meal would set me to't" (4.3.152–54). Surely this is part of the implication of the bed trick: that it is an emblem of the essential solipsism of sexuality in the play—sex in the darkness of self-imprisonment. Only Mariana may be exempted from the charge of self-involvement which touches all the other major figures in the action, but Mariana is less a figure in her own right than a secondary creation of the Duke's. She is Isabella's deputy, the one real cipher of the play, Echo to Angelo's Narcissus. By being compelled to acknowledge her, Angelo and Isabella create the means for a full social existence for them all.[44]

Self-love not sexual license is thus the essential social defect of the duke's Vienna, as the duke himself has to learn. In Angelo, self-love has preceded and caused sexual license. In Angelo, self-love is the obstacle to responsible self-restraint. Consequently, the deputy's prosecution of Viennese law is untarnished by his own sexual behavior, and the law itself has suffered no damage in Angelo's fall. His position—that men cannot temper the law in response to their own individuality; when the judge errs, he must submit to the same laws—has already taken his own behavior into account, as Angelo tells Escalus with respect to Claudio:

> You may not so extenuate his offence
> For I have had such faults; but rather tell me
> When I that censure him do so offend,
> Let mine own judgement pattern out my death,
> And nothing come in partial.   [2.1.27–31]

The similarity of Angelo's sexual behavior to that of his fellows is demonstrated not only in their shared culpability but also in the similarity of effect upon the women. Male sexuality in this city makes the categories that traditionally define female identity meaningless and make the women themselves sexually ambiguous—"nothing." The state is epitomized in Mariana and defines her real importance in the play: "Why you are nothing, then," the returned duke tells the veiled woman who appears before him, "neither maid, widow, nor wife" (5.1.178–79). But to describe Mariana is also to describe Juliet, Isabella, and Kate Keepdown. And thus the remaining category that Lucio tenders helpfully—"My lord, she may be a punk; for many of them are neither maid, widow, nor wife" (180–81)—is open to them all, thanks to an informal social code that has permitted engaged couples to bed together and to a law that exacts the death penalty of only one partner for getting caught. Only the minor female characters—Mrs. Overdone and the invisible Mrs. Elbow—escape the threat of sexual anomalousness, and then not completely. We learn of Mrs. Elbow that she was "respected" with her husband "before he married with her" (2.1.166–67), although her husband loyally denies it. Her presumably legitimate pregnancy offers no guarantee of sexual respectability since it only serves to bring her under somewhat mysterious circumstances to Mrs. Overdone's brothel where "there was nothing done to her once" (140). Thus Mrs. Overdone herself may be the play's sole triumphant case of clear female identity—as survivor, the widow of nine, "overdone by the last" (199). The firmness of her identity is equivalent to the permanence of her trade: "Double and treble admonition," Escalus exclaims, escorting her to prison, "and still forfeit in the same kind" (3.3.187–88). What counts for Madame Mitigation is less the constancy of identity than the constancy of appetite. Or, as Isabella remarks to Claudio: "Thy sin's not accidental, but a trade;/Mercy to thee would prove itself a bawd" (3.1.148–49).

All social distinctions in this city collapse into the two fundamental categories of gender.[45] Mrs. Overdone may protest to the assembled gallants in 1.2 that Signior Claudio is "worth five thousand of you all" (1.2.57). Yet his part in the transformation of Juliet to a semblance of Kate Keepdown, a woman less respectable even than Mrs. Elbow, turns Claudio into a version of Lucio and Master Elbow alike. And his desire to live by the seduction of Isabella turns him into a more poignant version of Pompey, "a poor fellow that would live" (2.1.220). From such a perspective, the difference between Claudio and Pompey becomes one of degree not of kind, and the distinction between the duke's two deputies becomes far more ambiguous. Pompey's trade, like Claudio's, would be lawful "if the law would allow it, sir" (2.1.224). It is precisely because the law as prosecuted by Angelo and Escalus will not allow the trades of Claudio and Pompey and because the play collapses distinctions between them and everyone else, that the worlds of this play meet in prison.[46] Indeed, the idea of the city as microcosm in this play contracts to the prison as a microcosm in which, in Pompey's full-blown account (1.3.1–20) of a new environment as familiar as the old, we find more social variety than we have experienced in the city-at-large.

As a symbol of restraint and compulsory withdrawal from the active life, the prison most obviously resembles Isabella's convent, another setting of stringent discipline. The comparison also strengthens the futility of Isabella's intention to withdraw from social engagement: the prison in this play does not interrupt or even order the rhythms of natural life. Rather it concentrates them, housing Juliet near her time, Claudio, Ragozine, and Barnardine near theirs, and turning bawd into hangman. Resolving in his own person Lucio's antithesis between the foppery of freedom and the morality of imprisonment, Barnardine demonstrates that prison in this play is a symbol not of external restraint but of self-imprisonment—the narcissism common to them all in its extremest form. His withdrawal from the external world is so complete that the Provost has neither reason nor capacity to imprison him further: "He hath evermore had the liberty of the prison: / give him leave to escape hence, / he would not" (4.2.145–47). Unlike Claudio, Barnardine is incapable of fearing death because he is incapable of imagining it. The essential Beckettian solipsist, he is impervious to command and thus to government: "I swear I will not die today for any man's persuasion. . . . If you have anything to say to me, come to my ward; for thence will not I today" (4.3.58–62). Could the duke—to paraphrase Pompey—take order for the Barnardines, he need not fear the drabs, the knaves, the bawds, or anyone else.

That imprisonment for Barnardine could only be self-imprisonment yields the most radical identification of the play—between Barnardine's cell and Juliet's womb. A sermon of Donne provides the context: "Wee are all conceived in close Prison; in our Mothers wombes, we are close Prisoners all; when we are borne, we are borne but to the liberty of the house; Prisoners still, though within larger walls; and then all our life is but a going out to the place of Execution, to death."[47] Willing prisoner of the womblike cell whose only choice is whether to go out to death, emblem of the issue of the womb in his infantile absorption in sleeping and drinking, Barnardine sums up in his person all the characters of the play—those who are brought to prison, like Claudio, Juliet, Mrs. Overdone, or Pompey; and those, like the duke, Isabella, and their two surrogates, who would retreat on their own to other enclosed spaces, convent, walled garden, moated grange, or the dark recesses of an enveloping hood.

Donne's sermon suggests no escape from the confinement of the womb of mortal existence. And like Barnardine's retreat, Angelo's orders for the execution of Claudio imply no release from the endless circularity and self-destructive consequences of Viennese narcissism. The duke's deputy has failed to act as the duke expected him to—as the duke himself would have acted in similar circumstances. If the creation of Angelo as substitute was part of the duke's effort to know himself in another, then Angelo's own self-absorption has defeated him. Far from loving his fault, Angelo hates it; it unshapes him quite. He has no reason to spare Claudio, since in seeing his image in Claudio, he can punish himself safely while executing another. He can fall back on his customary ambivalence and the contemptible comfort of another's shame:

> But that her tender shame
> Will not proclaim against her maiden loss,
> How might she tongue me!   [4.4.21–23]

The Duke has also not taken into account that, like Isabella, Angelo is particularly sensitive to the power of sexual shame, imagining Claudio capable of taking revenge "by so receiving a dishonour'd life / With ransom of such shame" (4.4.28–29).

Defeated by the intractability of Angelo and Barnardine, the duke must discover a means of redress that cures Angelo's tyranny by penetrating the self-love that is its cause. That there is one possible cure for the common solipsism—the cure provided by an alternate image of the city, not as prison but as theater—comes to the duke's notice less as something discovered than as something remembered, an evocation of the playmaking artifice so emphatic at the opening. As the duke's departure began the play, so his return must end it, in a fifth act whose internal structure recapitulates a five-act play.[48] If the prison contains the city, only the theater itself proves spacious enough to contain the prison. Even the duke's disguise as a friar—a black friar?—may contain a subtle visual reminder of the playhouse outside the dramatic frame.[49] The duke's beautiful enjoinder to the Provost—"look, th'unfolding star calls up the shepherd" (4.2.202–3)—requires us to look beyond the borders of the play world just when the prison seems most enveloping in Pompey's account of its universal contents. His vaguely sacramental allusion also suggests that the duke's "great injunctions" to enter the city publicly, especially since he refused to be accompanied in leaving it, are the moral injunctions from within born of his experience of the common narcissism, his own included. If his withdrawal exemplified the tendency toward self-involvement in the community, his public return will necessitate the emergence of the city's other narcissists. His technique is even more obviously theatrical in Elizabethan terms, given their traditions of street theater and ceremonial procession. The duke's initial instructions desire Angelo to meet him "at the consecrated fount" (4.3.97), although he actually meets him at the city gates; both would be places traditionally utilized for *tableaux vivants* during ceremonial entries. Friar Peter knows how to station Isabella "where you may have such vantage on the Duke / He shall not pass you" (4.6.11–12).

By bringing about the capsule reenactment of the events of the play, the duke acknowledges the dangerous irresponsibility of substitution as anything but a theatrical stratagem. He also reveals the providential limit to disorder which his disguised presence has always guaranteed. Discovering that Angelo does not behave as he himself would is to discover his own solipsism and to realize that power cannot be justly delegated in order to escape the imputations of tyranny.

The only justice the duke can count on is his own, as he hints to the Provost worried about the wisdom of sending Angelo the wrong head. This substitution, unlike the last one of Mariana for Isabella, will lead to justice; it is "not a resemblance, but a certainty" (4.2.187).

Unlike the crisis of the main action, which was precipitated by the duke's imperfect assessment of Angelo's behavior, the events in act 5 can only resolve themselves by the repudiation of substitution and by the duke's public acknowledgment of the unwise part he has created for himself—by staging himself directly and retrospectively to the eyes of the people.[50] All he need control is his own behavior in order to move Angelo and Isabella outside themselves and thereby experience the shame and consequences of their own narcissism.

The public setting takes on particular importance if we realize how easily Shakespeare could have set the entire fifth act, with all its overtones of judgment before the highest authority, in a council chamber.[51] Doubtless his choice here partly reflects Elizabethan reliance on public exposure as a judicial tool.[52] It also suggests Shakespeare's interest in using the silent onstage audience of citizens as representatives of the theatrical audience and in making us aware of the meaningful discrepancy between our knowledge and theirs. At every point in the fifth act before the duke's unmasking, this discrepancy allows us to identify the behavior of Angelo and Isabella as role-playing which, having reinforced their narcissism, is the only means of curing it. However, despite their essential similarity as the major self-admirers in the play, Angelo and Isabella are brought to an understanding of their solipsism by different means because Isabella's fault lies in what out of self-love she refused to do while Angelo's lies in what he actually did do. The duke therefore has Isabella assume the burden of the shame that was her central reason for denying Claudio by confessing to a dishonor that is not in fact hers. Crucial here is the fact of an audience: Isabella's narcissism, like Angelo's, might survive the deed itself, but it cannot survive the shame of it. Indeed, for Isabella feeling shamed does not even involve actual guilt, but it does require acknowledging the presence of others and the weight of their judgment.

By insisting on the improbability of Isabella's tale, the duke makes us attend specifically to the theatricality of this action and the earlier one it mirrors—a theatricality for which he is implicitly holding himself responsible. The duke's greater self-control here is largely manifested by the deliberate exaggeration of his language and gesture in condemning the women and praising the deputy. This overplaying of his part, obvious only to us, represents a retrospective self-criticism on the duke's part and a clue to the judgment we are to make of both men as they replay their hypocrisies—the duke by pretending again to withdraw so that Angelo can have the full scope of judicial power, Angelo by acting even more falsely to maintain his reputation for righteousness. This time, by correctly assuming the worst from Angelo, the duke can simultaneously reveal to Angelo and to the audience onstage the extent of Angelo's hypocrisy and guilt. But, since Angelo's unmasking can only happen after his own, the climactic moment also reveals the duke's share of responsibility for Angelo's crime, which is the theological meaning of vicariousness and the true morality of theater. If Angelo's primary fault lay, like Isabella's, in seeking to evade responsibility for Claudio's death (which is to say, for Claudio's sexuality), the duke can only atone for his evasion of responsibility by such a public unmasking. He too requires the presence of others. That this is a gesture of self-abnegation on his part surely explains why he so long delays the news of Claudio's survival—not only to test Isabella's newly won charity by seeing if she will plead to save the life of her brother's murderer but also to allow everyone onstage to see the profoundly dangerous implications of his withdrawal. The duke's release from narcissism lies in this implicit acceptance of his *felix culpa*. Like Angelo, he too may "become much more the better / For being a little bad" (5.1.438–39). However, one may regard Isabella's silence in response to the duke's offer of his hand—the gesture is especially meaningful for the duke himself—as the second climactic step in his joining the common life, the "apt remission" toward himself which does not diminish his unique authority but gives it the clear humanity it had hitherto lacked.

Our tendency to discredit Angelo's capacity to reform or Isabella's to marry argues powerfully for the depth of self-love in the play and the consequent unlikelihood of seeing true community in the symbolic marriages at the end. The duke's inability to control Lucio except punitively limits the perfectibility of this earthly city. For Lucio, the experience of shame and the sacramental benefit of matrimony are intelligible only at the level of bodily harm: "Marrying a punk, my lord, is pressing to death, / Whipping and hanging" (5.1.520–21). And even the duke cannot make Barnardine marriageable, in prison or out. Self-imprisonment seems to be the natural state for the individual in this city, from which only crisis precipitates him. Although the duke discovers in theatrical form and space the means for creating the image of community, the possibility remains at the end of the play that it may be only an illusion.

A Bounty of Contradictions

The city is not simply a dominant setting of English Renaissance drama. In classical tragedy and city comedy, as we have seen, it is the subject. What unites these various cities from ancient Rome to modern Venice is the playwrights' almost Augustinian sense of their doubleness. I summarized the doubleness in chapter 1 in the opposed figures of Cain and Amphion, in the city mother-mistress-muse as bride and whore, and in the opposed but interdependent forces of fratricide and creativity. In the plays it is the doubleness of Saturninus and Bassianus standing beneath the walls of Rome in *Titus Andronicus* or the doubleness of Catiline and Cicero as Rome's children in *Catiline;* it is the doubleness of Ephesus for the bewildered twin Antipholi and the doubleness of Shakespeare's Venice imaged in Shylock and Antonio. Like the urban theorists of ancient Rome or Renaissance Italy, Shakespeare, Jonson, and Middleton conceive of the city as more than a social aggregate. The city is not just the people. Rather it is a symbol, expressed in time, of human potentiality and desire in collective form—the *res publica* as central urban monument. But its most characteristic activity is to celebrate the predatory destruction or near-destruction of the individuals its mythic aspirations have nurtured.

This process of creation and destruction is clearest for the protagonists of classical tragedy, who find themselves engaged in conflict not simply with their societies but also with the myth of the cities in which they must act out their lives and deaths. The prominence of monumental imagery—Titus standing on a rock surrounded by a wilderness of sea; Caesar as a fountain spouting blood for Romans to bathe their hands in; Coriolanus as walking Colossus turned against Rome; even "pathic" Sejanus torn apart once as a statue and once as a man—suggests the contradictions in the bounty of the city. The hero and the city are competing monumentalities, each one creating and created by the other. Rome exacts self-sacrifice because it enshrines self-sacrifice as an ethical absolute. Titus uses one hand to cut off the other, for having hands means serving Rome. Rome is predatory womb and monumental tomb, biology becoming history, forming the monumental life in death. In these plays, the city offers the only terms and the only space in which characters may exist. Timon, the antitype of Orpheus and Amphion with his litany of curses, rejects Athens for his cave only to find Athens at his cave and the gold he gave away returned to him, uselessly, as inedible nourishment. He rejects the enshrinement other classical protagonists find they must accept, just as he refuses (as they do not) to save the city from the threat of destruction. He dies self-entombed and self-commemorated, taking on the customary duties of a city as his own. He is not Titus or Coriolanus: he has no mother and no sons; Athens is not Rome. His city, like Tiberius's Rome, has no redemptive self-image to set against its predatory consumption of the hero just as its hero fails to endow himself with the compelling, if severe, monumentality of Caesar, Coriolanus, and Titus Andronicus. Timon's desire for obscurity and death thus functions like Tiberius's desire for invisibility and survival— to deny the interdependence of city and self by depriving the city of normative social value. At the end of both plays, the city has become a necropolis.

The comic city too has a mythic doubleness and a contradictory bounty. In Jonson and Middleton, the predatory cycle that in the city tragedies serves to monumentalize the hero as a compensatory validation of the process of destroying him becomes what Middleton calls "the city powdering." The process, conditioned upon the fact of limit in conflict with the insatiability of appetite, turns the judicial comic convention of the biter bit, the guller gulled into summary proof of the unrelenting urban norm. For Jonson and Middleton, the obligation to praise city and court in the entertainments, to find in the two communities within and just without the walls a contemporary reflection of ideal community finds an effective counterweight in the negative urban portraiture of satire. Middleton's urban schemers, no less than Jonson's, take delight not just in their own ruthlessness but more importantly in the ruthlessness of others, which serves to universalize and thus to ratify their own. As Mosca has it, "almost / All the wise world is little else, in nature, / But Parasites or Sub-parasites" (*Volpone,* 3.1.11–13).

Satiric versions of the humanist city planners, Jonson's protagonists seek to command the human and material resources of the city through the strategic concentrations of design. They would contain the city in an alchemical house, in a treasury bedchamber, in a fairground, in a household filled with the sound of one voice. But appetitive urban man finally controls neither himself nor his city because his appetite for land, money, power or metamorphosis finally serves the larger appetite of the city itself, an appetite whose ultimate object like theirs is self-perpetuation. Social self-perpetuation, so joyfully celebrated in masque and pageant as born out of an earned abundance and a deserved centrality, has here become ironic in the attenuated, debased families and the predatory order of city comedy. The value of the city, though not the power of the city, has come into question.

To the polarized image of the city in Jonson and Middleton, Shakespeare promises a resolution. Rather than presupposing universalized self-interest as the basis of urban society, Shakespeare tests it by bringing the city in his three city comedies to self-examination through a crisis of law. The interconnectedness of urban life, imaged ironically in Jonson and Middleton in the cyclical operations of the predatory chain, is presented far more humanly in Shakespeare—in the contradictory experiences of the twin Antipholi, in the interdependence of Antonio and Shylock, in the painful narcissism of the dark duke's Vienna. The biggest difference between the Shakespearean comic city and the cities of Jonson and Middleton is thus the efficacy Shakespeare is willing to hypothesize for social love, for civic charity. Nevertheless, for these cities having law means something like what having hands means in *Titus Andronicus:* one hand cuts off the other. Love is inextricably yoked to hate. Just as Ephesus's charity to one twin occasions the persecution of his brother, so Antonio's love for Bassanio empowers Shylock's hatred for him. The narcissists of Vienna require the melodramatic theatrical law of fifth-act rescue and conversion to release them from the near-fatal contradictions of common self-hatred and self-love and of the inability to recognize another.

In each play, the contrivances of theater, in the form of improbable reunions and unlikely disguises and the substitutions of bedtrick and beheading, rescue Shakespeare's comic cities from the impasses to which exercise of the laws of their own being have brought them. From one point of view, these resources of theater are the Shakespearean city's own gift to itself, the drama as urban phenomenon. But, from another, the reciprocal mirroring of city and theater in Shakespeare's city comedies is more ambiguous because it self-consciously offers urban renewal and civic conversion as illusion. Perhaps we can ask no more of this playwright. Shakespeare is neither mayor nor monarch of the city of man, although he remains its most eloquent citizen.

Notes

Introduction

1. Raymond Williams, *The Country and the City* (New York: Oxford University Press, 1973), p. 1.

2. Maynard Mack, *The Garden and the City: Retirement and Politics in the Later Poetry of Pope, 1731–43* (Toronto: University of Toronto Press, 1969), p. 3.

3. Northrop Frye, *The Anatomy of Criticism* (Princeton: Princeton University Press, 1957), p. 141.

4. Northrop Frye, *The Stubborn Structure: Essays on Criticism and Society* (Ithaca: Cornell University Press, 1970), p. 126.

5. Thomas Dekker, *The Seven Deadly Sinnes of London*, ed. H. F. B. Brett-Smith (Oxford: Basil Blackwell, 1922), p. 9.

6. William Empson, *Some Versions of Pastoral* (London: Chatto and Windus, 1950), p. 6.

7. William S. Heckscher, "Goethe and Weimar," an address at the University of New Hampshire published as a pamphlet, 1961. I am indebted to Virginia W. Callahan for the loan of this material.

8. Quotations from *Hero and Leander* are from *The Poems of Christopher Marlowe*, ed. Millar Maclure (London: Methuen, 1968).

9. Rudolf Wittkower, *Architectural Principles in the Age of Humanism*, 3d ed. (London: Alec Tiranti, 1962), pp. 57–69.

10. James Dougherty, *The Fivesquare City: The City in the Religious Imagination* (Notre Dame: University of Notre Dame Press, 1980), p. ix.

11. Brian Gibbons, *Jacobean City Comedy: A Study of Satiric Plays by Jonson, Marston, and Middleton* (Cambridge: Harvard University Press, 1968).

Notes

12. Burton Pike, *The Image of the City in Modern Literature* (Princeton: Princeton University Press, 1981), p. 17.

Chapter One

1. Giovanni Botero, "The Greatness of Cities" in *The Reason of State and the Greatness of Cities,* trans. Robert Peterson (1606), ed. P. J. and D. P. Waley (New Haven: Yale University Press, 1956), p. 227.

2. George Puttenham, "The Art of English Poesie" in *Elizabethan Critical Essays,* ed. G. Gregory Smith (Oxford: Clarendon, 1904), 2:6.

3. The point is made by C. P. Jones, *Plutarch and Rome* (Oxford: Clarendon, 1971), pp. 90–91; the classical references come from this same book, p. 90n.

4. According to Numa Denis Fustel de Coulanges: "A city had nothing more at heart than the memory of its foundation"; from *The Ancient City: A Study of the Religion, Laws, and Institutions of Greece and Rome* (1864; reprint, Baltimore: Johns Hopkins University Press, 1980), p. 135.

5. St. Augustine, *The City of God* (15.5), trans. Henry Bettenson, ed. David Knowles (Harmondsworth: Penguin, 1972). All quotations from *The City of God* refer to this edition and will be cited hereafter parenthetically.

6. Helen Rosenau, *The Ideal City: Its Architectural Evolution* (London: Studio Vista, 1974), p. 29. Another, less architectural account of Jewish tradition is in Lidia Storoni Mazzolani, *The Idea of the City in Roman Thought: From Walled City to Spiritual Commonwealth,* trans. S. O'Donnell (Bloomington: Indiana University Press, 1970), pp. 77–79.

7. See Burton Pike's comments on this ambivalence and its appearance in Freud in *The Image of the City in Modern Literature* (Princeton: Princeton University Press, 1981), pp. 17–22.

8. Peter Brown, *Augustine of Hippo* (Berkeley and Los Angeles: University of California Press, 1967), p. 311.

9. Quoted by Edward R. Hardy, Jr., in "The City of God" from *A Companion to the Study of St. Augustine,* ed. Roy W. Battenhouse (New York: Oxford University Press, 1955), p. 259.

10. Storoni Mazzolani, *The Idea of the City in Roman Thought,* p. 266.

11. St. Augustine, *De catechizandis rudibus* (The First Catechetical Instruction), trans. Joseph P. Christopher, Ancient Christian Writers no. 2 (Westminster, Md.: Newman Press; and London: Longmans, Green, 1952), p. 61.

[226]

Notes

12. See Paul Shorey's introduction to the Loeb edition of Plato's *Republic*, trans. Paul Shorey (London: Heinemann, 1946) 2:xxviii.

13. C. Nicolet, *The World of the Citizen in Republican Rome*, trans. P. S. Falla (Berkeley and Los Angeles: University of California Press, 1980), p. 22.

14. Storoni Mazzolani, *The Idea of the City in Roman Thought*, p. 37; she quotes the passage from Seneca, p. 36.

15. The words belong to Rutilius Namatianus in *De reditu*, quoted in Donald R. Dudley, ed., *Urbs Roma: A Source Book of Classical Texts on the City and Its Monuments* (London: Phaidon Press, 1967), p. 227.

16. This is a recurrent theme in Aelius Aristides' *Panathenaic Discourse*, the text of which is translated by James H. Oliver in "The Civilizing Power: A Study of *The Panathenaic Discourse* of Aelius Aristides Against the Background of Literature and Cultural Conflict," *TAPhS*, n.s. 58, pt. 1 (1968): 45–90. All further references to this text will be cited parenthetically.

17. See Dudley, *Urbs Roma*, p. 5.

18. See Hans Baron's remarks on Aristides in *From Petrarch to Leonardo Bruni: Studies in Humanistic and Political Literature* (Chicago: University of Chicago Press, 1968), pp. 155–58.

19. Aelius Aristides, *The Roman Oration*, trans. James H. Oliver in "The Ruling Power: A Study of the Roman Empire in the Second Century After Christ Through the *Roman Oration* of Aelius Aristides," *TAPhS*, n.s. 43, pt. 4 (1953): 895–907.

20. See Storoni Mazzolani, *The Idea of the City in Roman Thought*, pp. 130–33.

21. Quoted in Dudley, *Urbs Roma*, p. 226.

22. *On the Consulship of Stilicho* (3.65–70, 130–37), quoted in Dudley, *Urbs Roma*, p. 226.

23. See Dudley, *Urbs Roma*, pp. 65–66.

24. William Heckscher, "Goethe and Weimar," an address at the University of New Hampshire, pp. 20–21.

25. The description of Cato is from Lucan, *Pharsalia* (2.388), quoted by Ernst H. Kantorowicz, *The King's Two Bodies: A Study in Mediaeval Political Theology* (Princeton: Princeton University Press, 1957), p. 214n.

26. For other discussions of Revelation, see Rosenau, *The Ideal City*, pp. 26–30; and James Dougherty, *The Fivesquare City: The City in the Religious Imagination* (Notre Dame: University of Notre Dame Press, 1980), pp. 17–20.

27. See Frank Granger's introduction to the Loeb Vitruvius, 2:36–37; for the prophet's historical context, see Storoni Mazzolani, *The Idea of the City in Roman Thought*, pp. 221ff.

28. From Remigio de Girolami, "Tractatus de bono communi," trans. and quoted in Heckscher, "Goethe and Weimar," p. 3.

29. *Ten Books on Architecture by Leone Battista Alberti*, trans. Giacomo Leoni, ed. Joseph Rykwert (London: Alec Tiranti, 1955), p. x. Although Leoni's translation first appeared in 1726, the editor has chosen to reprint the 1755 edition. I will follow customary practice in referring to Italian architectural treatises by their original titles; hence, *De re aedificatoria* for Alberti, hereafter cited parenthetically.

30. Itself quoted in Eugenio Garin, *Italian Humanism: Philosophy and Civic Life in the Renaissance*, trans. Peter Munz (Oxford: Basil Blackwell, 1965), p. 20. Cicero's text was a favorite of Petrarch's from whom its importance to Quattrocento humanism derives. See *Rerum familiarium libri I–VIII*, trans. Aldo S. Bernardo (Albany: State University of New York Press, 1975), 3:12, p. 146.

31. Garin, *Italian Humanism*, p. 42.

32. Roberto Weiss, *The Renaissance Discovery of Classical Antiquity* (Oxford: Basil Blackwell, 1969), pp. 59–72.

33. See Ricardo Quinones, *The Renaissance Discovery of Time* (Cambridge: Harvard University Press, 1972), pp. 163–64. Quinones quotes this letter from Petrarch on p. 164.

34. Joachim Du Bellay, *Les regrets et autres oeuvres poetiques*, ed. J. Jolliffe and M. A. Screech (Geneva: Droz, 1966). On Du Bellay's ambivalence toward the ruins, see Thomas M. Greene, *The Light in Troy: Imitation and Discovery in Renaissance Poetry* (New Haven: Yale University Press, 1982), pp. 220–41.

35. Dora and Erwin Panofsky, *Pandora's Box: The Changing Aspects of a Mythical Symbol*, Bollingen Series, no. 52 (New York: Pantheon, 1956), pp. 56–58.

36. Ibid., p. 63.

37. Peter Partner, *Renaissance Rome, 1550–1559: A Portrait of a Society* (Berkeley and Los Angeles: University of California Press, 1976), pp. 97–100.

38. Contarini, *The Commonwealth and Government of Venice*, trans. Lewis Lewkenor (1599; facsimile reprint, Amsterdam: Da Capo Press and Theatrum Orbis Theatrum, 1969), p. 1.

39. See William J. Bouwsma, *Venice and the Defense of Republican Liberty: Renaissance Values in the Age of the Counter-Reformation* (Berkeley and Los Angeles: University of California Press, 1968), pp. 145–51.

40. See Donald Weinstein, "The Myth of Florence," in *Florentine Studies: Politics and Society in Renaissance Florence*, ed. Nicolai Rubinstein (London: Faber and Faber, 1968), pp. 15–44; also, Marvin B. Becker, "Towards a Renaissance Historiography in Florence," in *Renaissance: Studies in Honor of Hans*

Baron, ed. Anthony Molho and John A. Tedeschi (Dekalb: Northern Illinois University Press, 1971), pp. 143–45.

41. Hans Baron, *The Crisis of the Early Italian Renaissance: Civic Humanism and Republican Liberty in an Age of Classicism and Tyranny*, 2d ed. (Princeton: Princeton University Press, 1966), p. 200.

42. Quoted by Baron in *The Crisis of the Early Italian Renaissance*, pp. 200–201.

43. Guilio C. Argan, *The Renaissance City*, trans. Susan Edna Bassett (New York: George Braziller, 1969), pp. 22–24.

44. Eugenio Garin, *Science and Civic Life in the Italian Renaissance*, trans. Peter Munz (Garden City, N.Y.: Doubleday, 1969), p. 25.

45. Lewis Mumford traces this development in *Culture of Cities* (New York: Harcourt Brace, 1938), pp. 13–139; see also "The Triumph of the Map," ch. 3 in Dougherty, *The Fivesquare City*, pp. 54–86.

46. Garin, *Science and Civic Life*, p. 25.

47. See James S. Ackerman, *Palladio* (Harmondsworth: Penguin, 1966), p. 160.

48. Pierre Lavédan, *Histoire de l'urbanisme: Renaissance et temps modernes*, 2d ed. (Paris: Henri Laurens, 1959), pp. 12–13; see also Rosenau, *The Ideal City*, pp. 51–55.

49. Rudolf Wittkower, *Architectural Principles in the Age of Humanism*, 3d ed. (London: Alec Tiranti, 1962), pp. 27 and 33.

50. Ibid., p. 8.

51. Ibid., p. 142.

52. Garin, *Science and Civic Life*, p. 36; on the Roman fora, see Dudley, *Urbs Roma*, pp. 77–78.

53. Garin, *Science and Civic Life*, pp. 21–33.

54. See John R. Spencer's note to his edition of Antonio Averlino Filarete, *Filarete's Treatise on Architecture*, 2 vols. (New Haven: Yale University Press, 1965), 1:25–26.

55. Bouwsma, *Venice and the Defense of Republican Liberty*, p. 63.

56. Castiglione, "The Booke of the Courtier," trans. Sir Thomas Hoby (1561), reprinted in *Three Renaissance Classics*, ed. Burton A. Milligan (New York: Scribners, 1953).

57. From a letter that prefaced the 1518 edition of Erasmus's *Enchiridion*, quoted and translated in *Christian Humanism and the Reformation*, ed. John C. Olin (New York: Harper and Row, 1965), p. 130.

58. For the conditions of this freedom and the general relations of *Utopia* with More's historical milieu, see the introduction by J. H. Hexter to *Utopia*,

ed. Edward Surtz, S.J., and J. H. Hexter, vol. 4 of *The Complete Works of St. Thomas More*, ed. Richard S. Sylvester (New Haven: Yale University Press, 1965), pp. xv–clxxxi. Quotations are from this text and are hereafter cited parenthetically.

Chapter Two

1. In Lewis Mumford, *The City in History: Its Origins, Its Transformations, and Its Prospects* (New York: Harcourt, Brace, 1961), p. 46.

2. M. J. McGann argues that Horace may have been attacked on the grounds of satiric eligibility because he lacked the high birth that seemed to confer authority on Lucilius and Varro; see "The Three Worlds of Horace's *Satires*," in *Horace*, ed. C. D. N. Costa (London: Routledge and Kegan Paul, 1973), pp. 84–85.

3. Maynard Mack, "The Muse of Satire," *Yale Review* 41 (1951): 86.

4. Niall Rudd, *The Satires of Horace* (Cambridge: Cambridge University Press, 1966), p. 37.

5. Ibid., 203–6.

6. Ibid., 214.

7. McGann, "Three Worlds of Horace's *Satires*," p. 60.

8. On the importance of the concept of the *bios*, see Charles Witke, *Latin Satire: The Structure of Persuasion* (Leiden: E. J. Brill, 1970), p. 77. There is a convincing account of autobiography in Horace in William S. Anderson, "Autobiography and Art in Horace," in *Perspectives of Roman Poetry: A Classics Symposium*, ed. G. Karl Galinsky (Austin: University of Texas Press, 1974), pp. 33–56.

9. Rudd, *The Satires of Horace*, p. 200.

10. On this difference between the two poets, see Ronald Paulson, *The Fictions of Satire* (Baltimore: Johns Hopkins University Press, 1967), p. 29.

11. Witke, *Latin Satire*, p. 120.

12. For a discussion of this general Roman attitude, see E. Courtney, *A Commentary on the Satires of Juvenal* (London: Athlone Press, 1980), pp. 24–26.

13. In Gilbert Highet, *Juvenal the Satirist* (Oxford: Clarendon Press, 1954), p. 50.

14. Witke, *Latin Satire*, p. 113.

15. Ibid., 151.

16. Courtney, *A Commentary on the Satires of Juvenal*, pp. 27–28.

17. Highet, *Juvenal the Satirist*, p. 66.

18. Alvin Kernan, *The Cankered Muse: Satire of the English Renaissance* (New Haven: Yale University Press, 1959), p. 35.

19. See Jérôme Carcopino, *Daily Life in Ancient Rome: The People and the City at the Height of the Empire,* trans. E. O. Lorimer, ed. Henry T. Rowell (New Haven: Yale University Press, 1940).

20. Courtney, *A Commentary on the Satires of Juvenal*, p. 29.

21. For a discussion of Horace's antiprimitivism, see Margaret E. Taylor, "Horace: 'Laudator Temporis Acti?'" *AJPh* 83 (1962): 23–43.

22. Anna Lydia Motto and John R. Clark, "The Mythos of Juvenal 3," *TAPhA* 96 (1965): 269.

23. This, according to H. B. Charlton, is the impression of these comedies on a modern or even on a Renaissance reader; see *Shakespearian Comedy*, 4th ed. (1938; London: Methuen, 1949), pp. 47–48.

24. See Erich Segal's brief account of Plautus's low reputation in *Roman Laughter: The Comedy of Plautus* (Cambridge: Harvard University Press, 1968), pp. 1–2. My comments in the rest of this paragraph, like my view of Plautus in general, are heavily indebted to Segal's book, throughout.

25. Of Plautus's twenty extant comedies, only *Rudens* has a nonurban setting. For characterizations of the country in Plautus, see *Mostellaria* (15ff.) or *Truculentus* (270ff).

26. For an introduction to Roman stage conventions, see George E. Duckworth, *The Nature of Roman Comedy: A Study in Popular Entertainment* (Princeton: Princeton University Press, 1952).

27. Segal, *Roman Laughter*, p. 13.

28. Segal (*Roman Laughter*, p. 17) also quotes these lines, but his analysis of their effect differs from mine.

29. The point that, in farce, the unacceptable becomes acceptable is Eric Bentley's, in *The Life of the Drama* (New York: Atheneum, 1967), but it is elaborated by Barbara Freedman, "Errors in Comedy: A Psychoanalytic Theory of Farce," in *Shakespearean Comedy*, ed. Maurice Charney (New York: New York Literary Forum, 1980), p. 235.

Chapter Three

1. J. Leeds Barroll demonstrates how closely Elizabethan historians linked civil war and Roman history in "Shakespeare and Roman History," *MLR* 53 (1958): 328–29.

Notes

2. W. Gordon Zeeveld, *The Temper of Shakespeare's Thought* (New Haven: Yale University Press, 1974), p. 139. The distinction between republic and empire is the central thesis of Paul Cantor's *Shakespeare's Rome: Republic and Empire* (Ithaca: Cornell University Press, 1976). He does not discuss *Titus* at all, presumably because Shakespeare is far less detailed about Roman institutions in that play.

3. See James Emerson Phillips, Jr., *The State in Shakespeare's Greek and Roman Plays* (New York: Columbia University Press, 1940), pp. 46–47.

4. Lawrence Stone argues that the sixteenth century marked the extreme development of primogeniture in the English family; see *The Crisis of the Aristocracy, 1558–1641* (Oxford: Clarendon, 1965), p. 591.

5. I take issue here with T. J. B. Spencer, who says of political institutions in the play, "The author seems anxious, not to get it right, but to get it all in." See "Shakespeare and the Elizabethan Romans," *Shak S* 10 (1957): 32.

6. John Velz has rightly noted the importance of the Roman wall in Shakespeare, although he overlooks this moment; see "The Ancient World in Shakespeare: Authenticity or Anachronism: A Retrospect," *Sh* 31 (1978): 11–12.

7. On Shakespeare's use of the Ovidian account of the four ages of the world, see Robert S. Miola, "*Titus Andronicus* and the Mythos of Shakespeare's Rome," *Sh St* 14 (1981): 89–90.

8. L. C. Knights, *Further Explorations* (London: Chatto and Windus, 1965), p. 59.

9. Reuben Brower has a nice discussion of this scene in the introduction to the Signet edition of *Coriolanus* (New York: Harcourt, Brace, 1966), p. xxxv.

10. Michael Goldman, *Shakespeare and the Energies of Drama* (Princeton: Princeton University Press, 1972), pp. 114–15.

11. Nicholas Brooke comments on the morbid aspect of Roman greatness, comparing it to Coriolanus's preoccupation with his wounds in *Shakespeare's Early Tragedies* (London: Methuen, 1968), p. 23.

12. Of all the critics of the play, A. C. Hamilton has stressed most strongly Titus as the devourer of his own children in *The Early Shakespeare* (San Marino, Calif.: Huntington Library, 1967), p. 67.

13. My count comes from Marvin Spevack, *A Complete and Systematic Concordance to the Works of Shakespeare*, 9 vols. (Hildesheim: Georg Olms, 1968), 3:161.

14. Maurice Charney notes, in a similar connection, that the 36 lines of soliloquy in *Coriolanus* represent minimal use of the device in Shakespeare; see *Shakespeare's Roman Plays: The Function of Imagery in the Drama* (Cambridge: Harvard University Press, 1961), p. 38.

15. In *The Story of the Night: Studies in Shakespeare's Major Tragedies* (London: Routledge and Kegan Paul, 1961), p. 130.

16. This phrase is Brower's, in his edition, p. xxxv.

17. In Knights, *Further Explorations,* pp. 36–37.

18. See G. K. Hunter, "Shakespeare's Earliest Tragedies: *Titus Andronicus* and *Romeo and Juliet,*" *ShakS* 27 (1974): 7.

19. Coppélia Kahn discusses Shakespeare's political understanding of rape in "The Rape in Shakespeare's *Lucrece,*" *Sh St* 9 (1976), especially pp. 56–58. Although she does not mention Lavinia, there are many similarities between the rapes of these two Roman wives and daughters.

20. Eugene Waith was the first to point this out in "The Metamorphosis of Violence in *Titus Andronicus,*" *ShakS* 10 (1957): 44; but see also, Albert H. Tricomi, "The Aesthetics of Mutilation in *Titus Andronicus,*" *ShakS* 27 (1974): 18.

21. René Girard, *Violence and the Sacred,* trans. Patrick Gregory (Baltimore: Johns Hopkins University Press, 1977), pp. 39–67.

22. See the *Standard Edition of the Complete Psychological Works of Sigmund Freud,* ed. James Strachey, 24 vols. (London: Hogarth Press, 1953), 13:142.

23. In G. Wilson Knight, *The Imperial Theme* (London: Methuen, 1954), p. 156.

24. In Leonard Barkan, *Nature's Work of Art: The Human Body as Image of the World* (New Haven: Yale University Press, 1975), pp. 95–108.

25. Charney, *Shakespeare's Roman Plays,* p. 143. See also Janet Adelman's fine essay, "'Anger's My Meat': Feeding, Dependency, and Aggression in *Coriolanus,*" reprinted in *Representing Shakespeare,* ed. Murray M. Schwartz and Coppélia Kahn (Baltimore: Johns Hopkins University Press, 1980), pp. 129–45.

26. Charney, *Shakespeare's Roman Plays,* p. 143.

27. For Eugene Waith, this is the chief effect of the play; see "The Metamorphosis of Violence," p. 46.

28. Hunter, "Shakespeare's Earliest Tragedies," p. 8.

29. For this argument, see J. L. Simmons, *Shakespeare's Pagan World: The Roman Tragedies* (Charlottesville: University Press of Virginia, 1973), pp. 16–17.

30. Barkan, *Nature's Work of Art,* p. 106.

31. For a discussion of this tradition in relation to Shakespeare, see William S. Heckscher, "Shakespeare in His Relationship to the Visual Arts: A Study in Paradox," *RORD* 13–14 (1970–71): 27–35.

Chapter Four

1. Larry S. Champion, *Shakespeare's Tragic Perspective* (Athens: University of Georgia Press, 1976), p. 201.

2. Alan C. Dessen, *Elizabethan Drama and the Viewer's Eye* (Chapel Hill: University of North Carolina Press, 1977), p. 154.

3. I quote here from Jonson's "Letter to the Readers" of *Sejanus* (Herford and Simpson, eds., 4:350). I have also relied more heavily than these notes will suggest on two editions: *Sejanus*, ed. Jonas Barish, Yale Ben Jonson Series (New Haven: Yale University Press, 1965); and *Catiline*, ed. W. F. Bolton and Jane F. Gardner, Regents Renaissance Drama (London: Edward Arnold, 1972).

4. For Shakespeare's brilliant economy of social portraiture here, see Una Ellis-Fermor, "*Timon of Athens:* An Unfinished Play," *RES* 18 (1942): 272.

5. The observation is Barkan's, *Nature's Work of Art*, pp. 90–95. The phrase quoted appears on p. 91. For a count of body images, see Christopher Ricks, "*Sejanus* and Dismemberment," *MLN* 76 (1961): 301–8.

6. Barkan, *Nature's Work of Art*, p. 92.

7. Gary D. Hamilton aptly sees Tiberius as the personification of Fortune here in "Irony and Fortune in *Sejanus*," *SEL* 11 (1971): 271–72.

8. Herford and Simpson note the parallels, *Catiline* (2:122–23).

9. See Geoffrey Hill, "The World's Proportion: Jonson's Dramatic Poetry in *Sejanus* and *Catiline*," in *Jacobean Theatre*, ed. John Russell Brown and Bernard Harris, Stratford-Upon-Avon Studies, no. 1 (London: Edward Arnold, 1960), p. 116.

10. The phrase quoted is from Herford and Simpson's introduction to *Catiline* (2:123).

11. For a discussion of cannibal imagery in *Timon*, see W. H. Clemen, *The Development of Shakespeare's Imagery* (Cambridge: Harvard University Press, 1951), pp. 169–70; also 1.2.40n.

12. Rolf Soellner, *"Timon of Athens": Shakespeare's Pessimistic Tragedy* (Columbus: Ohio State University Press, 1979), p. 83. But see also Richard Fly's description of Timon's bounty as enslaving self-aggrandisement, in *Shakespeare's Mediated World* (Amherst: University of Massachusetts Press, 1976), p. 128.

13. The first argument is Ellis-Fermor's; the second is J. C. Maxwell's, in "*Timon of Athens*," *Scrutiny* 15 (1948): 197.

14. The phrase in quotations belongs to David Cook, "*Timon of Athens*," *ShakS* 16 (1963): 87.

15. The more generous view indicated in the title of Jarold W. Ramsay's article, "Timon's Imitation of Christ," *Sh St* 2 (1966): 162–73, or in G. Wilson

Knight's influential notion of Timon as "the flower of human aspiration" in *The Wheel of Fire*, 4th rev. ed. (London: Methuen, 1949), p. 210.

16. See Maxwell, *"Timon of Athens,"* p. 197.

17. Soellner, *Shakespeare's Pessimistic Tragedy,* p. 112.

18. Arthur O. Lovejoy and George Boas, *Primitivism and Related Ideas in Antiquity* (1935; reprint, New York: Octagon Books, 1965), p. 10.

19. The quoted phrase belongs to Phillips, *The State in Shakespeare's Greek and Roman Plays,* p. 136, in his discussion of Timon's diatribes.

20. In Winifred Nowottny, "Acts 4 and 5 of *Timon of Athens,*" *SQ* 10 (1959): 496.

21. Ibid., p. 494.

22. Ibid., p. 496.

23. Ibid., pp. 494–95.

24. I am thinking particularly of Maxwell, who overestimates the curative potential of Alcibiades banishing usury, in *"Timon of Athens,"* p. 206; and Cook, who sees Athens as a metaphor for imperfect humanity with which Alcibiades comes to terms, in *"Timon of Athens,"* p. 94.

25. Soellner, *Shakespeare's Pessimistic Tragedy,* p. 11.

26. T. J. B. Spencer, " 'Greeks' and 'Merrygreeks': A Background to *Timon of Athens* and *Troilus and Cressida,*" in *Essays on Shakespeare and Elizabethan Drama in Honor of Hardin Craig,* ed. Richard Hosley (Columbia: University of Missouri Press, 1962), pp. 224–33.

27. See Bolton and Gardiner's introduction to *Catiline,* pp. xii–xiii.

28. The words are Geoffrey Hill's, "The World's Proportion," p. 120.

29. A typical satiric technique, according to Alvin Kernan, *The Cankered Muse: Satire of the English Renaissance* (New Haven: Yale University Press, 1959), p. 8.

30. Soellner makes this point, *Shakespeare's Pessimistic Tragedy,* p. 85.

31. Jonas Barish, following W. D. Briggs's 1911 edition of *Sejanus,* cites Machiavelli's *Discorsi* here; see *Sejanus,* 3.637 n.46.

32. Barish's introduction makes this point, ibid., p. 10.

33. Arthur F. Marotti, "The Self-Reflexive Art of Ben Jonson's *Sejanus,*" *TSLL* 12 (1970–71): 213.

34. This nice phrase comes from Bolton and Gardiner, eds., *Catiline,* p. xxii.

35. I follow Herford and Simpson's note here (X, p. 132); they cite Sallust, ch. 23.

36. These views belong, respectively, to John J. Enck, *Jonson and the Comic Truth* (Madison: University of Wisconsin Press, 1957), p. 187; Gabriele Bernhard Jackson, *Vision and Judgment in Ben Jonson's Drama* (New Haven: Yale

University Press, 1968), p. 151; and Joseph Allen Bryant, Jr., "Catiline and the Nature of Jonson's Tragic Fable," reprinted in *Ben Jonson: A Collection of Critical Essays,* ed. Jonas Barish (Englewood Cliffs, N.J.: Prentice-Hall, 1963), p. 154.

37. Bryant, "Catiline and the Nature of Jonson's Tragic Fable," pp. 149–50.

38. Ibid., p. 154.

Chapter Five

1. In David M. Bergeron, *English Civic Pageantry, 1558–1642* (Columbia: University of South Carolina Press, 1971), p. 66.

2. See, for instance, Jonas Barish, *Ben Jonson and the Language of Prose Comedy* (1960; reprint, New York: Norton, 1970), p. 242.

3. See Jonson's account of the form in the note prefacing *The Masque of Blackness* in Herford and Simpson's edition, 7:169. Although I have used the HS text and line numberings throughout, I am also indebted to Stephen Orgel's edition of *The Complete Masques,* Yale Ben Jonson Series (New Haven: Yale University Press, 1969).

4. This description of the social function of reveling comes from Enid Welsford, *The Court Masque: A Study in the Relationship Between Poetry and the Revels* (Cambridge: Cambridge University Press, 1927), p. 399.

5. George Kernodle, *From Art to Theater: Form and Convention in the Renaissance* (Chicago: University of Chicago Press, 1944), pp. 70–75.

6. T. E. Lawrenson, "Ville imaginaire, Décor Théâtral et Fête, autour d'un recueil de Geofroy Tory," in *Les Fêtes de la Renaissance,* ed. Jean Jacquot, 2 vols. (Paris: Editions du Centre National de la Recherche Scientifique, 1956), 1:427–29.

7. Sebastiano Serlio, "From 'The Second Book of Architecture,'" in *The Renaissance Stage: Documents of Serlio, Sabbattini, and Furttenbach,* ed. Barnard Hewitt (Coral Gables: University of Miami Press, 1958), p. 27.

8. Glynne Wickham, *Early English Stages, 1300 to 1600,* 2 vols. (London: Routledge and Kegan Paul, 1959), 1:86.

9. Kernodle, *From Art to Theater,* p. 90.

10. Gordon R. Kipling, "Triumphal Drama: Form in English Civic Pageantry," *Ren D,* n.s. 8 (1977): 38–39; on multiple audiences, see also Wickham, *Early English Stages,* pp. 59–61.

11. W. Todd Furniss, "Ben Jonson's Masques," in *Three Studies in the Renaissance: Sidney, Jonson, Milton* (New Haven: Yale University Press, 1958), p. 158.

12. Robert Withington, *English Pageantry*, 2 vols. (Cambridge: Harvard University Press, 1918), 1:180.

13. Per Palme, *Triumph of Peace: A Study of the Whitehall Banqueting House* (London: Thames and Hudson, 1957), pp. 152–53.

14. See Stephen Orgel, *The Illusion of Power: Political Theater in the English Renaissance* (Berkeley and Los Angeles: University of California Press, 1975), pp. 37–40.

15. John C. Meagher provides a summary of the dance as a Renaissance symbol in *Method and Meaning in Jonson's Masques* (1966; reprint, Notre Dame: University of Notre Dame Press, 1969), pp. 81–106.

16. See Stephen Orgel, *The Jonsonian Masque* (Cambridge: Harvard University Press, 1965), p. 139.

17. Ibid., p. 137.

18. Ibid., p. 159.

19. I am paraphrasing Pico della Mirandola's "Oration on the Dignity of Man," in *The Renaissance Philosophy of Man*, trans. Elizabeth L. Forbes, ed. Ernst Cassirer, Paul Oskar Kristeller, and John Herman Randall, Jr. (1948; reprint, Chicago: University of Chicago Press, 1956), p. 225.

20. D. J. Gordon sees this as Jonson's burlesque of Inigo Jones's claims to Vitruvian significance; see "Poet and Architect: The Intellectual Setting of the Quarrel Between Ben Jonson and Inigo Jones," *JWCI* 12 (1949): 162.

21. Stephen Orgel, "The Poetics of Spectacle," *NLH* 2 (1971): 387.

22. In Kipling, "Triumphal Drama," pp. 37–56.

23. I am quoting from Margot Heinemann's discussion of Middleton's city employments in *Puritanism and Theatre: Thomas Middleton and Opposition Drama under the Early Stuarts* (Cambridge: Cambridge University Press, 1980), p. 127.

24. Thomas Dekker, "The Magnificent Entertainment" (921–24), in *The Dramatic Works*, ed. Fredson Bowers, 4 vols. (Cambridge: Cambridge University Press, 1955), 2:281. But we ought to allow for some exaggeration from Dekker here. As Kipling notes, Dekker also called civic triumphs "the most choice and daintiest fruit that spring from *Peace* and *Abundance*"; see "Triumphal Drama," p. 38.

25. Quoted in John Nichols, *The Progresses, Processions, and Magnificent Festivities of King James the First*, 2 vols. (London: 1828), 1:360.

26. See Heinemann, *Puritanism and Theatre*, p. 131.

27. In *English Civic Pageantry*, Bergeron reproduces a drawing from manuscripts belonging to the Fishmongers' Company showing the bower and tomb of

William Walworth, a pageant car used in 1590 and 1616; see pl. 9, facing p. 150.

28. Heinemann, *Puritanism and Theatre*, p. 127.

Chapter Six

1. The phrase is Jonas Barish's in *Ben Jonson and the Language of Prose Comedy* (1960; reprint, New York: Norton, 1970), p. 244.

2. For this date, see Parker, ed., *A Chaste Maid in Cheapside*, p. xxviii–xxxv.

3. Gibbons, *Jacobean City Comedy: A Study of Satiric Plays by Jonson, Marston, and Middleton* (Cambridge: Harvard University Press, 1968), p. 30. The other standard treatment of city comedy is by Alexander Leggatt, *Citizen Comedy in the Age of Shakespeare* (Toronto: University of Toronto Press, 1973).

4. In seeing a significant thematic purpose to the induction, I disagree with Ruby Chatterji, "Unity and Disparity in *Michaelmas Term*," SEL 8(1968): 352.

5. See F. H. Mares, *The Alchemist*, Revels Plays (London: Methuen, 1967), p. xlvii.

6. Gibbons, *Jacobean City Comedy*, pp. 153–55.

7. Parker, ed., *A Chaste Maid*, p. xlvii. For other discussions of women in Middleton, see Caroline Lockett Cherry, "The Most Unvaluedst Purchase: Women in the Plays of Thomas Middleton," Institut für Englische Sprache und Literatur (Salzburg: Universität Salzburg, 1973), pp. 62ff. See also Leggatt's chapter, "Chaste Maids and Whores" in *Citizen Comedy*, pp. 99–124.

8. On the sex-money equation, see Richard Levin, *The Multiple Plot in English Renaissance Drama* (Chicago: University of Chicago Press, 1971), pp. 168–74; also George E. Rowe, Jr., *Thomas Middleton and the New Comedy Tradition* (Lincoln: University of Nebraska Press, 1979), p. 64.

9. Watson, ed., *A Trick to Catch the Old One*, p. xxi. All quotations refer to this edition.

10. Parker, pp. xlvii–lvi.

11. Barish, *Ben Jonson and the Language of Prose Comedy*, p. 181.

12. See Alvin Kernan, *The Cankered Muse: Satire of the English Renaissance* (New Haven: Yale University Press, 1959), pp. 168–70; also, Alvin B. Kernan, ed., *Volpone*, Yale Ben Jonson Series (New Haven: Yale University Press, 1974), pp. 9–10.

13. Samuel Schoenbaum, "*A Chaste Maid in Cheapside* and Middleton's City Comedy," in *Studies in the English Renaissance Drama: In Memory of Karl Julius Holzknecht*, ed. Josephine W. Bennett, Oscar Cargill, and Vernon Hall, Jr. (New York: New York University Press, 1959), p. 292.

14. I have treated the connections between Middleton and Plautus at length in "The City in Plautus and Middleton," *Ren D*, n.s. 6 (1973): 29–44.

15. Edward B. Partridge, *The Broken Compass: A Study of the Major Comedies of Ben Jonson* (London: Chatto and Windus, 1958), p. 85.

16. Ibid., p. 107.

17. Alvin B. Kernan, *The Plot of Satire* (New Haven: Yale University Press, 1965), p. 153.

18. I disagree, implicitly, with Rowe here who finds more evidence of urban change in this play than I do; see his *Thomas Middleton and the New Comedy Tradition*, p. 64.

19. See Levin, *The Multiple Plot in English Renaissance Drama*, pp. xvi–xvii; also Rowe, *Thomas Middleton and the New Comedy Tradition*, p. 66, and Chatterji, "Unity and Disparity," pp. 360–61.

20. See Alan C. Dessen, *Jonson's Moral Comedy* (Evanston, Ill.: Northwestern University Press, 1971), pp. 108–9.

21. See Levin, *Multiple Plot in English Renaissance Drama*, pp. 207–11.

22. Kernan, ed., *Volpone*, pp. 1–2.

23. See George R. Kernodle, "The Open Stage: Elizabethan or Existentialist?" *Shak S* 12 (1959): 3; see also Kernan, ed., *Volpone*, textual note to 2.2.2.

24. Barish, *Ben Jonson and the Language of Prose Comedy*, p. 183.

25. On the staging of *Bartholomew Fair*, see Eugene M. Waith's edition of the play for the Yale Ben Jonson Series (New Haven: Yale University Press, 1963), p. 214; and R. B. Parker, "The Themes and Staging of *Bartholomew Fair*," *UTQ* 39 (1969–70): 294–96.

26. A parallel pointed out by Leo Salingar, "Crowd and Public in *Bartholomew Fair*," *Ren D*, n.s. 10 (1979): 158.

27. Levin, *The Multiple Plot in English Renaissance Drama*, pp. 207–11.

28. See Mares' edition of *The Alchemist*, p. xlv.

29. John Mebane, "Renaissance Magic and the Return of the Golden Age: Utopianism and Religious Enthusiasm in *The Alchemist*" *Ren D* 10 (1979): 117–39.

30. I have treated the theme of Jonson's confined settings at more length in "Ben Jonson's Comedy of Limitation," *SP* 72 (1975): 51–71. See also a more recent discussion by Patrick R. Williams, "Jonson's Satiric Choreography," *Ren D*, n.s. 9 (1978): 121–45.

31. See Barish, *Ben Jonson and the Language of Prose Comedy*, pp. 181–82.

32. Waith, ed., *Bartholomew Fair*, p. 11.

33. Gabriele Bernhard Jackson, ed., *Every Man in His Humor*, Yale Ben Jonson Series (New Haven: Yale University Press, 1969), p. 15.

34. In "Crowd and Public in *Bartholomew Fair*," Salingar remarks that the characters "affect one another chiefly by contiguity" and concludes that "they are not a community but a crowd." Yet crowdedness is a chief characteristic of urban life then as now; it may be truer to say that the characters in the play are a crowd in the process of discovering themselves to be a community.

35. On the relationship of Jonson's platonizing beliefs in universal truth to the question of setting, see Gabriele Bernhard Jackson's discussion of the "truthful setting," in *Vision and Judgment in Ben Jonson's Drama* (New Haven: Yale University Press, 1968), pp. 77–94.

36. This is Rowe's observation in *Thomas Middleton and the New Comedy Tradition*, p. 64. He also ties this observation to the influence of the morality play tradition noticed by Gibbons in *Jacobean City Comedy*, p. 129.

37. Rowe comments that the youths' journeys from country to city symbolize "their acceptance of chaos," *Thomas Middleton and the New Comedy Tradition*, p. 65.

38. Watson, ed., *A Trick*, p. xix.

39. Levin, *The Multiple Plot in English Renaissance Drama*, pp. 194–202.

40. On this subject, see R. B. Parker, "Middleton's Experiments with Comedy and Judgement," in *Jacobean Theatre*, ed. John Russell Brown and Bernard Harris, Stratford-upon-Avon Studies, no. 1 (London: Edward Arnold, 1960), pp. 179–99.

41. Parker comments on the ambiguities of the portrayal of fertility in the play; see ibid., pp. l–li. He thus undercuts Arthur F. Marotti's account of the festive qualities of the play in "Fertility and Comic Form in *A Chaste Maid in Cheapside*," *Comp D* 3 (1969): 67.

42. Rowe comments that the induction associates "the country with purity and goodness," in *Thomas Middleton and the New Comic Tradition*, p. 63; but the play as a whole treats the country as irrelevant to the action except as it functions as an illusory goal for Quomodo and provides a supply of gulls.

43. See Rowe's excellent discussion of the allied subjects of prodigality and freedom in ibid., pp. 63–67.

Chapter Seven

1. This corollary is suggested, of course, by the change from Italy to England as the scene of the revised *Every Man in His Humour* and is only apparently contradicted by the Venetian setting of *Volpone*, which Jonson seems to have chosen for its special reputation of extraordinary luxuriousness and greed.

2. Anne Barton in a talk, "Shakespeare and Jonson," delivered at the Second Congress of the International Shakespeare Association/Shakespeare Association of America, Stratford-Upon-Avon, 1–7 August 1981.

3. On this point, see Leo Salingar, *Shakespeare and the Traditions of Comedy* (Cambridge: Cambridge University Press, 1974), pp. 59–61.

4. Ralph Berry comments that Syracuse and Ephesus are seen as identical, in *Shakespeare's Comedies: Explorations in Form* (Princeton: Princeton University Press, 1972), p. 26.

5. As Leonard Tennenhouse has done in "The Counterfeit Order of *The Merchant of Venice*," in *Representing Shakespeare*, ed. Murray M. Schwartz and Coppélia Kahn (Baltimore: Johns Hopkins University Press, 1980), p. 57.

6. In *The Crisis of the Aristocracy, 1558–1641* (Oxford: Clarendon Press, 1965), Lawrence Stone suggests a host of reasons why Elizabethan aristocrats were habitually overextended, adding that conspicuous consumption was "a cause of family decay second only to biological failure" (p. 184); see also his chapter 10.

7. For a different interpretation of this scene, see Tennenhouse's remarks on the system of dependence and trust in "The Counterfeit Order of *The Merchant of Venice*," p. 58.

8. Lever notes, for instance, that *institutions* was a new word in the sixteenth century and appears nowhere else in Shakespeare; see 1.1.10n.

9. See the excellent discussion of the questions of Angelo's surrogacy and dramatic function in A. D. Nuttall, "*Measure for Measure:* Quid Pro Quo?" *Sh St* 4 (1968): 235–37.

10. In A. P. Rossiter, *Angel with Horns*, ed. Graham Storey (New York: Theater Arts Books, 1961), pp. 152–53.

11. This is an effect that Michael Goldman has seen elsewhere in this play and in other Shakespeare plays; see *Shakespeare and the Energies of Drama* (Princeton: Princeton University Press, 1972), p. 164.

12. Sherman Hawkins, "The Two Worlds of Shakespearean Comedy," *Sh St* 3 (1967): 68.

13. I am quoting Ruth Nevo here, *Comic Transformations in Shakespeare* (London: Methuen, 1980), p. 26.

14. I feel that Shakespeare chooses place names like the Phoenix and the Centaur to play with notions of oneness and doubleness, an observation I am delighted to be seconded by Barbara Freedman in "Errors in Comedy: A Psychoanalytic Theory of Farce," *Shakespearean Comedy*, ed. Maurice Charney, New York Literary Forum, Vol. 5–6 (1980), p. 242.

15. Otto Rank, *The Double: A Psychoanalytic Study*, ed. and trans. Harry Tucker, Jr. (Chapel Hill: University of North Carolina Press, 1971). For two

recent discussions of doubling, fratricidal myths in Shakespeare, see Joel Fineman, "Fratricide and Cuckoldry: Shakespeare's Doubles" and Coppélia Kahn, "The Providential Tempest and the Shakespearean Family," both in *Representing Shakespeare*, ed. Schwartz and Kahn, pp. 70–109 and 217–43.

17. C. L. Barber has noticed that there is more of "daily, ordinary life" in *Errors* than in any other Shakespearean comedy except *The Merry Wives;* see "Shakespearian Comedy in *The Comedy of Errors*," *CE* 25 (1964): 493–97.

18. See Foakes, ed., *Comedy of Errors*, notes to 3.1.19–29.

19. The same point is expanded by Berry, *Shakespeare's Comedies*, pp. 35–37.

20. Nevo, *Comic Transformations in Shakespeare*, p. 26.

21. Foakes, ed., *Comedy of Errors*, p. xlvii.

22. Thomas H. Fujimura has discussed the different styles of the play in terms of three "worlds"—of Antonio, Portia, and Shylock—in "Mode and Structure in *The Merchant of Venice*," *PMLA* 81 (1966): 499–511. He sees Antonio's world mediating between the extremes represented by Portia and Shylock; I see the contrasts between Antonio and Shylock as more important in themselves, as two possibilities for Venice.

23. Meals often, of course, have sacramental associations for Shakespeare; see Marvin Felheim, "*The Merchant of Venice*," *Sh St* 4 (1968): 103–4.

24. This point has been made, in a slightly different way, by René Girard, "To Entrap the Wisest: A Reading of *The Merchant of Venice*," in *Literature and Society*, ed. Edward W. Said, Selected Papers from the English Institute, 1978, n.s. 3 (Baltimore: Johns Hopkins University Press, 1980), p. 104. Girard sees on both sides "the same obsession with displaying and sharpening a difference that is less and less real," while I see real but complementary differences.

25. For the view (which I do not share) that Antonio feels romantically betrayed by Bassanio's departure, see Graham Midgley, "*The Merchant of Venice*: A Reconsideration," *EIC* 10 (1960): 125.

26. See Lawrence Danson, *The Harmonies of "The Merchant of Venice"* (New Haven: Yale University Press, 1978), pp. 177–82, for a good summary of the reasons to excuse Jessica from condemnation here.

27. See Fujimura, "Mode and Structure in *The Merchant of Venice*," p. 503, for a discussion of this aspect of Bassanio's return to Venice, although with a more exalted view of Bassanio than my own.

28. R. F. Hill sees the uniqueness of the play in its treatment of the Antonio-Bassanio relationship coupled with this midway placement of the marriages; see "*The Merchant of Venice* and the Pattern of Romantic Comedy," *Shak S* 28 (1975): 75.

29. I am grateful to Lawrence Danson's measured comments on stage law in

Shakespeare, which seek to locate a middle ground between historical inquiry into contemporary English or Venetian law and dismissals of the entire question; see *The Harmonies of "The Merchant of Venice,"* pp. 83–86.

30. Ibid., p. 62.

31. In "Ideology and Class Conduct in *The Merchant of Venice*," *Ren D*, n.s. 10 (1979): 103, Frank Whigham also draws the parallel between these two scenes, but with different results.

32. See Barbara Lewalski's learned and influential article, "Biblical Allusion and Allegory in *The Merchant of Venice*," *SQ* 13 (1962): 340.

33. In Arnold Hauser, *Mannerism: The Crisis of the Renaissance and the Origin of Modern Art*, 2 vols. (London: Routledge and Kegan Paul, 1965), 1:115–17. I am indebted to Hauser's fascinating discussion of seventeenth-century forms of consciousness at many points here.

34. In James Trombetta, "Versions of Dying in *Measure for Measure*," *ELR* 6 (1976): 62.

35. For an example of Christian interpretations of the duke here, see Roy W. Battenhouse, "*Measure for Measure* and the Christian Doctrine of the Atonement," *PMLA* 61 (1946): 1029–59.

36. In Anthony Caputi, "Scenic Design in *Measure for Measure*," *JEGP* 60 (1961): 424.

37. I owe this characterization of vicariousness as the chief idea of the play to Nuttall, "Quid Pro Quo?" p. 232.

38. The parallel case of Cesare Borgia, whom Machiavelli mentions in *The Prince* as having temporarily delegated unpleasant magisterial chores, is often cited; see Nuttall, "Quid Pro Quo?" p. 238, and Trombetta, "Versions of Dying," p. 76.

39. See Nuttall, "Quid Pro Quo?" p. 240.

40. See Anne Barton's comments on this speech in *Shakespeare and the Idea of the Play* (1962; reprint, Westport, Conn.: Greenwood Press, 1977), p. 177.

41. Darryl J. Gless has noted that Luther objected to vows of chastity in part because they allowed clerics to think of themselves as a class apart, as Isabella does; see "*Measure for Measure*," *the Law, and the Convent* (Princeton: Princeton University Press, 1979), p. 76.

42. See Gless's remarks on this speech, ibid., p. 131; also Arthur Kirsch, "The Integrity of *Measure for Measure*," *Shak S* 28 (1975): 96.

43. Pointed out in another connection by René Girard, *Deceit, Desire, and the Novel: Self and Other in Literary Structure*, trans. Yvonne Freccero (Baltimore: Johns Hopkins University Press, 1966), p. 17.

44. On this attitude toward Claudio and Juliet, see W. L. Godshalk, "*Measure for Measure:* Freedom and Restraint," *Sh St* 6 (1970): 142.

45. Trombetta comments that the duke's "knowledge of Mariana is a little like having thought her up," in "Versions of Dying," p. 70.

46. Ibid., p. 67.

47. See Rossiter, *Angel with Horns,* p. 156, whose nice phrase I take over here.

48. Sermon 27, from *LXXX Sermons,* 1640; I owe this reference to E. Pearlman, "Shakespeare, Freud, and the Two Usuries; or, Money's a Meddler," *ELR* 2 (1972): 233.

49. See Josephine W. Bennett, *"Measure for Measure" as Royal Entertainment* (New York: Columbia University Press, 1966), p. 132.

50. I owe this suggestion to A. R. Braunmuller, professor of English, UCLA.

51. See Godshalk, "Freedom and Restraint," p. 147.

52. See Lever, ed., *Measure for Measure,* p. 3.

53. See Gless, *"Measure for Measure," the Law, and the Convent,* p. 149.

Index

Index

Index

Orpheus, 10; Titus Andronicus as
type of, 60; Lavinia as type of, 75;
Julius Caesar as antitype of, 79;
Timon as antitype of, 102, 221;
portrayed in civic pageantry, 147,
220
Ovid, 10, 75

Pageantry, civic: 124–29, 138–49
Palladio, Andrea, 27, 28
Palme, Per, 128
Pandora, as Rome, 24
Panofsky, Dora and Erwin, 24
Parker, R. B., 154
Partridge, Edward, 157, 164
Pericles, 19
Petrarch, 20, 22–23, 24, 25
Pico della Mirandola, 134
Pike, Burton, 8
Plato, *Republic*, 12–13, 66, 138, 167
Plautus, 8, 34; comedies discussed,
50–57; comedies compared to
Shakespeare's, 51–52; compared
to *Timon of Athens*, 104; compared
to Jacobean city comedy, 52, 156;
Amphitruo cited with *Comedy of
Errors*, 189
Plutarch, 10
Pope, Alexander, 1
Predation: in cities, 3; in *Julius
Caesar*, 76, 77–79, 85; in
Coriolanus, 80–82, 87–89; in city
comedy, 152–77
Primitivism: in Horace and Juvenal,
49–50; in *Timon of Athens*, 103–5
Puttenham, George, 9

Quinones, Ricardo, 23

Rank, Otto, 187
Revelation, Book of: 20–21, 24–25,
75; echoed at James I's coronation
entertainment, 140. *See also* John
of Patmos
Romanitas, 114, 123; in Juvenal, 50;
in *Titus Andronicus*, 60; in
Coriolanus, 67–69, 71, 86; in *Julius
Caesar*, 70–71, 85–86; in *Sejanus*,
94–96, 109
Rome, 2–3, 20, 34; in *City of God*,
12–14; classical praises of, 15–18;
ruins of, 18, 22–25; in Revelation,
20–21, 25; compared to Venice
and Florence, 25–26, 28; in
Horace, 35–44; in Juvenal, 44–
50; in Shakespeare's Roman
tragedies, 58–90, 220–21; in
Jonson's Roman tragedies, 91, 93–
99, 108–23, 220–21; as mother in
Coriolanus, 87–90; as mother in
Catiline, 96–97, 116–21;
compared to London in pageants,
127–28, 142–44, 147
Romulus and Remus, 10
Rosenau, Helen, 8
Rossiter, A. P., 184

Sallust, used by Jonson in *Catiline*,
116, 121
Segal, Erich, 51
Seneca, 14
Serlio, Sebastiano, 126–27
Shakespeare, William, 2, 7–8, 34,
125, 220–23; compared to
Plautus, 51–52; idea of Rome in,
58–90; Roman tragedies compared
to Jonson's, 91–94, 96, 122–23;
"city comedies," 178–219